Temporality and Progress in Victorian Literature

Nineteenth-Century and Neo-Victorian Cultures
Series editors: Ruth Heholt and Joanne Ella Parsons

Recent books in the series
Domestic Architecture, Literature and the Sexual Imaginary in Europe, 1850–1930
Aina Martí-Balcells
Assessing Intelligence: The Bildungsroman and the Politics of Human Potential in England, 1860–1910
Sara Lyons
The Idler's Club: Humour and Mass Readership from Jerome K. Jerome to P. G. Wodehouse
Laura Fiss
Michael Field's Revisionary Poetics
Jill Ehnenn
Narrative, Affect and Victorian Sensation: Wilful Bodies
Tara MacDonald
The Provincial Fiction of Mitford, Gaskell and Eliot
Kevin A. Morrison
Women's Activism in the Transatlantic Consumers' Leagues, 1885–1920
Flore Janssen
Queer Books of Late-Victorian Print Culture
Frederick D. King
British Writers, Popular Literature and New Media Innovation, 1820–45
Alexis Easley
Philanthropy in Children's Periodicals, 1840–1930: The Charitable Child
Kristine Moruzi
Temporality and Progress in Victorian Literature
Ruth M. McAdams

http://www.edinburghuniversitypress.com/series-nineteenth-century-and-neo-victorian-cultures

Temporality and Progress in Victorian Literature

Ruth M. McAdams

EDINBURGH
University Press

Edinburgh University Press is one of the leading university presses in the UK. We publish academic books and journals in our selected subject areas across the humanities and social sciences, combining cutting-edge scholarship with high editorial and production values to produce academic works of lasting importance. For more information visit our website: edinburghuniversitypress.com

© Ruth M. McAdams 2025

Edinburgh University Press Ltd
13 Infirmary Street
Edinburgh EH1 1LT

Typeset in 11/13pt Sabon
by Cheshire Typesetting Ltd, Cuddington, Cheshire, and
printed and bound in Great Britain

A CIP record for this book is available from the British Library

ISBN 978 1 3995 3284 6 (hardback)
ISBN 978 1 3995 3286 0 (webready PDF)
ISBN 978 1 3995 3287 7 (epub)

The right of Ruth M. McAdams to be identified as the author of this work has been asserted in accordance with the Copyright, Designs and Patents Act 1988, and the Copyright and Related Rights Regulations 2003 (SI No. 2498).

Contents

List of Figures	vi
Acknowledgements	vii
Series Preface	ix
Introduction: The Unfashionable Age	1
1. In Search of Progressive Time	28
2. Disraeli's Frenetic Stasis	59
3. Thackeray's Persistent Fashion	97
4. Progressing in Harriette Wilson and Harriet Martineau	131
5. Stuck in Hardy	169
Conclusion: Fashionable Aging in Margaret Oliphant's *Kirsteen*	210
Bibliography	218
Index	238

Figures

3.1 Vignette in footnote, by William Makepeace Thackeray. *Vanity Fair*. Published at the Punch Office, 1847. Number 2, chapter 6, p. 56. Image provided by Chapin Library, Williams College.   107

5.1 Napoleon caricature by Johann Michael Voltz, adapted by Rudolf Ackermann, 1814. Image provided by Cornell University, PJ Mode Collection of Persuasive Cartography.   186

Acknowledgements

The ancient ancestor of this book was my dissertation in the Department of English Language and Literature at the University of Michigan, Ann Arbor. I owe a great debt to my dissertation committee—Danny Hack, Tina Lupton, and especially Adela Pinch—for astute feedback, professional guidance, and ongoing moral support. My friends and classmates at Michigan offered encouragement and camaraderie in that formative period that has continued in the years since. I am grateful for the material support I received at Michigan, secured by generations of activists at the Graduate Employees Organization, Local 3550 of the American Federation of Teachers.

The origins of my interest in nineteenth-century British literature stretch back even further. From my time at the University of Pennsylvania, I want to thank Michael Gamer, Sean Keilen, and Rachel Buurma, and from my time at the University of Edinburgh, Bill Bell and Peter Garside. I also want to thank my former colleagues and students at Boğaziçi University in Istanbul, especially Leyla Kayhan Elbirlik.

Over the years, my thinking has been nourished by scholarly conferences and seminars, including the North American Victorian Studies Association, Interdisciplinary Nineteenth-Century Studies, the Modern Language Association, the Dickens Project, the Nineteenth Century Studies Association, the Association of Canadian College and University Teachers of English, the Victorians Institute, the Midwest Victorian Studies Association, and the CUNY Victorian seminar—thank you to Sophia Hsu for the invitation. My friends and colleagues in the field have offered insightful feedback on drafts of the entire manuscript. I owe a great debt especially to Meg Dobbins, Jayne Hildebrand, Mimi Winick, and Priyanka Jacob.

As a non-tenure-track faculty member at Skidmore College, I have received limited institutional support for this project. The focus of this book changed dramatically after I completed my PhD, with my interest in non-progressive temporalities shaped by the lived experience of cyclical precarity that has characterised my employment. I would like to thank the attendees of the Scholarly and Creative Endeavors lunch groups sponsored by the Center for Leadership, Teaching, and Learning; my non-tenure-track colleagues in English; and, especially, my fellow organizers of Skidmore Faculty Forward, SEIU Local200 United. Their solidarity has helped make this book possible.

Early versions of pieces of the book appeared in *Victorian Studies*, *Victorian Literature and Culture*, and *Nineteenth-Century Contexts*. At Edinburgh University Press, Emily Sharp and Elizabeth Fraser have brilliantly shepherded the project through the publication process. I also want to thank series editors Ruth Heholt and Joanne Ella Parsons, as well as two anonymous readers of the manuscript for their generous and thoughtful feedback.

I am deeply grateful to my parents, Dan McAdams and Rebecca Pallmeyer, who have supported and encouraged me in many ways over the years, while modeling intellectual curiosity and egalitarian marriage. Finally, with love, to my partner Andrew Bozio, who has always valued my career as much as he values his own.

Series Preface

Nineteenth-Century and Neo-Victorian Cultures
Series Editors: Ruth Heholt and Joanne Ella Parsons

This interdisciplinary series provides space for full and detailed scholarly discussions on nineteenth-century and Neo-Victorian cultures. Drawing on radical and cutting-edge research, volumes explore and challenge existing discourses, as well as providing an engaging reassessment of the time period. The series encourages debates about decolonising nineteenth-century cultures, histories, and scholarship, as well as raising questions about diversities. Encompassing art, literature, history, performance, theatre studies, film and TV studies, medical and the wider humanities, Nineteenth Century and Neo-Victorian Cultures is dedicated to publishing pioneering research that focuses on the Victorian era in its broadest and most diverse sense.

For my parents

Introduction
The Unfashionable Age

This book's method and argument can be sketched in miniature through a brief comparison of three passages. In the first two, Victorian historical writers each use the metaphor of old clothes to illustrate a larger point about historical change. In "The Spirit of the Age" (1831), John Stuart Mill observes, "Mankind have outgrown old institutions and old doctrines, and have not yet acquired new ones. When we say outgrown, we intend to prejudge nothing. A man may not be either better or happier at six-and-twenty, than he was at six years of age: but the same jacket which fitted him then, will not fit him now."[1] For Mill, the size contrast between the child's jacket and the adult's body reflects the inevitability and the visibility of change over time. Notwithstanding the trajectory of growth seemingly implied by the development from childhood to adulthood, Mill emphasizes that change is at least potentially neutral: "when we say outgrown, we intend to prejudge nothing." Bagehot's *The English Constitution* (1867), by contrast, uses clothing to suggest that change over time is not readily visible, observing:

> As a man's family go on muttering in his maturity incorrect phrases derived from a just observation of his early youth, so, in the full activity of a historical constitution, its subjects repeat phrases true in the time of their fathers, but now true no longer. Or, if I may say so, an ancient and never-altering constitution is like an old man who still wears with attached fondness clothes in the fashion of his youth: what you see of him is the same; what you do not see is wholly altered.[2]

For Bagehot, the old man's fondness for the fashions of his youth suggests a subtler vision in which the appearance of continuity

I

belies the reality of change. The old man's body and the style of his clothes have remained externally consistent, while the man himself and the fashionability of those styles have altered substantially.

These two texts reveal three common ways that Victorian historical writers use the idea of old clothes to illustrate the passage of time. First, for both Mill's jacketless twenty-six-year-old and Bagehot's aging man, the stable size and shape of the individual garment throws into relief the continuity or change of the body itself. Second, the continual novelty of fashion ruthlessly renders older styles obsolete, such that Bagehot's old man's consistent wardrobe indexes his ever-increasing distance from youth and fashion. And third, the individual garment itself experiences wear and tear. As Bagehot acknowledges, the old man's clothes are only in the *fashion* of his youth—the actual garments are probably gone. In these ways, the interplay between clothing and the body-in-time can suggest multiple trajectories, often neutral or non-developmental, richly illustrating the perceptual difficulties of registering continuity and change. Bagehot furthermore suggests the role of a fleeting and iterative orality in marking the passage of time. The family "go on muttering" "repeat[ed] phrases" that are no longer apt.

Yet, as we see in Mill's unconvincing disavowal of the developmental narrative implied by the outgrowing of a child-sized jacket, the two passages also disclose a tension between what writers intend to illustrate through old clothes and what careful attention reveals: that clothing persistently frustrates its instrumental use in historical narrative. The third passage I will discuss illustrates the way that Victorian fiction often exploits clothing's temporal complexity in order to defamiliarize the idea of change over time. Here is how Charles Dickens's *Little Dorrit* (1857) introduces the minor character of Mr. Nandy as a holdover from a bygone past:

> Anybody may pass, any day, in the thronged thoroughfares of the metropolis, some meagre, wrinkled, yellow old man ... This old man is always a little old man. If he were ever a big old man, he has shrunk into a little old man; if he were always a little old man, he has dwindled into a less old man. His coat is of a colour, and cut, that never was the mode anywhere, at any period. Clearly, it was not made for him, or for any individual mortal. Some wholesale contractor measured Fate for five thousand coats of such quality, and Fate has lent this old coat to this old man, as one of a long unfinished line of many old men.

It has always large dull metal buttons, similar to no other buttons ....
Yet this old man wears these clothes with a certain unaccustomed air
of being dressed and elaborated for the public ways; as though he
passed the greater part of his time in a nightcap and gown.[3]

The passage presents an apparently straightforward contrast
between the modernity of the city and the antiquity of Mr. Nandy.
What is particularly striking, however, is how Dickens expresses
this point through clothes. The coat is both a metonym and a
metaphor for Mr. Nandy's advanced age. It throws into relief
the latter half of the trajectory whose beginnings Mill sketches.
That is, Mr. Nandy's steady diminution of size—from big to little,
little to less—seems to indicate his ever-shrinking relevance to the
contemporary world. The coat, like age itself, is a deindividuating uniform. Victorian fiction trains us to look away from figures
like Mr. Nandy in order to see the world as progressive and progressing. Yet his quietly perplexing coat fits this narrative poorly.
The coat is out of style, but in a strange way—"of a colour, and
cut, that never was the mode anywhere, at any period." Whereas
Bagehot's old man's clothes embody an identifiable past style of
his youth, Mr. Nandy's coat is in a style that was never in style.
The garment is glaringly non-contemporary, but it baffles efforts
to historicize it.

Were Mr. Nandy's coat real, we could fairly assert that
although it may never have been fashionable among clothes-conscious people, it must at least have been suitable at a time and
place, among a particular group. Indeed, the passage acknowledges the coat's ubiquity, distinguishing "the mode" from what
people actually wear. The fashion historian Elizabeth Wilson goes
further, arguing with Bagehot and against Dickens's narrator that
all styles of clothing originated as high fashion, though time can
easily erase this history.[4] Mr. Nandy's coat is thus not only confusingly old-fashioned and ill-fitting because second-hand, ready-made, and a stable size atop a shrinking body. It is also strangely
resilient—unlike many real garments, this coat will survive its
wearer. The passage envisions the coat as mass-manufactured,
a phenomenon that does not truly get started until later in the
century, rendering it also more modern than we might expect.
Thus, Mr. Nandy's clothes are both a holdover of the past and
a harbinger of the future—their aesthetic, size, and condition
static despite the changes around them. This interplay between

the garment, the aging body, and time itself that we see in Mill, Bagehot, and Dickens is an invitation to rethink questions about the theorization, representation, and experience of progress in Victorian literature. These readings of clothing point to a broader tension that I analyze in this book between what the ideology of progress wants to do with these indices of non-progressive time—I'll call them irregular survivors—and what these survivors themselves seem to say. Progress would ignore them, code them as vestigial, or imagine their inevitable, imminent decline. And yet they show us that rather than a rapid, orderly march of progress, history is layered and multiple, characterized by stasis, regress, cyclicality, and rupture.

∽

Temporality and Progress in Victorian Literature argues that Victorian literature uses traces of a lingering past to theorize time as non-progressive and discontinuous. For decades, the dominant view in Victorian studies has been that the period's economic, political, and intellectual developments led to a broad sense that time was defined by continuous improvement, an argument outlined in Jerome H. Buckley's influential *The Triumph of Time* (1966). Moreover, scholars held, this master narrative of progress was both substantiated by positivistic or empirical analysis and evident across Victorian writings. Yet Buckley himself hints at the complexity of the issue when he argues that the writings of Thomas Babington Macaulay, Lord Acton, and Bagehot, "supported by the somewhat less emphatic avowals of Dr. Arnold, Mill, Morley, Kingsley, Huxley, and many others, reaffirmed the eighteenth-century idea of progress as a primary dogma of the Victorian period."[5] In this account, Buckley brushes past the "less emphatic" nature of many of the "avowals" of progress and suggests, furthermore, that the idea is paradoxically quintessential of both the Victorian period and the eighteenth century, a telling sign of the way that theories of progress repeatedly rely on forms of repetition and return.

In recent years, historians have qualified the idea that the Victorians unilaterally embraced progressive history, or what, following Herbert Butterfield's early twentieth-century formulation, we have called the "whig interpretation of history."[6] J. W. Burrow's *A Liberal Descent* (1981) nuances Buckley's thesis in observing that whig history was not simply the belief in continuous progress but rather the result of what Burrow calls "the

Whig compromise," in which writers appeal to an ancient English constitution that was born perfect but is nonetheless always improving.[7] Peter J. Bowler's *The Invention of Progress* (1989) identifies a cyclical model of progress embraced in the Liberal Anglican tradition, in which the rise and fall of individual civilizations contributes to an overarching divine plan.[8] Yet despite revisionist work, Buckley's thesis remains essentially intact. Michael Bentley's *Modernizing England's Past* (2005) observes broadly that what came to be known as whig history "so dominated the way in which the Victorians' past became framed that it becomes hard to think of anybody writing then who did not in some sense reflect its preoccupations."[9] Martin Hewitt (2006) observes that the Victorian chronotype was characterized, among other things, by a "grand whiggish narrative of progress" that was challenged only at the end of the century.[10] Likewise, Mark Bevir (2017) describes the Victorian period as "the heyday of what might be called 'developmental historicism,'" in which history was treated "as a progressive unfolding of principles such as character, sociability, reason, and liberty."[11]

Literary scholarship reflects the same view. Citing Burrow, Bowler, and Bentley, Billie Melman (2012) observes that "a notion of onward progress and its adjacent belief that history had a direction, from the past to the future via an ameliorative present, predominated in Victorians' senses of their own and other people's pasts."[12] Similarly, Sue Zemka (2018) asserts that "a belief in progress was so deeply embedded in nineteenth-century Britain that it was one of those beliefs for which there was no outside," and that "the nineteenth-century *idea* of history was unthinkable apart from the *form* of progress."[13]

At the same time, literary scholars have long observed the non- and anti-developmental trajectories within fiction that is typically associated with progressive development. For example, Mary Mullen observes that, particularly in colonial Ireland but also elsewhere, nineteenth-century "realism's contradictory dynamic itself counters development through anachronisms that create anti-developmental narratives."[14] Elisha Cohn argues that "lyrical moments" of non-purposive stasis regularly interrupt the *Bildungsroman*.[15] For both Mullen and Cohn, the departure from progress is the prerogative of literature, and yet careful readings of nineteenth-century philosophy of history have observed that here too, the idea of progress is not theorized unproblematically. In a more recent chapter, Bentley comments that in the period between 1815 and 1870, progressive history "has a paradigmatic force, but it requires equally forceful containment,"[16] while Helen Kingstone similarly remarks that the evidence "does not support any monolithic narrative of progress" in Victorian history writing.[17] I join these scholars in arguing that both literature and philosophy of history in the Victorian period repeatedly fail to theorize progressive linear temporality.

My book contributes to a broader scholarly challenge of the Buckley thesis by considering how the irregular life-cycles of individuals and objects undermine Victorian progress. The ideology of progress requires continuity, and yet it permits only very particular forms of endurance over time, rendering progress difficult to experience or narrate. Victorian literature richly stages the challenges of representing progress—challenges that are already evident in history writing, as we saw in Mill and Bagehot above. On the one hand, writers and characters repeatedly confront holdovers—like the aging person or the formerly fashionable object—that insist on the essential sameness of past, present, and future. On the other, they encounter evidence of the radical disconnection of individual moments from each other—in the form of fleeting conversations or sudden deaths. In texts by Thomas Babington Macaulay, Benjamin Disraeli, William Makepeace Thackeray, Harriet Martineau, Thomas Hardy, and others, I find numerous alternative conceptions of time theorized against the emerging dominance of a progress narrative. The book thereby uncovers the heterogenous shapes of time imagined by Victorian literature—regress, cyclicality, stasis, and rupture. These shapes are not simply progress's others, but rather constituent elements of progress's theorization. They reveal progress narratives to be ideological and inadequate, suggesting that there can be no history (things happening), only historiography (ways of understanding things that happen).

My readings demonstrate, first, that rejections of the progressive vision are possible throughout the century, and second, that attempts to represent or imagine progress repeatedly falter, becoming more fraught than writers seem to anticipate. This latter proposition reflects that for the Victorians, as perhaps for Victorianists, the idea of progress remains appealing even when closer scrutiny—of history, of literature, or of people's own lives—does not support it. As I show in Chapter 1, the commitment to linear progress among historians and theorists of history is certainly strengthening over the course of the century, notwithstanding the apparent challenge presented by the non-progressive temporalities of evolutionary theory. Yet even historians' strongest assertions are footnoted by caveats and bounded by limitations. In the subsequent chapters, I argue that literary writers were confronting and even exploiting similar problems. This book analyzes texts written between approximately 1825 and 1890, the period during which the ideology of liberal progress is thought to be ascendant. And I do not look at lyric poetry, a genre or mode generally associated with temporal suspension, notwithstanding recent work by Monique Morgan, Irmtraud Huber, and Mark Canuel that emphasizes the lyric's complex temporalities and reliance on developmental forms.[18] Rather, I examine precisely those genres—history writing, the historical novel, the *Bildungsroman*, life-writing—in which we would expect the ideology of progress to be evident. *Temporality and Progress in Victorian Literature* identifies a canon of literary texts that not only represent but also embody non-linearity, in that they are particularly difficult to place in the "parade model" of literary history, in which writers or texts march past in an orderly, linear procession.[19] Whether immediately considered old-fashioned (Hardy's *Wessex Tales*, analyzed in Chapter 5), or stirring up decade-old gossip (Harriette Wilson's *Memoirs*, Chapter 4), or published many years after being written (Martineau's *Autobiography*, also Chapter 4), or recursively revised after publication (Disraeli's *Vivian Grey*, Chapter 2), these texts confound the timelines of literary history. This book began from an attempt to find for myself the basis in Victorian history writing of the progressive history that is supposedly dominant in the period—and its expressions in nineteenth-century literature. What I found instead was that the history writing itself was puzzled and ambivalent while the literature either enthusiastically detracted from or struggled to represent progress.

In order to illustrate the difficulty of representing progress in Victorian literature, I track instances of irregular survival—individuals and objects who linger or evanesce on a timeline that is hard to reconcile with a progress narrative. Smooth and continuous progress requires that after someone or something implicates the larger narrative, they recede and are replaced. As Victorian literature shows us, such a trajectory is rare. These unsynchronized lifespans present two complementary problems for the representation of continuous progress. First, there is the question of how to account for holdovers of the past that continue to command attention, refusing to be coded as vestigial. Raymond Williams theorizes this concept as the residual, that which "has been effectively formed in the past, but it is still active in the cultural process ... as an effective element of the present."[20] These occur on a number of registers—formerly fashionable objects, powerful elderly figures, and architectural ruins. Second, there is the issue of how to understand sudden losses that reveal the disconnectedness of individual moments in time. These are experiences like unexpected death, which breaks time into discrete segments of before and after, or conversation, which seems to reflect the ephemerality of the present. The topics I touch on in this book—unfashionable waistcoats, aging courtesans, remembered conversations—are united in that their temporal duration suggests that time is non-progressive and discontinuous. Their seemingly disparate nature reveals how such a subversion of progress saturates Victorian literature. Recognizing these irregular survivors as a coherent category of analysis allows us to see both the appeal and the challenge of apprehending progress on a disaggregated or personal level.

Taking up the residual, my readings trace the way that Victorian texts represent two apparent embodiments of a lingering past: the aging person and the formerly fashionable or aesthetically dated object. These individuals and things can seem different, but progress would treat them similarly, as antiquated holdovers of the past, or what Williams calls the archaic.[21] In Victorian literature, however, older people and things often prove profoundly disruptive, much more like Williams's residual, that which is formed in the past but active in the present. The texts I analyze in this book trouble the logic of gradual decline and generational replacement by which a progress narrative would dispense with the elderly, who reveal instead the multiplicity of time. These texts see old and young as engaged either in protracted and inconclusive contestations (as in Disraeli's *Coningsby* or Oliphant's *Kirsteen*), or in moments of storytelling that lead nowhere and reveal the monumentality of loss (as in Hardy's *The Trumpet-Major*). In the texts I study, the personal experience of time, whether the individual is elderly or simply reflecting on their earlier life (as in Wilson's *Memoirs*), often suggests a discontinuous or segmented temporality—time as stasis punctuated by untheorizable rupture.

Introduction: The Unfashionable Age

Like the elderly person, the formerly fashionable or aesthetically dated object might easily be understood as archaic and imminently disappearing. Yet in Victorian literature such objects often outlive their moment in vogue and experience rediscovery or reinterpretation. In real life, the trajectory of the quotidian object is nearly always one of decline. In the Victorian texts I analyze, however, such objects remain remarkably resilient—like the propaganda print, a "hieroglyphic profile of Napoleon" that survives in an old woman's attic in *The Trumpet-Major*.[22] The elderly individual and the out-of-date object thus undermine any narrative of uniform, continuous change, let alone one of growth or improvement. These embodiments of endurance often suggest instead a temporality in which past and present are indistinguishable. My Introduction's title, "The Unfashionable Age," thus reflects both a growing alienation in the Victorian period from the shrinking present of fashionable temporality and a gnawing anxiety about the looming obsolescence of later life.

Yet the ideology of progress is challenged not only by these forms of temporal continuity but also by discontinuities that rupture and segment time. Victorian writers often explore this phenomenon through conversation, which serves as a reminder of what is instantaneously lost to posterity. In "On History Again," Thomas Carlyle calls the tongue a "historic organ" and contrasts the vast number of words that can be spoken with the smaller number that can be written, using speech as synecdoche for time's fleeting, uncapturable excess.[23] As we see in Disraeli's later revisions to his early silver-fork novel *Vivian Grey* (1826), for example, Victorian writers are fascinated by the idea that the past was constituted by unrecorded, sparkling conversations of a kind that is no longer possible under the social strictures and literary conventions of modernity. This literary interest in a lost spoken past develops just as direct speech is increasingly rejected in history writing. In "History," Macaulay criticizes Herodotus and especially Thucydides for inventing historical speech and, conflictingly, for misrepresenting its style.[24] Macaulay's twofold objection reflects not only a nascent disciplinary norm but also a growing sense in the nineteenth century that speech—its patterns, cadences, or words—is subject to historical changes that exceed the progressive narrative. Too brief, too fleeting to implicate progress, speech requires writers to theorize historical rupture or suspension.

Taken together, these indices of irregular survival in Victorian literature make visible temporal inertia and fleetingness that complicate Walter Benjamin's famous account of the nineteenth century as the era of "homogeneous, empty time."[25] In that paradigm, time moves forward at a steady pace, witnessing linear progress or development. Such a vision was theorized as a historical and cultural aberration—Benedict Anderson traces its emergence in the West around the end of the eighteenth century, when it displaced an earlier Christian sense of temporal simultaneity;[26] Reinhart Koselleck identifies a similar moment "at which eager expectations" began to "diverge and remove themselves from all previous experience."[27] And progress is generally understood to have died in the early twentieth century, whether it "met its Waterloo on the Somme,"[28] or with the breakup of European empires, or with Einsteinian relativity.[29] A parallel narrative associates literary Modernism or the avant-garde with temporal experimentation, rupture, shock, and a radical break from a bourgeois, liberal past.[30] Yet I demonstrate that even in the time and place of progress's apparent heyday, continuous improvement was appealing conceptually but remained difficult to experience, narrate, or represent. Surrounded by historical trajectories that exceed or are inconsistent with progress, Victorian writers theorize a range of alternatives.

The argument provides an important supplement to critiques of Victorian liberal progress from the political left—within the period and in modern scholarship—and, for that matter, to recent defenses of liberalism from such critiques, like Amanda Anderson's *Bleak Liberalism*.[31] Notwithstanding the value of these debates, I use irregular survivors to highlight Victorian literary critiques of progress that are coming from the political right. In this way, I offer a counterpoint to scholarship that has emphasized the politically radical uses of nostalgia in Victorian literature, such as Carolyn Lesjak's *The Afterlife of Enclosure: British Realism, Character, and the Commons*.[32] As Alex Murray also notes, "the desire to conserve the past, or more specifically to mine it for alternatives to the (capitalist) present, has been an intrinsic feature of the British radical tradition since its inception."[33] This slippage between pure conservation and something more like mining reflects, as Williams observes, that residual elements can be either oppositional to or incorporated into the dominant paradigm. The survivors I trace in this book are certainly oppositional to the dominant paradigm of progress. In this way, they are inconsistent with what John Skorupski calls a "practical conservatism" that seeks to preserve or maintain a status quo through limited reforms and modernizations.[34] Even Edmund Burke acknowledges that "a state without the means of some change is without the means of its conservation."[35] Rather, the non-progressive temporalities I trace in this book are best understood as anti-liberal, seeking radical breaks, returns, and suspensions inconsistent with moderate conservatism. As I'll show, these texts reflect dogmatic reaction rather than radical critique.

Three conversations about progress: Liberal history, the object, and the person

In order to advance my argument that irregular survivors of the past in Victorian literature undermine the progress narrative, I synthesize three ongoing critical conversations: the reconsideration of nineteenth-century liberal history; the analysis of the temporalities of objects in material culture studies and fashion theory; and the examination of the trajectories of the life by age studies and queer temporality. These three disparate conversations share an interest in the way that change over time is reified, witnessed, or experienced. I draw upon their structural similarity: in each of these areas, scholarship highlights experiences of irregular survival in which temporal duration or ephemerality troubles the specific model of rise, fall, and replacement that progress demands. Triangulating these methodologies allows me both to reveal the conceptual difficulties of narrating progress and to establish the range of alternative temporal shapes imagined by Victorian literature.

Postcolonial scholarship on nineteenth-century liberal history has rightly emphasized the extent to which progress was always imagined as limited to white European men. In *The Intimacies of Four Continents* (2015), Lisa Lowe describes liberalism as "a project that includes at once both the universal promises of rights, emancipation, wage labor, and free trade, as well as the global divisions and asymmetries on which the liberal tradition depends, and according to which such liberties are reserved for some and wholly denied to others."[36] Such denials have a temporal dimension as well. Dipesh Chakrabarty famously observes that the key texts of liberal progress "consigned Indians, Africans, and other 'rude' nations to an imaginary waiting room of history."[37] Amy Allen, citing James Tully, similarly remarks that "the language of progress and development is the language of oppression and domination for two-thirds of the world's people."[38] Accordingly, work in Victorian studies has considered the imperialist and racist discursive formulation of nineteenth-century progress as well as the rhetorical strategies of writers responding to their own exclusion from it, particularly from the late nineteenth century onward. Nasser Mufti and Jed Esty have each charted the resistance to progressive temporality in imperial contexts in the historical novel and modernist *Bildungsroman* respectively, though Esty acknowledges that modernist writers "violate a progressive logic they presume to have existed, resist linear historicism that is in part projected back onto Victorian realism by writers eager to assume the mantle of an experimental literary future."[39] Feminist scholarship has similarly considered representations of women's distinctive experience of the lifespan in the novel of development.[40] Recent theorists of queer temporality have explored the complex relationship between queer identity and progress, whether theorizing the antifuturity of queerness or observing the forcible conscription of queer subjects into the narrative that "it gets better" over time.[41]

Temporality and Progress in Victorian Literature complements these efforts by focusing on a different problem with progress, observing that beyond its social limitations, progress proves inherently difficult to experience, narrate, or theorize, raising foundational questions about what it means to live in time. Chakrabarty notes the role of Mill's "On Liberty" and "On Representative Government" in denying political rights to Black and brown subjects of the British Empire by suggesting that they were not ready for progress.[42] But as I discuss in Chapter 1, Mill's other work struggles to imagine what historical progress might look like even for white people. Of course, this empty center amplifies just how violent the ideology of progress is, but it also reveals conceptual problems at the heart of the idea of progress that are not simply the result of its racist and sexist exclusions, but rather a sign that progress is impossible to disaggregate to the level of the subject, no matter who that subject is.

As a critical analysis of hegemonic linear time that finds it intact nowhere, with internal cracks in its foundations, *Temporality and Progress* makes two interventions. First, it works to nuance our understanding of the liberal progressive temporality to which

Introduction: The Unfashionable Age 13

postcolonial, feminist, and queer theorists are responding, showing how progress often cannot accommodate any individual's experience and is difficult to narrate in detail. To that end, although I discuss texts like *Vanity Fair* and *Wessex Tales* that are on the margins of the historical novel, I move also beyond that genre to life-writing and the *Bildungsroman* to consider what Victorian writers thought progress might look and feel like in the present.[43] Complicating the view of Victorian literature as suffused with a sense of progressive time, I argue that while the question of progress was indeed central, progress often eludes apprehension.

My second intervention highlights a particular strand of resistance to Victorian liberalism, one associated with conservative or reactionary politics. The writers and characters who detract from liberal progress in this book do so not because they are excluded from it on the basis of their identity. Rather, they see as decline what others see as progress, reflecting a conservative desire to preserve the status quo or resurrect the past, *or* they understand the appearance of progress as an illusion that belies a fundamental stasis—a politically prismatic lens. In this way, I depart from another node of recent scholarship on nineteenth-century liberal history that has considered how contingency and chance spurred writers to imagine proliferating alternative possibilities. Work by Catherine Gallagher, Jason Jones, Anders Engberg-Pedersen, Michael Tondre, and Adam Grener has examined how new developments in military history, cartography, mathematics, and probability theory led to literary explorations that resist determinism.[44] I trace a different, anti-contingent strain in nineteenth-century history and literature, one that closes down lateral alternatives in favor of a vertical sense of unified time. In this way, I build upon recent scholarship—by Edward Adams and Miriam Elizabeth Burstein, for example—that has emphasized the persistence of older ways of thinking about history in the nineteenth century.[45]

In making these two interventions into our understanding of how nineteenth-century progressive history is theorized and represented, I have drawn upon a second critical conversation: the analysis of the complex temporalities of clothing and other aesthetically dated material objects. In this way, I extend the method Elaine Freedgood develops in *The Ideas in Things*. Whereas in Freedgood's readings, attention to "the things of realism" results in "a return of the imperial repressed," I focus on material details that open up a rich and layered sense of time.[46] Clothing proves to be a particularly fruitful example of the category of irregular survival in Victorian literature, and its conceptual framework provides a portable model for thinking about a broad range of survivors.

Following Thorstein Veblen and Virginia Woolf, Victorian literary scholarship most often analyzes fictional clothing in relation to gender and class—recent work inspired by Thing Theory and New Materialism has rarely considered clothing, since as Celia Marshik observes, Thing Theory "tends to prioritize things that are around, but not *on*, the body."[47] In considering clothing as epiphenomenal of social oppression, scholarship has drawn upon powerful economic and sociological theories, like Veblen's influential argument that dress "functions as an index of the wealth of its wearer—or, to be more precise, of its owner," with this distinction reflecting the special role of women's clothing in displaying male economic power and ensuring female subservience.[48] Woolf throws cold water on the idea that clothing might prove additionally meaningful, arguing in "Modes and Manners of the Nineteenth Century" (1910) that "to discover soberly how far thought has expressed itself in clothes, and manners as we call them, is ... difficult. There is the temptation to hook the two together by the most airy conjectures."[49] This specter of "airy conjectures" haunts scholarly analyses of nineteenth-century fashion. Even Rebecca N. Mitchell's comments on the cultural significance of Victorian fashion concede that "it can be tempting to think of fashion as a linear progression evolving alongside but independent of major political, social and industrial movements, with only sporadic imbrication."[50] Yet both recent fashion theorists and nineteenth-century writers insist upon fashion's meaningfulness. Fashion theory observes that Veblen "cannot account for the form that fashion changes take. Why did the bustle replace the crinoline, the leg of mutton sleeve the sloping shoulder?"[51] Writing around the turn of the twentieth century, Veblen and Woolf are responding to a significant strand of Victorian thinking that understands fashion's changes as significant, if in abstract and uncertain ways.

Veblen's legacy also ascribes to fashion the temporality of continual novelty—he argues that "flux and change and novelty are demanded by the central principle of dress—conspicuous waste."[52] Yet fashion's relationship to progressive time is complex. Lauren Gillingham emphasizes "fashion's dual temporality—its inflection as transient and intransigent."[53] That is, on one level, fashion is associated with modernity and progress as a "vehicle for articulating a new consciousness of the unprecedented rapidity of social change."[54] Daniel Leonhard Purdy likewise observes that "fashion's obsession with change, its constant search for the newest design, gave it a formal similarity with other systems that demanded continuous innovation."[55] Yet on another level, fashion tends to reveal both the limitations and the ambivalent character of change over time. Gillingham comments that "far from promoting change, fashion serves to preserve the power and privilege of the ruling class."[56] The anonymous article "Modern Beau Brummellism" (1867) bemoans that "the lowest menials endeavor to imitate, to the best of their powers, the grandest lords and ladies in the land"[57]—reflecting a sense that imitative clothing rightfully fails to level natural hierarchies. Like nineteenth-century whig history itself, as I will demonstrate in Chapter 1, fashion is understood to have originated in the departure from a feudal paradigm in which clothes were dictated by profession or class,[58] a tradition still lingering at least into the eighteenth century.[59] Thus, fashion could be associated with social mobility and democracy or alternately with the stable or increasing social stratifications of industrial capitalism. The link between fashion and progress is thus intimate but paradoxical.

Clothing's complex temporalities in Victorian discourse are especially evident in Carlyle's *Sartor Resartus* (1833–4). Perhaps exemplifying the airy conjectures Woolf had in mind, the enigmatic German philosopher Diogenes Teufelsdröckh asserts that clothes embody abstract or spiritual ideas: "Matter exists only spiritually, and to represent some idea, and *body* it forth. Hence Clothes, as despicable as we think them, are so unspeakably significant."[60] Yet that significance remains elusive and the temporality of clothing vexed. For Teufelsdröckh, clothes embody time's phoenix-like spirit of death and rebirth. Referring to the dandy, he asks "is there not in this Life-devotedness to Cloth, in this so willing sacrifice of the Immortal to the Perishable, something (though in reverse order) of that blending and identification of Eternity with Time, which, as we have seen, constitutes the Prophetic character?"[61] Yet clothes do not just connect past and present but also reflect our postlapsarian state, our fallen departure from Edenic nakedness. In contrast to the author of "Modern Beau Brummellism," Teufelsdröckh laments that clothing is a precondition of economic inequality. He asks "Are we Opossums; have we natural Pouches, like the Kangaroo? Or how, without Clothes, could we possess the master-organ, soul's-seat, and true pineal gland of the Body Society: I mean a PURSE?"[62]

Later in the century, Oscar Wilde likewise reflects a keen sense of the temporal richness of clothing—he briefly resurrected knee-breeches. In "The Suitability of Dress" (1882), he affirms Teufelsdröckh's or Carlyle's sense of the significance of clothing, claiming "A history of dress would be a history of minds; for dress expresses a moral idea; it symbolizes the intellect and disposition of a nation."[63] He also observes with ambivalence the ostensible shift away from more rigid sartorial mores, suggesting that "dress and vocation should be in harmony."[64]

As these writers begin to reflect, Veblen's paradigm of continual novelty grossly oversimplifies fashion history's cycles of repetition and periods of stasis. On the level of the specific style, there is a "cyclical process whereby individual designs gain currency only to be abandoned and replaced," but then perhaps rediscovered.[65] Purdy suggests that, already in the eighteenth and nineteenth centuries, fashionability manifested as connoisseurship of fashion history, an anticipation of the heterogeneity of styles we associate with postmodernism.[66] Timothy Campbell's *Historical Style: Fashion and the New Mode of History, 1740–1830* (2016) has shown the imbrication of fashion with modern conceptions of temporality in the Romantic period.[67] As Wilde's knee-breeches indicate, later nineteenth-century fashion, too, often had a historical consciousness and retro sensibility.

This book recovers a Victorian tradition of using clothing in robust ways to meditate on history's unfolding. I build on Gillingham's recent analysis of how nineteenth-century novels "draw from fashion's citational practices a model for conceptualizing the present's relationship with the past."[68] In *Vanity Fair*, for example, as I discuss in Chapter 3, Jos Sedley's sustained commitment to colorful waistcoats has a shifting meaning over the course of his life, suggesting a form of queer maturation through stasis, a version of what we see in Bagehot's aging man. As this example reflects, the irregular survival of clothes often suggests that time is static, repetitive, and uneven. Yet rather than focus on clothing alone, I situate it within a wider Victorian interest in the uneven lifespans of material culture, using insights from the study of clothing to illuminate the non-progressive temporalities of other irregular survivors in Victorian literature. Looking at objects that seem clearly dated—like propaganda prints, medieval ruins, and ceremonial weapons—I observe how they thematize their relationship to time by appearing to crystalize a particular moment. And then I uncover how they ultimately complicate the narratives they initially appear to support.

This insistent incongruity between a progress narrative and the unpredictable temporal trajectory of the isolated object is not limited to objects but rather applies to people too. For this reason, my reconsideration of the representation of nineteenth-century progress draws upon scholarship that examines the temporal trajectories of the individual life. Whereas theorists of queer temporality have interrogated how the coercive expectations of the normative life-course are construed positively as growth or progress, scholars in age studies have emphasized that individual aging is often imagined as a process of decline. Simone de Beauvoir quotes the nineteenth-century French critic Sainte-Beuve using a horticultural metaphor to encapsulate this ideology: "We harden in some places and rot in others: we never ripen."[69] Recent studies by Helen Small, Kay Heath, Karen Chase, and Andrea Charise have analyzed the theorization of aging as decline in the wake of nineteenth-century biopolitical and industrial developments—and the resistance of individuals and texts to that ideology.[70] Complicating this picture, Rebecca Rainof argues that mid-life adults are in fact central to nineteenth-century progress narratives because they experience "gradualist plots of maturity," in which change is so slow as to be imperceptible.[71] This gradualism is not an anathema to progress but rather a sign of the slow and smooth development central to British national identity, forged in contrast to the political upheavals of France.[72] I join Rainof in pushing back against the idea that the aging individual is discarded by the progress narrative, considering texts in which older characters experience a static vitality that challenges the assumption of change over time.

My book brings an age studies critique to bear on the analysis of nineteenth-century ideas about history, considering writers' use of the categories of "youth" and "age" in imagining progress. To that end, although I spotlight minor older characters like *Vanity Fair*'s Lord Steyne, I focus not on the elderly per se, but rather on the uneven movement of the individual through time, following Devoney Looser's advocacy for a dynamically conceived "ag*ing* studies" that considers the whole life course.[73]

The normative experience—from birth through death—is sometimes called the "life-*cycle*" for its perceived symmetry, and though I prefer the more neutral "life*span*," the idea of a cycle suggests the life's subversion of linearity. Following this insight, I explore how Victorian texts complicate youth's association with growth and development. The *Bildungsroman* and the marriage plot appear to narrate a vision of progress that culminates in early adulthood, "channeling the chaotic energies of youth into the normative containers of middle-class employment and domestic life," as Jacob Jewusiak puts it.[74] I analyze texts that avoid and rewrite these plots. In Hardy's *Wessex Tales* (Chapter 5), for example, courtship fails and stalls. In *Vanity Fair* (Chapter 3), plots extend beyond marriage or refuse it. In Disraeli's *Vivian Grey* (Chapter 2) and Wilson's *Memoirs* (Chapter 4), narratives of professional development refuse to develop. Certainly, texts like Disraeli's *Coningsby* evince ageism, but youth, too, is a mixed and not wholly enviable state—just as likely to be going nowhere as to be on the rise. The texts I analyze in this book reveal how assumptions about the shape of the life repeatedly destabilize linear progress narratives that are possible only when abstracted from the individual.

Beyond the question of the temporal shape or direction of the life, aging also unfolds within a shifting dialectic of continuity and rupture. Observing that the organization of the lifespan into discrete stages is the product of "capitalist stratification" aided by the "demographic imagination," Jewusiak provides a "theory of the duration of aging that resists the sedimentation of life into analytical categories."[75] Jewusiak offers here an important contribution to understanding personal time as messily processual. Drawing upon his work, I observe that segmentation and discontinuity nonetheless routinely characterize the long life in nineteenth-century fiction and life-writing and are sometimes instrumentalized to undermine the idea that identity is inert or genealogical. In sedimentation and retrospective accumulation, texts like Martineau's *Autobiography*, as I explain in Chapter 4, find destabilizing multiplicity and potentiality that threaten to fracture her mature adult self.

Identifying commonalities among scholarly conversations on the lifespan of the individual, the trajectory of the fashion, and the mechanics of liberal progress itself, has allowed me to reveal how the irregularity of historical survival presents a foundational problem for the idea of continuous improvement. Taken together, the unsynchronized lifespans of objects and individuals in nineteenth-century literature provide diverse models for understanding non-progressive shapes of time, the way these shapes are perceived or experienced, and the question of time's continuity.

Overview of chapters

Chapter 1 establishes that the influential historical writings of the Victorian period struggle to theorize linear progress. Through a close analysis of essays on history by Macaulay and Carlyle as well as Mill's *System of Logic* (1843 and 1862) and a passage from Walter Scott's *Waverley* (1814), I argue that the dominance of the progressive theory of history and the positivist historical method has been consistently overstated in Victorian studies. Even at its most strident, the idea of progress is hemmed in by narrow limits, assailed by detractors, and torn between continuous and segmented models. The positivist method is similarly fraught and, moreover, proves difficult to reconcile with the period's most compelling history writing. This chapter sets the stage for the rest of the book by tracing the fault lines in historical discourse that are exploded in the literary texts I consider in the remaining chapters.

After Chapter 1's analysis of nineteenth-century historical writings whose influence on literature is often oversimplified, this book is organized roughly chronologically (even though the texts themselves thematize the complexity of linear chronology). Building on the previous chapter's account of the debate between continuous and segmented progress, Chapter 2 argues that Disraeli's fraught vision of progress-through-regress ultimately effects a stasis in which time is hyperactive but going nowhere, as we see in Disraeli's extensive use of topical, sparkling dialogue. Although scholars have read *Coningsby* (1844) and *Sybil* (1845) as novelizations of the Tory radical history Disraeli outlines in his nonfiction, I emphasize how these novels segment time, reading their aesthetics of immediacy in dialogue with his notorious *roman-à-clef*, *Vivian Grey* (1826 and 1853). In both his public persona and his fiction, Disraeli seemed to have a paradoxical relationship to time—undergoing successive sartorial transformations eerily reflective of the zeitgeist, while also defying expectations for the trajectory of a career. His novels feature older men who resist their reading as representatives of a debauched past being inexorably overtaken by a moral present. I argue instead that for Disraeli, the arc of the life ultimately challenges linear history, suggesting a vision of time as stasis punctuated by unseen rupture.

The book then shifts to consider not only the difficulty of narrating progress but also the rejection of it. Chapter 3 analyzes Thackeray's *Vanity Fair* (1848), focusing on the novel's representations of fashionable clothing and high-society life. I argue that Thackeray uses the temporal multiplicity and ambiguity of fashion to depict time as striated and multidimensional. In so doing, I challenge the critical paradigm that has long maligned attention-grabbing clothing in historical fiction as a kind of facile historicism. In dramatizing the persistence of older styles, offering multiple interpretations of apparently fashionable garments, and depicting the unsynchronized life cycles of clothes, *Vanity Fair* undermines the idea that to be historically situated is to keep pace with a rapid linear narrative. In a reading that draws upon the novel's interest in intergenerational power and aristocratic privilege as embodied by older men, I uncover similarities in Thackeray's and Disraeli's depictions of the overlaps, repetitions, and redundancies of temporal continuity. Moving between the poles they represent—between theorizing progress and rejecting it—has allowed me to survey the intractable rhetorical challenges to conceptualizing the continuous unfolding of time, challenges that encompass all sides of the debate over progress as time's direction.

My readings of aristocratic older men in Chapters 2 and 3 highlight the always strained relationship between historical progress and the trajectory of the individual life, even among powerful subjects. In Chapter 4, I turn to women's life-writing to trace diverging responses to the rhetorical dilemma posed by the patriarchal sense that a woman's social and sexual capital declines precipitously with age. Through an unusual comparison between the courtesan Harriette Wilson's *Memoirs* (1825) and Harriet Martineau's serious, canonical *Autobiography* (1877), I argue that these contrasting texts share an interest in an orality that breaks time into discrete, discontinuous pieces. Whereas Wilson's *Memoirs* use cyclical and static temporality to avoid grappling with aging, Martineau's *Autobiography* defiantly asserts her personal and professional development, informed by Comtean positivism. Although scholarship has emphasized Martineau's adoption of a male vision of *Bildung*, I query this picture by uncovering how she, like Disraeli, struggles to narrate individual development, and instead represents her life as radically split into distinct phases.

Focusing on the case of women's autobiography, this chapter explores the way that generic, ideological, and gender difference can collapse in representations of personal time. While the book is otherwise organized chronologically, Chapter 4's juxtaposition of historically overdetermined texts contributes to my recovery of a Victorian critique of linear literary history.

The final chapter returns to a more resistant response to progress, one that resembles the stasis and repetition of Wilson. Whereas scholarship has generally dismissed Hardy's *The Trumpet-Major* (1880) and *Wessex Tales* (1888) as failed historical fiction on the model of Walter Scott, I read these texts as using their historical settings to theorize stasis rather than Scott-style development. In their iterative and unresolvable courtship plots, their strange references to dates and years, and their interest in the continuity of the landscape, these texts represent time as inert and changeless. They use objects that have a deceptively straightforward temporality—clothing, propaganda, monuments—to reveal unexpected complexities. In their fascination with the young person's death, or its narrow avoidance, these texts re-signify old age as contingent rather than inevitable and find a reparative relationship between young and old, though one of shared loss rather than successive contestation. Analyzing Hardy's interest in the mechanisms through which things stay the same over time, my reading brings out unexpected connections to Thackeray, finding in these ideologically and generically contrasting texts a shared project in conceptualizing stasis.

The brief conclusion offers a glimpse of synthesis between women's professional development and the cycles of fashion in Margaret Oliphant's *Kirsteen* (1890). Returning to women's distinctive, ambivalent embrace of the idea of progress over the course of a long life, I read the relationships among clothing, family pedigree, and career trajectory in this novel as revealing that the appearance of passive continuity must be effortfully and retroactively constructed through creative anachronism. In so doing, I complicate the view of *fin de siècle* literary culture as interested in decadence, degeneration, or decline while historical culture confidently asserted progress.[76] Instead, I emphasize both the ongoing appeal of progress for literary writers and the perceptual difficulties of experiencing or narrating it. Thus, the Conclusion suggests some of the ways that progress endures as a privileged, and desired, conceptualization of personal time.

Coda

Throughout these readings, I demonstrate that progress was not as dominant or straightforward an idea in the Victorian period as scholars have assumed, pointing to the way that irregular survivors make progress difficult to register or represent. In the process, I also reject an implicit corollary assumption that popular consciousness or scholarship has since dispensed with progress narratives. Such a view is ironically something of a progress narrative itself. In *The Fate of Progress in British Romanticism* (2022), Mark Canuel traces a meta-history of Romanticist scholarship—and a parallel development in literary and cultural theory—in which each new analytical paradigm critiques the progress narratives inherent to the old paradigm, only to replace them with subtler progress narratives.[77] As Canuel observes, an "anti-progressive position ... does not actually produce alternatives to progressive discourses but rather offers new, but decidedly more covert, progressivisms."[78] Thus, he deftly outlines a widespread and persistent tendency in scholarship to be both implicitly progressive and explicitly hostile to the idea of progress. I make a related point in Chapter 1, demonstrating that the twenty-first century remains, if anything, more rather than less committed to the idea of empirically documented gradual improvement than was the Victorian period. Thus, my project traces not only nineteenth-century theories of historical simultaneity but also the simultaneity of historical theories, in the nineteenth century and today.

In its engagement with unspoken assumptions about change over time, this study's final contribution is methodological and answers calls for engaged presentism in Victorian literary studies. The 2015 "Manifesto of the V21 Collective," for example, argues that the field has problematically adopted a positivist historicism, characterized as "a mode of inquiry that aims to do little more than exhaustively describe, preserve, and display the past."[79] In critiquing the Manifesto, I build on work by Wai Chee Dimock and Eleanor Courtemanche that has observed the mutual constitution of historicism and presentism—Courtemanche has identified multiple "shadow presentisms" that lurk behind specific historicist approaches.[80] I argue that presentist and anachronistic modes of thought arise from and have ongoing resonance with the nineteenth-century historical theory that the V21 Manifesto caricatures. As I document in Chapter 1, presentist thinking develops in the nineteenth century alongside and in dialogue with self-conscious historical detachment. That is, both the engaged stance toward the past and the diversity of sophisticated theories of time that we associate with our modernity are theorized in the Victorian period in conjunction with linear progress.

Thus, my book contributes to and intervenes in a movement in Victorian studies that understands the period as profoundly contiguous with our present. This insight has led to important work emphasizing the nineteenth-century genealogies of many twenty-first-century problems, from climate change to white supremacy. Yet in the process it has, first, assumed that presentism is a modern critical insight rather than an integral feature of nineteenth-century thought, and second, often posited a flat sameness over time as the only alternative to triumphalist liberal progress. I seek to complicate this outlook by establishing the diverse ways that Victorian writers imagined the shapes of time. These shapes reflect several of progress's others—not only stasis, but also regress, cyclicality, and rupture—*and* they prove mutually constitutive of linear progress. To some extent, I draw upon the proliferating but unstable critical vocabulary of the "new time studies"—terms Susan Stanford Friedman catalogues as follows: "coexisting, collapsing, conjoined, crisscrossing, crumbled, deferred, discontinuous, disjunctive, disruptive, dissident, doubled, enmeshed, entangled, foreshortened, fractured, heterogeneous, interwoven, multidimensional, multidirectional, multiplanar, multiple, plural, simultaneous, stretched, and so forth."[81] Although I use a more limited selection of terms, I nonetheless challenge Friedman's claim that such temporalities were first "anticipated by early twentieth-century Euro-American modernism."[82] That is, I join Jim Reilly in arguing that nineteenth-century writers shared the insights about history and historical representation that are typically associated with a post-WWI episteme.[83] In the process, I suggest that a nagging sense of liberal progress's unfeasibility is not a late-breaking development, but a Victorian inheritance.

To be sure, my method is inevitably historicist, one of what Courtemanche has called the "self-reflexive critical historicisms" of Victorian studies.[84] That is, I consider texts within a thick context of their histories of composition, publication, and reception. Yet both in method and argument, I will emphasize that historicism registers not only change but also continuity. Historicism is the way to study how things endure, a vital project. By historicizing presentism, I reveal it as a way of living in time whose politics are multiple and vexed. Through a broad and nuanced sense of what historicism has done and can do, my work aims to model a kind of scholarship that is attentive to past-ness for the sake of the present.

There may appear a temptation to celebrate some of the temporalities I examine in this book for their resistance to an increasingly hegemonic progress associated with the violence of Victorian liberalism and imperialism—a desire to see progress's others as feminist, queer, crip, anti-colonial, or anti-racist. Yet I will demonstrate repeatedly that the politics of these modes is a mixed bag at best. In this way, I build on Michael Tondre's observation that temporal "multitudinousness ... does not necessarily lead to a politics of liberation."[85] Even when they detract forcefully from visions of liberal progress, texts like Hardy's *Wessex Tales* do not critique or offer alternatives to the elements of progress that are most problematic: progress's exclusions, its violence, or its calm complacency to existential threat. Instead, these texts either evince a conservative resistance to change or assert the impossibility of progress in ways that are arguably defeatist and self-fulfilling. As I discuss especially in Chapter 2 with respect to Disraeli, the others of progress evident in my texts prefigure the temporal theories of post-liberal political thought, not only on the left but also the right.

At its widest point, *Temporality and Progress* speaks to a modern longing for progress under bleak circumstances. Within higher education, funding cuts, adjunctification, and right-wing political attacks have resulted in a precarious present and future for scholars who critically analyze the past. Outside higher education, appeals to the past that reject gradual liberal progress have characterized the best and worst of political rhetoric. From where we stand—from a layered and uneven now—gradual linear progress has both been discredited as history and proven manifestly inadequate to our urgent problems, from authoritarianism and state violence to economic inequality and climate catastrophe. And yet despite the mainstream popularity of declinist rhetoric lamenting or trying to forestall the loss of American or Western global hegemony,[86] a quiet faith in gradual improvement still informs so many conversations about the future's horizons of expectation. Were true incremental progress possible, it might be better than the future we seem to face. This book traces the shape of the alternatives to progress, the visions of past, present, and future that reject continuous, gradual change in favor of something dramatically different. As history lives on, *Temporality and Progress* examines Victorian responses to never-more-relevant questions about the shapes of historical time, the dialectic between continuity and rupture, and the uses of the past in the present.

Note

1. Mill, "Spirit," 53.
2. Bagehot, *English Constitution*, 5.
3. Dickens, *Little Dorrit*, 363.
4. Wilson, *Adorned in Dreams*, 5.
5. Buckley, *Triumph*, 41.
6. Butterfield, *Whig Interpretation*, 4.
7. Burrow, *Liberal Descent*, 33.
8. Bowler, *Invention of Progress*, 50–1.
9. Bentley, *Modernizing*, 5. Following Bentley, I will use a lowercase w to refer to the historiographical outlook and practitioners of whig history as distinct from the capital-W Whig political party and its adherents. See Bentley, *Modernizing*, 6.
10. Hewitt, "Why the Notion," 432.
11. Bevir, *Historicism*, 2.
12. Melman, "Power of the Past," 467.
13. Zemka, "Progress," 812–13, 813.
14. Mullen, *Novel Institutions*, 11.
15. Cohn, *Still Life*, 5.
16. Bentley, "Shape and Pattern," 209.
17. Kingstone, *Victorian Narratives*, 20.
18. See Morgan, *Narrative Means*; Huber, *Time and Timelessness*; and Canuel, *The Fate of Progress*.
19. St. Clair, *The Reading Nation*, 2.
20. Williams, *Marxism and Literature*, 122.
21. Ibid.
22. Hardy, *Trumpet-Major*, 151.
23. Carlyle, "On History Again," 17–18.
24. Macaulay, "History," 388–90.
25. Benjamin, "Theses," 205.
26. Anderson, *Imagined Communities*, 24.
27. Koselleck, *Futures Past*, 284.
28. Bentley, *Modernizing*, 7. See also Bevir, *Historicism*, 18.

29. Friedman, "Alternatives to Literary History," 380.
30. See Friedman, "Alternatives to Literary History," but see also Schoenbach (*Pragmatic Modernism*) for a recent challenge to this reading of Modernism.
31. Anderson, *Bleak Liberalism*.
32. Lesjak, *The Afterlife of Enclosure*.
33. Murray, "Conservative," 372.
34. Skorupski, "The Conservative Critique," 401.
35. Burke, *Reflections on the French Revolution*, 19–20.
36. Lowe, *Intimacies of Four Continents*, 3.
37. Chakrabarty, *Provincializing Europe*, 8.
38. Allen, *End of Progress*, 3.
39. Esty, *Unseasonable Youth*, 18. See also Mufti, *Civilizing War*.
40. See Fraiman, *Unbecoming Women* and Abel, Hirsch, and Langland, *The Voyage In*.
41. See Edelman, *No Future* and Love, *Feeling Backward*.
42. Chakrabarty, *Provincializing Europe*, 8.
43. Notwithstanding the tradition analyzed by Burstein's *Victorian Reformations*, the historical novel tends to tell a narrative of development from one thing to another, whereas I highlight those texts that struggle to imagine progressive change. Also, like nineteenth-century history writing more broadly, as Kingstone has demonstrated, the historical novel tends to avoid the recent past and its perspectival challenges.
44. See Gallagher, *Telling It Like It Wasn't*; Jones, *Lost Causes*; Engberg-Pedersen, *Empire of Chance*; and Tondre, *The Physics of Possibility*.
45. Adams (*Victorian Practice of History*) charts the ongoing vitality of the epic tradition well into the twentieth century, whereas Burstein (*Victorian Reformations*) analyzes the adaption of an earlier Christian sense of temporal simultaneity to the new nineteenth-century genre of the controversial historical novel.
46. Freedgood, *Ideas in Things*, 1, 3.
47. Marshik, *At the Mercy of Their Clothes*, 13. For rich connections between clothing, gender, and class, see Hatter and Moody, *Fashion and Material Culture*; Shannon, *The Cut of His Coat*; and Mitchell's introduction to *Fashioning the Victorians*. For work inspired by Thing Theory and New Materialism, see Freedgood, *Ideas in Things*; Plotz, *Portable Property*; and Lutz, *Relics of Death*.
48. Veblen, "Economic Theory," 54.
49. Woolf, "Modes and Manners," 224.
50. Mitchell, *Fashioning*, 24.

51. Wilson, *Adorned in Dreams*, 50.
52. Veblen, "Economic Theory," 57.
53. Gillingham, *Fashionable Fictions*, 16.
54. Gillingham, "Novel of Fashion Redressed," 62.
55. Purdy, *Rise of Fashion*, 1.
56. Gillingham, *Fashionable Fictions*, 14.
57. "Modern Beau Brummellism," 137.
58. Gillingham, *Fashionable Fictions*, 3–4.
59. Davidoff and Hall, *Family Fortunes*, 410.
60. Carlyle, *Sartor Resartus*, 56.
61. Ibid., 207.
62. Ibid., 51.
63. Wilde, "Suitability of Dress," 137.
64. Ibid., 233.
65. Purdy, *Rise of Fashion*, 15.
66. Ibid., 15–16.
67. Campbell, *Historical Style*.
68. Gillingham, *Fashionable Fictions*, 23.
69. Beauvoir, *Coming of Age*, 380.
70. See Small, *The Long Life*; Heath, *Aging by the Book*; Chase, *The Victorians and Old Age*; and Charise, *Aesthetics of Senescence*.
71. Rainof, *Victorian Novel of Adulthood*, 6.
72. Ibid., 3.
73. Looser, "Age and Aging Studies," 27–8.
74. Jewusiak, *Aging, Duration, and the English Novel*, 4.
75. Ibid., 5, 7, 15.
76. See, for example, Arata, *Fictions of Loss* and Greenslade, *Degeneration, Culture, and the Novel*.
77. Canuel, *The Fate of Progress*, 10–12.
78. Ibid., 12.
79. "Manifesto," para. 1.
80. Courtemanche, "Beyond Urgency," 463; see also Dimock, "Editor's Column."
81. Friedman, "Alternatives to Literary History," 388.
82. Ibid., 379.
83. Reilly, *Shadowtime*.
84. Courtemanche, "Beyond Urgency," 462.
85. Tondre, *Physics of Possibility*, 17.
86. Esty, *Future of Decline*.

1

In Search of Progressive Time

This chapter argues that despite its apparent conceptual simplicity, progress proves difficult to theorize or imagine in nineteenth-century history and philosophy of history. Even the most confident Victorian theories of progress are beset by four temporal structures—regress, cyclicality, stasis, and rupture—that appear to oppose progress but that ultimately mutually constitute it. Like progress, regress is smoothly unidirectional, suitable to a grand narrative of transformation—as we see in famous decline narratives like Edward Gibbon's *Decline and Fall of the Roman Empire* (1776–89) or Allan Bloom's *The Closing of the American Mind* (1987). Both books are premised on an earlier rise, reflecting that cyclicality often presumes periods of progress followed later by stagnation and decline—as in the fourteenth-century North African philosopher Ibn Khaldun's *Muqaddimah* (1377) or Giovanni Arrighi's *The Long Twentieth Century* (1994). Victorian thinkers, too, confronted the possibility that progress was bounded or encompassed by cyclicality. For example, Duncan Bell notes the "intellectual dexterity" with which nineteenth-century imperial boosters attempted to exempt the British Empire from the "monitory teaching of the historical record" that "empires followed a predetermined trajectory: they rose, they declined and ultimately they fell."[1] Likewise, Peter J. Bowler observes a cyclical model of progress embraced in the Liberal Anglican tradition, in which the rise and fall of individual civilizations contributes to an overarching divine plan.[2] Whether progress subsumes cyclicality or cyclicality subsumes progress quickly becomes a speculative matter of scale and perspective.

Theories of progress also rely on stasis—or, in its more positive construction, continuity—usually in one of two ways. First, theories of smooth, gradual progress sometimes acknowledge that the experience can feel like stasis—on this basis Rebecca Rainof understands mid-life adults as emblematic of the extreme gradualism that progress favors. Second, and conversely, segmented theories of progress envision periods of stasis punctuated by great leaps forward. Thus, for segmented progress, rupture is also a necessary component. In its resistance to narration or theorization, rupture lurks behind all the other temporal forms, suggesting the power of instantaneous break. Sue Zemka has argued that the moment of sudden rupture is the "primary temporal unit and a central artistic conceit of industrial culture."[3] Yet as I will go on to show, nineteenth-century theories of progressive history avoid representing or theorizing rupture, just as they rely on it.

In the first section of this chapter, through readings of Thomas Babington Macaulay, John Stuart Mill, and Henry Thomas Buckle, I demonstrate that Victorian historians saw progress as limited in scope and constituted through its others. Focusing on the paradoxical role of the individual in progressive history, I demonstrate that although a positivist historical method and a vision of progress often appear to go hand in hand, they prove difficult to reconcile. The fundamental incommensurability of positivism and progress leads to the questions of methodology and experience that animate the rest of the chapter. In the second section, I consider nineteenth-century and modern theories of "presentism"—the active embrace of present concerns in the study of history—in order to show that Victorian progressive history was self-consciously presentist. I outline two mutually inconsistent kinds of presentism that whig history attempts to combine: a discontinuous or appositional model and a continuous or genealogical model. In so doing, I argue that presentism is by no means a correction to the delusion of objectivity that plagued nineteenth-century historians. Instead, presentism is actively theorized in Victorian history writing, underscoring the basic presentist insight that past and present are commensurable.

Departing from the earlier analysis of the paradoxical role of the individual in progressive history, the final section considers the more literary questions of how progress writ large is witnessed and how it relates to the individual life. I use Walter Scott's influential account, at the end of *Waverley*, of the different ways to perceive historical progress, whether diachronically through one's own experience or synchronically through intergenerational contact. Scott's model reveals that the life course serves as a rich but problematic metaphor for philosophy of history. For that reason, I end the chapter by analyzing the way that Jean-Jacques Rousseau and Friedrich Nietzsche attempt to use the trajectory of the individual life to explain the impossibility of civilizational progress. Although, as Bowler demonstrates, broad models of progress could encompass localized patterns of rise and fall, the structural parallel between the individual and the society tends to reveal the two as out of sync. I draw Rousseau and Nietzsche together with recent theories of queer temporality, which have also considered the challenges of intergenerational communication and solidarity. I use queer temporality to throw into relief hegemonic progressive temporality—"straight" time—revealing the instability of its theorization even in its clearest formulations. Throughout this chapter, I argue that the basic structure of progress narratives is more complex than it appears, that progress requires rhetorical and intellectual paradoxes, and that it seems to disappear under close scrutiny.

Positivist progress at its limits

As Reinhart Koselleck argues, "progress is a modern category whose content of experience and whose surplus of expectation was not available before the eighteenth century."[4] Progress has a complex relationship to earlier Christian temporalities. On one level, it constitutes an Enlightenment revision of the Christian conception of linear time established by Augustine's rejection of cyclicality in *The City of God*.[5] On another level, it rejects the Christian historiography of earthly societal decline leading to apocalypse and a "divine Jerusalem ... that would only be realized after the end of history."[6] Yet even in the eighteenth century, major thinkers are divided on the question of progress, with the Marquis de Condorcet more sanguine but David Hume and Immanuel Kant more skeptical.[7] Koselleck observes that Diderot "saw a catastrophe, analogous to the cycles of antiquity, threatening on the horizon," and argues that "even Voltaire ... remained entirely reserved with respect to any optimism."[8]

In the Victorian period, the idea that history unfolds as gradual, gentle, and inexorable progress evolved into what, following Herbert Butterfield, we have called the "whig interpretation of history."[9] Subsequent scholarship complicated Butterfield's account of whig history as simply continuous progress. J. W. Burrow has established that whig history initially reflected a paradox he calls "the [w]hig compromise," in which writers both appeal to an ancient ideal English constitution and identify ongoing, continuous progress.[10] Although the progressive vision became dominant, Victorian whig history could still emphasize the ancient constitutionalism, as it does in the work of Tories like William Stubbs and Benjamin Disraeli, as I discuss in this next chapter. This more conservative vision of progress undergirds what Mary Mullen has called a path-dependent temporality, "which claims that organizations make decisions at 'critical junctures' and that subsequent developments reinforce these decisions."[11] Thus, the Victorian idea of progress—like the modern idea of progress—is a two-edged sword that can provide the impetus to pursue change or the complacency of understanding the world as advanced and advancing. Hayden White has even suggested that a certain degree of underlying progressive faith in the superiority of the present over the past is an inherent element of all historical consciousness,[12] and as Mark Canuel has compellingly argued, even explicitly antiprogressive positions are often implicitly progressive.[13] Progress can be hard to avoid.

Despite its diffuse appeal, the idea of progress was independent of and difficult to reconcile with the historical methods—concerned with evidentiary and epistemological questions—that were developed and debated in the nineteenth century. Mill acknowledges that the doctrine of universal improvement is "not a question of the method of the social science, but a theorem of the science itself."[14] Given Mill's agenda in Book VI of the *System of Logic* (1843 and 1862) to describe how physical science methodologies can be adapted to the social sciences, his digression on historical progress is a change of both topic and tone. At first, he attempts to define progress neutrally, as any consistent directional change: "The words Progress and Progressiveness are not here to be understood as synonymous with improvement and tendency to improvement."[15] Yet the sense that progress is not inherently good disappears almost immediately:

> It is conceivable that the laws of human nature might determine, and even necessitate a certain series of changes in man and society, which might not in every case, or which might not on the whole, be improvements. *It is my belief indeed* that the general tendency is, and will continue to be, saving occasional and temporary exceptions, one of improvement; a tendency towards a better and happier state.[16]

Its many caveats aside, this rare invocation of "belief" admits that Mill's personal commitment to the idea of progress is neither strictly an extension of his methodological argument nor fully supported by historical evidence. Although, as Butterfield notes, the whig historian's presumption of progress serves in practice as "an implicit principle of selection" for historical evidence, in Mill and elsewhere it remains an unspoken ideological commitment rather than a self-conscious methodological argument.[17]

Because the presumption of inevitable improvement necessarily circumscribes individual agency, progress might seem most consistent with the historiography of systematic dialectical unfolding theorized by G. W. F. Hegel or Karl Marx. And indeed, those highly individualist philosophies of Carlyle, Nietzsche, Arthur Schopenhauer, or Søren Kierkegaard widely reject whig history.[18] Yet paradoxically, whig history tends to emphasize rather than de-emphasize the agency of individuals, unconvincingly crediting them with developments whose causes are plainly more complex. For example, Butterfield particularly objects to how whig historians valorize Martin Luther for setting in motion a process of secularization—an outcome Luther certainly did not intend.[19]

Yet whig history's awkward individualism emerged falteringly over the course of the century. Macaulay's 1828 essay "John Dryden" hews closely to the idea that individuals are incidental to larger historical progress:

> Society indeed has its great men and its little men, as the earth has its mountains and its valleys. But the inequalities of intellect, like the inequalities of the surface of our globe, bear so small a proportion to the mass, that, in calculating its great revolutions, they may safely be neglected. The sun illuminates the hills, while it is still below the horizon; and truth is discovered by the highest minds a little before it becomes manifest to the multitude. This is the extent of their superiority. They are first to catch and reflect a light, which, without their assistance, must, in a short time, be visible to those who lie far beneath them.[20]

In this passage, Macaulay figures the great man as a mountain or hill, passively reflecting the sun's rays just a few moments before they reach the valley below, and thus as a modest harbinger of inevitable change. Of course, Macaulay's globe metaphor also suggests larger cyclical narratives of rotation and revolution that occur independent of human agency, reflecting his softer vision of gentle and depersonalized progress over time.

In the *System of Logic*, Mill pointedly disagrees, adapting Macaulay's metaphor to suit a different argument. Mill reconciles general progress with individual greatness by suggesting that "the influence of remarkable individuals is decisive ... in determining the celerity of the movement."[21] After quoting Macaulay, Mill contests:

> So it would be, if truths, like the sun, rose by their own proper motion, without human effort; but not otherwise. I believe that if Newton had not lived, the world must have waited for the Newtonian philosophy until there had been another Newton, or his equivalent .... Eminent men do not merely see the coming light from the hill-top, they mount on the hill-top and evoke it; and if no one had ever ascended thither, the light in many cases might never have risen upon the plain at all.[22]

We might note first that, for Macaulay, the great man is not *standing at* but rather *is* the summit. By contrast, for Mill, the great man effortlessly ascends the mountain, apparently penetrating what must be a thick cloud covering just below the summit that will prevent light from ever reaching the plain. Once there, the great man actively "evokes" the sun's light. In this way, Mill essentially abandons the metaphor of a sunrise, developing instead the mountain element of Macaulay's passage, perhaps, as the mountaineer George Mallory said of Everest, "because it's there."

Furthermore, Mill's comments on Newton and Butterfield's on Luther reflect not only progressive history's strange individualism, but also its strict cultural and historical limits, what Lisa Lowe has called "the economy of affirmation and forgetting that structures and formalizes ... liberal ways of understanding."[23] Indeed, whig history's canon of heroes heavily represents not only white Anglo-Saxon Protestant men, but also the sixteenth and seventeenth centuries, reflecting that progressive history was first advanced as a specific historical claim about the origin of "Western modernity." This sense of a major historical break in early modernity emerged gradually, however. In fact, the influential early formulation of Macaulay's 1828 essay, "History," focuses instead on the break between antiquity and the Middle Ages. Macaulay contrasts modern history writing favorably with even the best ancient writers, who are limited by the stasis of their cultures.[24] For Macaulay, antiquity's "torpor was broken by two great revolutions, ... the victory of Christianity over Paganism" and the Viking invasion of Europe.[25] These having been accomplished, "the second civilisation of mankind commenced, under circumstances which afforded a strong security that it would never retrograde and never pause."[26] Macaulay thus suggests only indirectly, by eliminating the possibilities of reversal or stagnation, that modern (white, Christian) civilization is moving continually forward. Yet despite its uniqueness, modernity is reiterative, a "second" civilization distinct from a first, with a doubled causality in religious change and migration. In offering a positive construction on the fall of Rome and the invasion of Germanic tribes in 476 CE, Macaulay's early essay anticipates the historical periodization of later nineteenth-century "English Teutonic circle" of historians, as Oded Y. Steinberg has traced.

It is worth pausing here to note the attenuated nature of Macaulay's theorization of progress in the early essays. As the Victorian writer most strongly associated with progressive history, Macaulay is initially circumspect, theorizing modern progress as reiterative, modest, and undergirded by cycles. Admittedly, thirty years later, in the *History of England from the Accession of James II* (1859) Macaulay's claims for progress are far more confident, though explicitly limited in national scope and inaugurated in early modernity. Macaulay identifies the distinct origin point of progress in the "Glorious Revolution" of 1688, which he famously interprets as a triumph of parliamentarianism over absolutism. Although the text's opening passage promises "faithfully to record disasters mingled with triumphs, and great national crimes and follies," Macaulay firmly concludes:

> Yet, unless I greatly deceive myself, the general effect of this chequered narrative will be to excite thankfulness in all religious minds, and hope in the breasts of all patriots. For the history of our country during the last hundred and sixty years is eminently the history of physical, of moral, and of intellectual improvement.[27]

The development of Macaulay's work from a mitigated and indirect theorization of progress in "History" and "John Dryden" to an assertive and concrete account in *History of England* begins to indicate the growing confidence in progress as a paradigm during the nineteenth century and its increasing emphasis on a distinct historical break in early modernity.

Yet the precise location and causality of this historical rupture remains disputed, with some writers pinpointing the Protestant Reformation rather than the 1688 Revolution. For example, Lord Acton's 1895 inaugural lecture as Regius Professor of Modern History at Cambridge asserts: "this constancy of progress, of progress in the direction of organized and assured freedom, is the characteristic fact of modern history."[28] Like Macaulay, Acton understands progress as delimited by an untheorized rupture, an "unheralded" transition, the Protestant Reformation, which is "marked off by an evident and intelligible line from the time immediately preceding."[29] Although Acton locates the turning point around 1517, and Macaulay first in 476 and then in 1688, their accounts of progress have the same structure: time was basically static until, for debated reasons, progress suddenly began, inaugurating Western modernity, and it has continued ever since.

A segmented structure, relying on unseen moments of rupture, also governs the positivist historicism that developed following Auguste Comte's *Cours de Philosophie Positive* (1830–42). Comte argues that civilization has unfolded in three distinct phases, the theological, the metaphysical, and finally the positive, in which humanity recognizes that history, like other social scientific fields, is subject to invariable natural laws.[30] Although Comte himself was not particularly interested in the empirical verification of historical laws, positivist historicism became associated with statistical empiricism through Mill's *System of Logic* and Henry Thomas Buckle's *History of Civilization in England* (1857, 1861).[31] Buckle makes explicit positivist historicism's central self-referential premise: that the insight that human behavior is rule-governed constitutes progress itself, and that this progress sets in motion further progress through the gradual determination of those rules. Surveying recent advances across branches of knowledge, Buckle argues:

> Whoever is at all acquainted with what has been done during the last two centuries, must be aware that every generation demonstrates some events to be regular and predictable, which the preceding generation had declared to be irregular and unpredictable: so that the marked tendency of advancing civilization is to strengthen our belief in the universality of order, of method, and of law.[32]

This sense of the progressively expanding dominion of orderly knowledge nonetheless depends on the earlier historical rupture—again in the seventeenth century—in which the metaphysical paradigm was rejected whole cloth in favor of positivism. Only afterward are "the discoveries of genius ... essentially cumulative."[33]

Yet the progressively accumulating knowledge that positivism celebrates is limited not only in time but also in scope. Buckle argues at length that human advancements are the result of intellectual rather than moral developments, because moral truths are stable and universal.[34] For example, he claims—in a text published the same year as the 1857 Indian Rebellion—that the decline in warfare over the preceding few centuries is the result of advances in technology and political economy rather than a change in ethics.[35] Buckle thus theorizes intellectual progress and its consequences specifically in opposition to the stasis of human morality. Leopold von Ranke similarly limits progress to certain arenas by rejecting it in others.[36] Whereas Buckle studies economic, scientific, and intellectual histories and Ranke the histories of church and state, they nevertheless agree that progress does not apply to "all branches of human nature and skill."[37] Ranke explains that progress "is to be assumed in the realm of material interests in which retrogression will hardly be possible unless there occurs an immense upheaval. In regard to morality, however, progress cannot be traced."[38] Thus, both Ranke and Buckle assert a distinction between different kinds of history, identifying limited areas of accumulative progress—for Buckle, these are intellectual, whereas for Ranke, they are material, despite the lurking threat of rupture—only to distinguish them from moral progress, which is impossible. Canuel has argued that whereas eighteenth-century writers understood political, scientific, and cultural progress as necessarily coextensive and interlinked, Romantic writers imagined political progress as separate from and independent of progress in other realms. As we see in Ranke and Buckle, such a division between different kinds of history that follow different trajectories is evident even in the most strident nineteenth-century positivist thought.

The strong link between progressive history and positivist historicism, whether today or in the nineteenth century, ultimately eludes a full explanation. In fact, the historian Michael Bentley understands them as entirely different historiographical paradigms, with the detached empirical positivism of "modernist" history writing—whose heyday was the beginning and middle of the twentieth century—forged in rejection of nineteenth-century whig history. Moreover, as Thomas Piketty's *Capital in the Twenty-First Century* (2014) and the entire field of climate science demonstrate, statistical analysis can equally reveal narratives of cyclicality, decline, or apocalypse. Although positivist historicism and the progressive vision are often considered distinctly Victorian, both ideas have intensified in subsequent years.[39] As Bentley puts it, "the whigs did not die: they survived science, ... they found ways to survive the First World War and by keeping their heads either down, or at least out of the universities, they survived the twentieth century."[40] As Bentley suggests, progressive history is thriving, often in combination with positivism, in popular intellectual work. The Big Data-driven positivism of the twenty-first century vastly exceeds what Buckle could have dreamed. And if Acton is a high-water mark for the Victorian doctrine of progress, sea levels have since risen. Despite the foundational challenges of postcolonial, anti-racist, and anti-capitalist scholarship and activism, and despite the popularity of declinist rhetoric that Jed Esty's *The Future of Decline* has recently documented, confident expressions of the inevitability of progress apparently remain viable. We might contrast Acton's relative restraint with Steven Pinker's best-selling *The Better Angels of Our Nature: Why Violence Has Declined* (2011) or even Hans Rosling's slightly more measured *Factfulness: Ten Reasons We're Wrong about the World—And Why Things Are Better than You Think* (2018). Pinker spends hundreds of pages using statistics to support the same premise as Buckle, that violence has consistently declined over the *longue durée*—from the earliest hunter-gatherer civilizations to the present, in every human culture, on every scale of reference. The book may trace progress on this one metric only, but it is staggeringly universal in scope. Although humanists as well as statisticians have criticized Pinker's work, its success is a testament to the tremendous modern appetite for data-driven progress narratives that make the claims of Macaulay or even Acton look strikingly modest by comparison.

Presentism, then and now

Thus far, I have demonstrated that nineteenth-century accounts of progressive history are heavily footnoted by caveats that incorporate other temporal structures. At this point, I want to suggest that progressive history is also a kind of presentism—an active embrace of the way that present conditions always inform historical engagements. In fact, presentism was developed in the nineteenth century alongside the self-conscious critical detachment more often associated with historical discourse in the period. The case of nineteenth-century progressive history reflects a basic division between two different kinds of presentism—a genealogical model and an appositional model. The way that progress narratives try to combine these two presentisms helps reveal competing theories of progress and the perceptual challenges of registering it.

Wai Chee Dimock defines presentism, in its original negative valence, as:

> a fallacy that deforms the past in our own image. To be a 'presentist' is to allow the concerns of the moment to color all our perceptions. It is to be blithely unaware of historical specificities, to project our values onto past periods without any regard for the different norms then operative. Such narcissism erases the historicity of texts, their conditions of production and reception.[41]

Yet as Eleanor Courtemanche has observed, presentism has undergone a broad resuscitation in Anglo-American literary studies since around 2016, spurred by what Dimock calls the "enormity of a calamitous present [that] requires the closeness rather than the distance of the past."[42] Advocates of presentism often assume that it is a radical modern correction to the delusion of objectivity that plagued nineteenth-century historians, with Nietzsche the shining exception—despite Bentley's account of how historiographical detachment is more characteristic of twentieth- than of nineteenth-century British history writing.[43] Nonetheless, Nietzsche's injunction in *On the Uses and Disadvantages of History for Life* (1873) to "employ history for the purpose of *life!*" is often credited as the origin of an engaged historicism, a lone early detractor from the dominant paradigm of detached neutrality.[44]

Of course, like all stances, detached neutrality has an implicit politics shaped by present concerns. Courtemanche observes that "each particular historicist approach contains within itself an image of the present moment against which this past is posited—a 'shadow presentism' that usually remains untheorized."[45] Yet even beyond the shadow level, nineteenth-century philosophy of history explicitly debated the historiographical tension between ethical engagement and studied neutrality. To begin with, the engaged approach precedes Nietzsche in the work of Carlyle, for whom history was, as Chris R. Vanden Bossche puts it, "never simply about the past in itself but about the past speaking to the present and intervening in the social and political realm."[46] Carlyle's 1830 essay "On History" begins by defining its subject in presentist terms: "It is a looking both before and after; as, indeed, the coming Time already waits, unseen, yet definitely shaped, predetermined, and inevitable, in the Time come; and only by the combination of both is the meaning of either completed."[47]

Indeed, in the long history of studying history, the most ambitious claims of detachment are a brief aberration from a general tendency toward avowedly presentist analysis. Nietzsche's argument stems from a period of intense contestation between the two approaches: the detached view is being theorized best (by Ranke, whose relevant work remained unpublished until 1888 or later, and by the second edition of Mill's *System of Logic*, in 1862) and first reaching a wide audience (through Buckle's *History of Civilization in England*, 1857–61) around the same time that Nietzsche wrote the *Uses and Disadvantages* in 1873. Furthermore, Nietzsche argues that a presentist engagement *already* animates the three existing kinds of history that he discusses—monumental, antiquarian, and critical history.

Scholarship tends to focus on Nietzsche's innovative and politically powerful idea of critical history, a history for the oppressed that can achieve restorative justice. Nietzsche explains its necessity and purpose as follows:

> For since we are the outcome of earlier generations, we are also the outcome of their aberrations, passions and errors, and indeed of their crimes; it is not possible wholly to free oneself from this chain .... The best we can do is to confront our inherited and hereditary nature with our knowledge, and through a new, stern discipline combat our inborn heritage and inplant in ourselves a new habit, a new instinct, a second nature, so that our first nature withers away.[48]

This assertion that history can be marshalled to redress historical crimes has rightfully been celebrated, inspiring "many critical projects [that] seek to *fix or heal* the past."[49] Yet scholars attend less often to the politically ambiguous epistemological component of Nietzsche's critical history. Anthony K. Jensen compares Nietzsche's critical historians to "forensic detectives whose primary concern is not what happened but whether and to what extent what is claimed to have happened can be proven."[50] Carlyle again prefigures this element of Nietzsche, arguing that the historical record is profoundly incomplete and hopelessly biased to the point that many established claims are baseless.[51] Although Jason Jones sees Nietzsche to "endorse"[52] critical history at the expense of its foils, the seemingly more conservative monumental and antiquarian histories, Nietzsche's attitude toward each of the three modes is mixed, and he advocates using them in concert to restore the link between history and life that is severed by the positivistic "demand that history should be a science."[53]

I understand Nietzsche's monumental and antiquarian histories as reflecting two alternative and mutually inconsistent forms of presentism that are variously evident across both nineteenth-century history writing and modern presentist analysis. Monumental history reflects a discontinuous or appositional model and antiquarian history a continuous or genealogical model. Nietzsche's monumental history, in the "great men" tradition of Plutarch, Machiavelli, or Carlyle's *On Heroes* (1840), approaches the past as an archive of emulable models that can inspire future greatness: "Satiate your soul with Plutarch and when you believe in his heroes dare at the same time to believe in yourself."[54] Although Courtemanche notes the association of "the direct model approach" with the neoconservative movement, the idea of emulating past individuals has a politically broad applicability.[55] Monumental history thus tends not only to find greatness in the past but also to assume a basic similarity between past and present. This kind of presentism is discontinuous, insofar as a linear connection between past and present is unnecessary. Instead, monumental history relies on the idea of discrete repetition or resonance—past and present are structurally parallel, existing in formal apposition. In this way, monumental history does not require that certain challenges or issues be universal across time, but rather simply some form of temporal cyclicality, repetition, or return. In this vein, Walter Benjamin's "Theses on the Philosophy of History" theorizes historical materialism, in which individual historical moments are "blasted out of the continuum of history" in order to be juxtaposed with the present.[56] The force is required because, for Benjamin, history is a sedimentary process in which individual moments become hard to separate. Benjamin's famous backward-propelled angel "sees one single catastrophe which keeps piling wreckage upon wreckage and hurls it in front of his feet."[57]

Nietzsche's antiquarian history offers an alternative model of presentism, one grounded in the idea of sustained continuity over time. Courtemanche observes that many presentist engagements, including those of the V21 Manifesto, presume that "the present is constructed by a disavowed yet persistent *material continuity with the past*."[58] Although such efforts often think big, asserting broad continuities on the level of carbon emissions, imperial structures, or wealth inequality, Nietzsche describes antiquarian history as highly localized. Because of its intimate connection to the historian's immediate context, it has a limited outlook: "The antiquarian sense of a man, a community, a whole people, always possesses an extremely restricted field of vision; most of what exists it does not perceive at all, and the little it does see it sees much too close up and isolated."[59] This account of restricted perception strongly resembles Nietzsche's description of the desirable unhistorical state as "enclosing oneself within a bounded horizon."[60] In the essay "Nietzsche, Genealogy, History," Michel Foucault similarly defends the hyperlocalization of what he calls "the historical sense," arguing that it "shortens its vision to those things nearest to it—the body, the nervous system, nutrition, digestion, and energies."[61] Thus, antiquarian history is particularly good at implicating the historian in the narrative. This continuous presentism appears to reflect Nietzsche's own method in *On the Genealogy of Morals* and Foucault's in *Discipline and Punish*—not a "history of the past in terms of the present" but rather a "history of the present."[62] In both works, insights about the present prompt an investigation of how they came about. In "On History Again," Carlyle similarly anticipates "that men permanently speak only of what is extant and actively alive beside them. Thus do the things that have produced fruit, nay whose fruit still grows, turn out to be the things chosen for record and writing of."[63]

The continuous presentism of antiquarian history or genealogy exists in irresolvable tension with these same writers' intense resistance to the totalizing of historical narrative. Foucault's "Nietzsche, Genealogy, and History," for example, advocates "an indispensable restraint" that "must record the singularity of events outside of any monotonous finality," a radically anti-narrative approach that is notably absent in *Discipline and Punish*.[64] Similarly, Carlyle argues:

> It is not in acted, as it is in written History: actual events are nowise so simply related to each other as parent and offspring are; every single event is the offspring not of one, but of all other events, prior or contemporaneous, and will in turn combine with others to give birth to new: it is an ever-living, ever-working Chaos of Being, wherein shape after shape bodies itself forth from innumerable elements.[65]

Scholars have long observed that Carlyle's history writing, as Christopher Parker puts it, presents "a grand interpretation of the course of modern history [that] is a remarkably confident tracing of the causes and consequences in history for somebody who had thought it a chaos of being."[66]

This tension between genealogical presentism and historiographical skepticism begins to suggest that strategies for resisting overconfident and status-quo bolstering historical narrative can strangely resemble the positivist emphasis on data accumulation—reflecting, again, the fundamental tension between progress and positivism. Benjamin, for example, claims that "*nothing that has ever happened* should be regarded as lost for history," because we cannot know until Judgment Day what was significant and what was not.[67] He goes on to praise the "chronicler who recites events without distinguishing between major and minor ones," reflecting that presentism can strategically reclaim the neutral stance toward the historical record more often associated with positivist empiricism.[68] Foucault similarly writes that genealogy "requires patience and a knowledge of details, and it depends on a *vast accumulation of source material*."[69] In this emphasis accumulating information, Foucault shares something with Buckle or Ranke, reflecting that genealogy and positivism both use their attention to detail to distinguish themselves from grand progress narratives.

This strange resonance between the presentist and the positivist emphases on detail helps to illuminate how nineteenth-century accounts of historical progress have a sort of doubled presentism. That is, these progress narratives reflect a discontinuous presentism, in that each past moment offers a separate, legible example of the historically universal struggle for progress. And they also reflect a continuous presentism, in that the past triumphantly culminates in the present. Rather than revealing the drawbacks of a self-monitored detachment, nineteenth-century progressive history is better understood as an intense presentism in which the discontinuous and continuous modes short-circuit each other. Butterfield describes whig history as the study of the past "with *direct and perpetual* reference to the present" through a "system of *immediate* reference to the present-day."[70] In fact, Butterfield objects to whig history's insistently ethical stance—his critique contributes to a new, "modernist" approach in British history writing in the early twentieth century. As we saw, for example, in Mill's acknowledgement that progress is a "theorem" supported by his "belief," nineteenth-century theorists of history were flickeringly aware of the ideological nature of their commitment to progress. Brian W. Young argues that progress appealed to religious historians as an alternative to the secularizing impulse of positivist detachment, and that nineteenth-century progress was conceived in religious terms.[71]

Acton makes explicit that his faith—not in statistical data but in Christianity—motivates his belief in progress. Justifying his contention that the historian should err on the side of harshness in judging historical actors by Christian principles, Acton explains:

> There is a popular saying of Madame de Stael, that we forgive whatever we really understand. The paradox has been judiciously pruned by her descendant, the Duke de Broglie, in the words: "Beware of too much explaining, lest we end by too much excusing." History, says Froude, does teach that right and wrong are real distinctions. Opinions alter, manners change, creeds rise and fall, but the moral law is written on the tablets of eternity.[72]

This typically Actonian tissue of quotation reveals nascent awareness of the ideological nature of his own historical practice. Shifting vertiginously from the potentially destabilizing relativism of Staël and Broglie to the ostentatious certainty of Froude, Acton's argument rests on a vague distinction between, on the one hand, opinions, manners, and creeds, which rise and fall cyclically over time, and, on the other hand, changeless moral law. In a lecture whose thesis, again, is that "progress ... is the characteristic fact of modern history," Acton must delimit the domain of progress from the domains of cyclical change and eternal changelessness—yet another example of how progressive history incorporates and relies on non-progressive temporalities.[73]

Although Acton's investments are different, his passionate call for an ethically engaged historical study evinces a political urgency shared by recent arguments for presentism in literary studies. The particular way that nineteenth-century progress narratives often unconvincingly combine appositional/discontinuous and genealogical/continuous models of presentism reflects the theoretical question of whether progress requires an unbroken line traced from past to present or can instead occur in fits and starts. As we will see in the next section, this theoretical question about continuity also implicates how progress can be witnessed by the individual.

Progress, the generation, and the individual life

With all its caveats and limits, how could progress be felt or registered in the Victorian period? How did a wider sense of progress over time relate to the individual's temporally unfolding experience of a long life? How could progress accommodate experiences that did not at least initially appear to be progressive? These questions hover on the periphery of the nineteenth-century philosophy of history I have considered thus far, but they come to the center in the literary texts I analyze in later chapters. Answers to these questions often hinge on assumptions about whether the individual can change over time. In one common view, the individual witnesses progress diachronically, observing or experiencing wider material, intellectual, or ideological changes as they happen. Yet in another, competing view, the older individual is not a witness to change but rather a static vestige who still embodies the attitudes and practices of an earlier moment. In that latter case, the older person can reveal progress synchronically, through encounters between young and old that reflect contrasting outlooks or attitudes.

Although these two visions of aging contrast with one another, Walter Scott suggests both possibilities in the "Postscript, which should have been a preface" to *Waverley* (1814). Remarking on social change in Scotland over the preceding "sixty" (actually closer to seventy) years, he observes, "But the change, though steadily and rapidly progressive, has, nevertheless, been gradual; and, like those who drift down the stream of a deep and smooth river, we are not aware of the progress we have made until we fix our eye on the now-distant point from which we set out."[74] Yoon Sun Lee reads this passage, floating peacefully down the lazy river of history, as an example of "vection," or the "sensory uncertainty about one's own movement in space," which in Scott's novels "becomes a trope of historical change."[75] The imperceptibility of progress—the fact that it feels like stasis—becomes ironically its defining experience. As Maia McAleavey notes, the passage also "articulates a tension, embedded in progressive models of history, between a sense of continuity (the deep and smooth river) and a sense of dramatic upheaval (the awareness of historicity, or the gulf between the present and the past)."[76] Yet as I traced above in Macaulay, Mill, Acton, and others, progress reflects not just a historiographical tension *between* rupture and continuity but also a trajectory *from* rupture *to* continuity—progress began with a radical break, but thereafter has been smooth. In one sense, then, rupture remains in the past, while the distance between one's present and one's past is the way to perceive what is otherwise imperceptible.

Thus, this part of the "Postscript" suggests the possibility that the individual can perceive progressive change diachronically, albeit in limited and disorienting ways. Through the backward glance to the point of departure, the individual can also apprehend change synchronically. Scott goes on to describe how this synchronic way of marking historical time can take on an interpersonal dimension:

> Such of the present generation as can recollect the last twenty or twenty-five years of the eighteenth century, will be fully sensible of the truth of this statement, especially if their acquaintance and connexions lay among those who, in my younger time, were facetiously called "folks of the old leaven," who still cherished a lingering, though hopeless attachment, to the house of Stuart. This race has now almost entirely vanished from the land .... It was my accidental lot ... to reside, during my childhood and youth, among persons of the above description; and now, for the purpose of preserving some idea of the ancient manners of which I have witnessed the almost total extinction, I have embodied in imaginary scenes, and ascribed to fictitious characters, a part of the incidents which I then received from those who were actors in them.[77]

As we see here, the shift from rupture to continuity results in an uneven texture of time characterized by shifting configurations of intergenerational dialogue. In Scott's account, the Jacobite rebellion destroys the continuity represented by the "old leaven," though it is temporarily survived by the "*folks of* the old leaven," the individual loaves raised by it. In this initial formulation, the historical novel arises from an act of intergenerational communication that preserves experiences just beyond the point of living memory, perhaps. Scott noticeably hedges, explaining that the "race has now *almost* entirely vanished," that he has "witnessed the *almost* total extinction" of their "ancient manners," suggesting the unknown endpoint of living memory. Thus, Scott positions himself as a mediator, not only between past and present, but also between one group of people and another, offering an influential understanding of the texture of time as defined by the possibilities of cross-generational dialogue.

The nineteenth century did not have this sense of the word "generation," as I have been using it, meaning a group defined by membership in an age cohort. Astrid Erll has recently updated Karl Mannheim's influential argument that the modern concept of the generation emerged only after the triggering event of the First World War, with its idea of a lost generation. Erll demonstrates that in the early twentieth century, generationality was posited as an alternative social identity category that united all individuals of a particular age cohort—cutting across gender, race, and class.[78] Other scholars, however, have suggested that the modern concept of the generation slowly emerged in the nineteenth century— though still following Mannheim, through the idea of uneven death. Richard Cronin has observed how the "premature" deaths of "second generation" Romantic poets shape scholarly accounts of the end of Romanticism, whereas Devoney Looser notes that Maria Edgeworth and Frances Burney are strangely understood as forerunners to Austen, despite surviving her and continuing to publish well into the nineteenth century.[79] Tom Mole goes farther to claim that "the idea of a break between two generations with different attitudes and concerns emerges in the first half of the nineteenth century, and the first historical shift to be described in those terms is the shift from Romantic to Victorian generations."[80] Perhaps due to its unique association with the monarch's life, the Victorian period in particular is often conceived as constituted by individuals who were themselves Victorians, perhaps "eminent Victorians," following Lytton Strachey.[81]

Age studies scholar Margaret Morganroth Gullette persuasively argues that generational identity has often problematically undercut intergenerational feminist, anti-racist, and anti-capitalist solidarity, observing that the "Boomer–Xer War" of the 1990s, for example, "explains major historic, economic, and social changes in postindustrial capitalism in a way that reduces resistance to them."[82] A similar dynamic today shapes debates over educational debt, affordable housing, and climate change. In the next two chapters, I explore how generational identity in *Coningsby* and *Vanity Fair* serves as a proxy for access to power—the two novels offer contrasting responses to the question of whether generational renewal might bring about meaningful change.

Scott's "Postscript" does not use "generation" in the modern sense, but it does demarcate Scott's age cohort indirectly through its relationship to another age cohort. Elsewhere in his work, Scott uses "generation" in its broad early nineteenth-century sense of referring to any group of individuals.[83] Here, when he refers to "*such of* the present generation as can recollect" the last years of the eighteenth century, he acknowledges that some will not, indicating that "the present generation" encompasses the entire reading public. Nonetheless, Scott suggests a shared consciousness limited to his age cohort because of their remembered relationship to another cohort. Whereas Erll observes that generations are often defined against each other—"no generationality without its genealogical other"[84]—Scott suggests a more reparative but still relational conception in which his cohort is defined through their connection to the "folks of the old leaven."

Scott's *Waverley* enacts what Richard Terdiman has described as the nineteenth-century's "shift in the mode of conservation (and awareness) of the past, from the activity of live, organic memory to what might be termed artificial or archival memory."[85] Yet the "Postscript" offers a more detailed account of how this shift happens, with an intermediary step in which cross-generational contact provides a synchronic mode of sensing change over time. In this figuration of the elderly as the past, Scott begins to suggest how literary texts imagine the relationship between progress and the potential duration of the human life. As Reinhart Koselleck puts it, contemporaneous, coexisting individuals "did live in the same experiential space, but their perspective was interrupted according to political generation and social standpoint."[86] Scott is not alone in identifying a shift in the late eighteenth century in which time started to seem layered and multiple. Per Koselleck, "the one process of time became a dynamic of a coexisting plurality of times."[87] This multiplicity can ultimately work to evacuate the present by removing most people from it. From the perspective of the individual, a younger person can look like one's past, and an older person one's future. From the perspective of the collective, however, younger people can look like the future and older people the past. Thus, interactions between contemporaneous individuals of different ages are overlaid with a doubled sense that one is speaking both backward and forward across time.

Whereas in Scott's "Postscript" the "folks of the old leaven" have a privileged relationship to the history of the Jacobite Rebellion because they lived during it, nineteenth-century writers also reify the elderly person as a symbol of heightened historical consciousness and a metaphor for civilizational development. Andrea Charise has observed an "insistent rhetoric of 'life-course' so often used to characterize the culture and literature of this period."[88] The tendency to use the life-course as a metaphor for the trajectory of a community, society, or civilization is distinct from Recapitulation Theory (the idea that the development of the embryo mirrors the stages of the species' earlier evolution) and long precedes its initial theorization in the 1820s. In fact, Koselleck identifies this natural metaphor as a longstanding element of conceptions of time, one that modern progress ultimately rejects: since "every metaphor of natural growth contains the inevitability of eventual decay, … the course from youth to old age always excludes the sense of progress to an open future."[89] Bowler similarly observes that the parallel between individual and civilizational development tends to suggest a cyclical account of time in which both individuals and civilizations first grow and mature, then decline and die.[90]

For this reason, the parallel between the individual life and the trajectory of history remains an alluring metaphor for nonprogressive historical unfolding. In the "Discourse on the Origin and the Foundations of Inequality among Men" (1755), Jean-Jacques Rousseau posits that what distinguishes humans from animals is

> the faculty of perfecting oneself; … which … successively develops all the others, and resides in us, in the species as well as in the individual, whereas an animal is at the end of several months what it will be for the rest of its life, and its species is after a thousand years what it was in the first year of those thousand.[91]

Thus, for Rousseau, the extended period of individual human development and the capacity for species-wide development are parallel phenomena. Of course, Rousseau ultimately espouses a form of stadialism in which certain racial groups advance while others remain fixed in a "primitive" state. Although the extent and implications of Rousseau's valorization of the state of nature are debatable, I want to draw attention to how his account of the "civilizing process" as degeneration and decline relies on a similar vision of the trajectory of the human life:

> Why is man alone liable to become imbecile? Is it not that he thus returns to his primitive state and that, whereas the Beast, which has acquired nothing and also has nothing to lose, always keeps its instinct, man again losing through old age or other accident all that his *perfectibility* had made him acquire, thus relapses lower than the Beast itself?[92]

Quite unlike a *Bildungsroman*, in which the protagonist's arrival at adulthood is the triumphant culmination of the maturation process, Rousseau fixates on the decline, or cyclical return, that sometimes characterizes late life—notwithstanding the way that progressive history can absolutely accommodate individual aging by envisioning mechanisms of generational succession and renewal, as I discuss in the next chapter. For Rousseau, however, this cyclicality of the individual life is the result of having left the state of nature, in which time is truly static. Describing the shift from a hunter-gatherer to an early agricultural lifestyle, he concludes:

> The example of the Savages, almost all of whom have been found at this point [i.e., as hunter-gatherers], seems to confirm that Mankind was made always to remain in it, that this state is the genuine youth of the World, and that all subsequent progress has been so many steps in appearance toward the perfection of the individual, and in effect toward the decrepitude of the species.[93]

Thus, once humans establish settled societies, individual and species development diverge—progress for the individual is cyclical return or even regress for the species. Yet the stasis of the state of nature is hard to describe—it has no corollary in the individual life and can only exist for the group. Whereas a civilization might, presumably, experience periods of meaningful stasis, the individual largely cannot—they (singular) inherently experience time and leave the period of "genuine youth," albeit in variable ways.

Similarly, Nietzsche laments the celebrated rise of historical consciousness in the nineteenth century by comparing it to civilizational aging: "Historical culture is indeed a kind of inborn grey-hairedness, and those who bear its mark from childhood must instinctively believe in the *old age of mankind*."[94] The specter of gray hair remains Nietzsche's choice metonym for the spiritual consequences of age. For Nietzsche, youth should be the peak of life, free from an overbearing historical consciousness and imbued with energies necessary for personal and community success. Yet he observes with alarm a "premature grey-beardedness of our present day youth."[95] In this way, he establishes the rhetorical framework of recent anxiety in some circles about the economic and social consequences of an aging society.

We might even see Nietzsche's prematurely gray beard as a symbol of queer temporality, a disconnection from normative developmental expectations. In rejecting the idea of aging into wisdom, Nietzsche and Rousseau anticipate the anti-futurist strand of queer temporality. The status of futurity in queer studies is debated, with José Esteban Muñoz arguing that queerness is "essentially about the rejection of a here and now and an insistence on potentiality or concrete possibility for another world."[96] Nonetheless, theories of queer temporality often reject the heteronormative cherishing of the future and longevity. Jack Halberstam describes the vision of time that queer temporality pushes against:

> we chart the emergence of the adult from the dangerous and unruly period of adolescence as a desired process of maturation; and we create longevity as the most desirable future, applaud the pursuit of long life (under any circumstances), and pathologize modes of living that show little or no concern for longevity. Within the life cycle of the Western human subject, *long periods of stability* are considered to be desirable, and people who live in rapid bursts (drug addicts, for example) are characterized as immature and even dangerous.[97]

As Halberstam observes, straight time has a lopsided shape: once maturation is achieved, the goal becomes stasis rather than growth.[98] This unevenness reflects how progressive time itself is theorized, as I demonstrated above, involving moments of unseen rupture, and periods in which slow progress and stasis are perceptually indistinguishable. Halberstam's "immature" drug addict and Nietzsche's prematurely gray-bearded youth both reveal that normative temporality has dramatically shifting expectations for different points along the life course.

Thus, the life's shifting normative temporalities and the specter of aging as decline strain the potential parallel between the individual life and the progressive unfolding of history. But since the achievements of one cohort must pass to the next in order for progress to survive individual deaths, additional questions arise around the mechanisms and consequences of intergenerational communication. Whereas Scott envisions picturesque scenes of storytelling from old to young, Rousseau argues that the impossibility of intergenerational dialogue ensures the stasis of life under the state of nature:

> If by chance he made some discovery, he was all the less in a position to communicate it as he did not recognize even his Children. The art perished with the inventor; there was neither education nor progress, generations multiplied uselessly; and as each one of them always started from the same point, Centuries went by in all the crudeness of the first ages, the species had already grown old, and man remained ever a Child.[99]

Rousseau's account of a species both "already grown old" and "ever a Child" anticipates Nietzsche's concern over the pernicious paradox of a prematurely gray beard, reflecting that this metaphor tends to reveal the civilization as not only headed toward the grave but also developmentally stunted. I will return in a moment to Rousseau's assumption that the older inventor is looking for *his own* children rather than simply haranguing any passing wedding guest or young Walter Scott. For the moment, I want to observe that the failure of communication Rousseau describes—in which potential progress is lost with each death—also worries a broad range of nineteenth-century philosophy of history. Even those theorists who generally envision progress express skepticism regarding the ability to pass knowledge from old to young.

In 1854, during what must have been a particularly stressful question-and-answer session following his lecture "On the Epochs of Modern History," Ranke was pressed on the issue of moral progress by an audience member, King Maximilian II of Bavaria.

As I explain above, Ranke explicitly excludes the realm of morality from his larger argument about historical progress. In the exchange with Maximilian, he justifies this exclusion by asserting that it is impossible to transfer wisdom downward through the generations. As documented in the reconstruction of the lecture completed by Ranke's student in the 1880s, Maximilian asks pointedly "whether[,] when the individual raises himself to a higher moral level" over the course of a life, "this progress does not also encompass all of mankind."[100] Ranke replies, "The individual dies. His existence is finite .... I believe that every generation is equal in moral greatness to every other generation and that there is no higher potential for moral greatness."[101] If individual moral progress takes place (and, unlike Rousseau or Nietzsche, Ranke assumes that it often does), that progress is lost with individual death. As I discuss above, progressive history already treats the individual historical actor paradoxically, both emphasizing and de-emphasizing their agency. It evinces similar uncertainty about how individual development might structurally parallel or implicate a larger progress narrative. Although even King Max can guess how the course of a human life might contribute to moral progress, the connection between these two registers remains problematic.

Lee Edelman's withering critique of "reproductive futurism" offers another fraught vision of the intergenerational relations dictated by a progress narrative—one that similarly emphasizes the failures of cooperation or solidarity.[102] In American politics, Edelman argues, the ostensible interests of "the Child" as a reified, abstract concept are pitted rhetorically against demands for rights by queer adults.[103] Because "the Child" represents the future, their alleged needs take precedence. Whereas civilizational progress in Rousseau's state of nature is prevented by the obviously surmountable logistical hurdle of locating *one's own* children, Edelman argues that the model of reproductive futurity impedes progress by its very design. If progress is a "constantly anticipated future reality," it can be deferred into a never-realized future, with no need to take action to bring it about.[104]

∽

As I have been demonstrating, the approach to and even the desirability of intergenerational communication is implicated by whether the writer sees age, like Scott, as an archive; like Ranke, as wisdom; like Nietzsche, as lassitude; or like Rousseau, as imbecility. Normative ideas about what it means to be young or old underlie these theories of history. The issues I have traced regarding the anxiety of cross-generational contact seem to have played out in a literary studies conference on "The Contemporary" held at Princeton University in March 2016. This conference is a particularly illuminating example of the state of cross-generational dialogue in literary studies not only because the field of contemporary literature has a unique relationship to time that has fostered the theorization of contemporaneity, but also because the conference organizers published a frank reflection on the experience of curating the event.[105]

Their account of the process of selecting participants suggests an abiding concern over the pitfalls of cross-generational contact in the scholarly conference setting. The organizers explain:

> We limited the invitation to early and mid-career scholars for two reasons. First, we wanted to create an atmosphere of equality. We didn't want graduate students or junior faculty to feel pressure to impress senior scholars—or worse, to avoid offending senior scholars. Second, we wanted scholars to be able to change their minds, to participate without the weight of their past opinions.[106]

Such an approach is perhaps understandable given the hierarchies that shape academic communication. Yet if this account reflects reasonable concerns about the difficulties of speaking across differences of power, it does so by replicating the assumption that older scholars are both powerful and intellectually inflexible. In assuming that such an approach would result in more equality, the organizers reveal concern about inequalities not only between early and late-career scholars, but also inequalities *within* each cohort, acknowledging that the career trajectory is one of increasing inequality over time. Thus, in attempting to exclude the powerful senior scholar, they also exclude the senior scholar who does not command obsequious deference from cowering graduate students, nor do they acknowledge that adjunctification has exploded career inequalities and foreclosed paths to professional development for most scholars. For these conference organizers, as for Nietzsche, the contemporary is the province of the (relatively) young—though, of course, the academy demands many years of study before one achieves the rank of an early-career scholar.

In this final comment on the temporal trajectories of the scholarly career, I aim to suggest that normative ideas about the life course and anxieties about cross-generational contact contain implicit and unexamined historical claims that tend to complicate any progress narrative. The surprisingly poor fit between progress writ large and the individual life long precedes the current reconsideration of the basic idea of hope for a better future and the demand for intergenerational solidarity in the face of climate catastrophe, runaway capitalism, and global pandemic. Nineteenth-century historians and philosophers of history were naggingly aware of the internal contradictions and paradoxes of progress, trying and usually failing to find ways around them. In the book's remaining chapters, I trace the different ways that Victorian literary writers identified and exploited the fault lines in this body of work.

Notes

1. Bell, "Empire," 236, 211.
2. Bowler, *Invention of Progress*, 50–1.
3. Zemka, *Time and the Moment*, 1.
4. Koselleck, *Practice of Conceptual History*, 219.
5. Augustine, *City of God*, 528–32.
6. Koselleck, *Practice of Conceptual History*, 223.
7. Burns and Rayment-Pickard, *Philosophies of History*, 32.
8. Koselleck, *Practice of Conceptual History*, 231.
9. Butterfield, *Whig Interpretation*, 4.
10. Burrow, *Liberal Descent*, 33.
11. Mullen, *Novel Institutions*, 4.
12. White, *Metahistory*, 2.
13. Canuel, *Fate of Progress*, 12.
14. Mill, *System of Logic*, 914 (VI.x.3).
15. Ibid., 913 (VI.x.3).
16. Ibid., 913–14 (VI.x.3); my italics.
17. Butterfield, *Whig Interpretation*, 25.
18. White, *Metahistory*, 13–14; Burns and Rayment-Pickard, *Philosophies of History*, 131.
19. Butterfield, *Whig Interpretation*, 34–63.
20. Macaulay, "Dryden," 324.
21. Mill, *System of Logic*, 938 (VI.xi.3).
22. Ibid., 937–8 (VI.xi.3).
23. Lowe, *Intimacies of Four Continents*, 3.

24. Macaulay, "History," 393.
25. Ibid., 416, 417.
26. Ibid., 417.
27. Macaulay, *History of England*, 14.
28. Acton, "Study of History," 517.
29. Ibid., 507.
30. Bourdeau, "Auguste Comte"; Burns and Rayment-Pickard, *Philosophies of History*, 100.
31. Burns and Rayment-Pickard, *Philosophies of History*, 101.
32. Buckle, *History of Civilization*, 5.
33. Ibid., 163.
34. Ibid., 130.
35. Ibid., 146–62.
36. Ranke is not truly a positivist, though his emphasis on evidence has long resulted in the misunderstanding that he sees historical knowledge in the bare accumulation of facts (Iggers, "Introduction," xi–xii; Burns and Rayment-Pickard, *Philosophies of History*, 68). The difficulty of translating Ranke's famous instruction that the historian should "zeigen wie es eigentlich gewesen" ("show [history] as it actually/essentially was") has contributed to the confusion (Burns and Rayment-Pickard, *Philosophies of History*, 69). Iggers notes that Ranke's call for an unwaveringly impartial stance toward historical conflicts should logically preclude progress narratives. Indeed, Ranke asserts that "every epoch is immediate to God" (Ranke, *Theory and Practice of History*, 21). Yet Ranke's self-policed impartiality functions alongside an ideological commitment to the superiority of the Western and Protestant perspectives (Iggers, "Introduction," xxxi–xxxiii; White, *Metahistory*, 169). Iggers as well as Burns and Rayment-Pickard conclude that on balance, Ranke does affirm historical progress (Iggers, "Introduction," xxxii; Burns and Rayment-Pickard, *Philosophies of History*, 69), albeit limited to the "Latin and Germanic peoples" (Ranke, *Theory and Practice of History*, 20).
37. Ranke, *Theory and Practice of History*, 21.
38. Ibid., 22.
39. Nineteenth-century positivists were notably ambivalent about the unity of all knowledge, a presumption more fully embraced by the early twentieth-century movement of logical positivism (Burns and Rayment-Pickard, *Philosophies of History*, 98–100; Bourdeau, "Auguste Comte").
40. Bentley, *Modernizing England's Past*, 7.

41. Dimock, "Editor's Column," 257.
42. Courtemanche, "Beyond Urgency," 475; Dimock, "Editor's Column," 259.
43. Dimock calls Nietzsche a "key figure in [the] heady genealogy" of presentism (Dimock, "Editor's Column," 259). His "Uses and Disadvantages" was singled out for discussion at the inaugural symposium of V21, an avowedly presentist organization, in Chicago in October 2015.
44. Nietzsche, "Uses and Disadvantages," 66; Jensen, *Nietzsche's Philosophy of History*, 120.
45. Courtemanche, "Beyond Urgency," 463.
46. Vanden Bossche, "Introduction," xxix.
47. Carlyle, "On History," 3.
48. Nietzsche, "Uses and Disadvantages," 76.
49. Courtemanche, "Beyond Urgency," 470.
50. Jensen, *Nietzsche's Philosophy of History*, 84.
51. Carlyle, "On History," 6.
52. Jones, *Lost Causes*, 5.
53. Nietzsche, "Uses and Disadvantages," 78.
54. Ibid., 95.
55. Courtemanche, "Beyond Urgency," 466.
56. Benjamin, "Theses on the Philosophy of History," 205.
57. Ibid., 201.
58. Courtemanche, "Beyond Urgency," 465.
59. Nietzsche, "Uses and Disadvantages," 74.
60. Ibid., 120.
61. Foucault, "Nietzsche, Genealogy, History," 361.
62. Foucault, *Discipline and Punish*, 31.
63. Carlyle, "On History Again," 21.
64. Foucault, "Nietzsche, Genealogy, History," 351.
65. Carlyle, "On History," 7.
66. Parker, *English Idea of History*, 53.
67. Benjamin, "Theses on the Philosophy of History," 197, italics mine.
68. Ibid.
69. Foucault, "Nietzsche, Genealogy, History," 351, italics mine.
70. Butterfield, *Whig Interpretation of History*, 11, italics mine.
71. Young, "History," 159.
72. Acton, "Study of History," 550–1.
73. Ibid., 517.
74. Scott, *Waverley*, 363.

75. Lee, "Vection, Vertigo, and the Historical Novel," 182.
76. McAleavey, "Behind the Victorian Novel," 237.
77. Scott, *Waverley*, 363.
78. Erll, "Generation in Literary History," 395.
79. Cronin, *Romantic Victorians*, 7; Looser, *Women Writers and Old Age*, 1–2; Franco Moretti has also claimed that the generational turnover of readers every 25–30 years shapes the regular and coordinated rise-and-fall pattern of novelistic subgenres in the eighteenth and nineteenth centuries (Moretti, *Graphs, Maps, Trees*, 20–2).
80. Mole, *What the Victorians Made of Romanticism*, 38.
81. Bristow, "Why 'Victorian'?," 2. A tradition of scholarship has even attempted to carve out a "mid-Victorian generation," its middleness conveniently avoiding lives that spanned established historical periods, theorizing a cohort squarely positioned in one place. See Burn, *Age of Equipoise*; Hoppen, *Mid-Victorian Generation*; and Young, *Victorian Eighteenth Century*.
82. Gullette, *Aged by Culture*, 58, 53.
83. Mole, *What the Victorians Made of Romanticism*, 38.
84. Erll, "Generation in Literary History," 396.
85. Terdiman, *Present Past*, 30.
86. Koselleck, *Futures Past*, 282.
87. Ibid.
88. Charise, *Aesthetics of Senescence*, xxiv.
89. Koselleck, *Practice of Conceptual History*, 226.
90. Bowler, *Invention of Progress*, 11.
91. Rousseau, "Discourse on the Origin," 141.
92. Ibid., 141, italics original.
93. Rousseau, "Discourse on the Origin," 167.
94. Nietzsche, "Uses and Disadvantages," 101, italics original.
95. Ibid., 116.
96. Muñoz, *Cruising Utopia*, 1.
97. Halberstam, *In a Queer Time and Place*, 4–5, italics mine.
98. In disability studies, there is a similar ambivalence toward futurity with some scholars celebrating "crip time" as freedom from the future orientation of an ableist culture, while others make powerful demands for a future for disabled people. In a reading of this passage, Alison Kafer departs from Halberstam in noting the limits for disability studies of the queer opposition to the fetishization of longevity, given, first, the institutional structures that foreshorten crip lives, and second, the pressure on crips to perform compulsory

nostalgia for a lost able body/mind (Kafer, *Feminist, Queer, Crip*, 40–2).
99. Rousseau, "Discourse on the Origin," 157.
100. Ranke, *Theory and Practice of History*, 23.
101. Ibid.
102. Edelman, *No Future*, 2.
103. Ibid., 19–21.
104. Ibid., 8–9.
105. I did not attend this conference. I have chosen this example—from outside of my home field of Victorian studies—to avoid personalizing the issue.
106. Chihaya, Kotin, and Nishakawa, "The 'Contemporary' by the Numbers."

2

Disraeli's Frenetic Stasis

Over the course of his life, Benjamin Disraeli underwent several transformations. As a young man, he modeled his persona on Byron and wrote fashionable silver-fork novels. In middle age, he led an upstart parliamentary faction, "Young England," despite being already nearly forty and several years older than his colleagues. As prime minister—in his sixties and seventies, exemplary of what Karen Chase calls "gray power" or gerontocracy[1]— Disraeli was "a major architect of the late-Victorian imperial program."[2] Disraeli is easily read as a shapeshifting reflection of the zeitgeist. Take for example Daniel Schwartz's 1979 monograph, which begins by contrasting two portraits that bookend Disraeli's trajectory of dramatic change:

> The first, ... after an 1840 painting by A. E. Chalon, shows Disraeli with long, somewhat unkempt hair, an arrogant look approaching a sneer on his lips, inflamed eyes as if he had been up all night, a sloppy, creased coat, and an open shirt, his neck hardly concealed by a cravat .... In the second portrait, flatteringly painted by Sir John Everett Millais in 1881, the last year of Disraeli's life, the former Prime Minister, in formal dress and bow tie ..., is the picture of propriety. Looking very much younger than his years, confident and poised, with arms folded, neat, stern without being unduly severe, and clearly in complete control of his emotions, he is the embodiment of the successful statesman. His taut self-control and his polished manner (every hair of beard and head is in place) contrast so strikingly with the earlier portrait that it reminds us that Disraeli, more than most men, consciously created the public self that stares so imposingly at us.[3]

Schwartz's contrast is typical in emphasizing that Disraeli masterfully manipulated his self-image to reflect cultural transformations in styles of dress, attitudes toward the body, and standards of propriety. Rachel Teukolsky similarly remarks that Disraeli's "life story models all the appeal of ambition, self-making, and an irrepressible rise to power."[4] And yet, in Schwartz's account, Disraeli's intimate relationship to contemporaneity is ultimately estranging. Disraeli looks strangely old when young and strangely young when old, a jarring asynchrony akin to Nietzsche's image of the prematurely gray beard.

As this passage suggests, throughout his political and literary careers, Disraeli seemed to have a confounding relationship to time—both disconnected from and too beholden to normative temporality. Disraeli troubled expectations for the aging process and the career arc when, between premierships, he returned to fiction after a twenty-three-year gap. The reception of *Lothair* (1870) reflected, as Sandra Mayer puts it, that the "frivolous activity of novel-writing," which might be tolerated in a younger man, now "seemed incompatible with the dignified solemnity of respectable statesmanship."[5] Moreover, although Disraeli's fiction evolved aesthetically over the years, he remained committed to frenetic topicality and descriptive exuberance—the soon-maligned generic features of the silver-fork novel in which Disraeli first made his name in the 1820s.[6] As Teukolsky observes, *Coningsby* (1844) "blend[s] the silver fork genre with the political—in an era when politics itself was a silver fork affair."[7]

Inspired by the ironies of Disraeli's and his novels' relationships to time, this chapter argues that Disraeli rejects a vision of gradual continuous change and instead imagines history as periods of stasis punctuated by rupture. He consistently asserts a form of progress on this segmented model, but then struggles to imagine what change might look like, defaulting to a broader sense of stasis. As I suggested in the previous chapter, the stasis-and-rupture model of progress offers a more flexible system for incorporating and subsuming seemingly non-progressive developments within a larger progress narrative. Disraeli uses this system both to accommodate what he understands as long periods of decline and also, paradoxically, to suggest the broad sameness of the past and the present. In this way, Disraeli strongly emphasizes the ancient constitutionalism that is one pole of what J. W. Burrow identifies as the "[w]hig compromise."

I demonstrate this argument through an analysis of three novels in which Disraeli experiments with continuous and segmented models of progress, *Vivian Grey* (1826 and 1853), *Coningsby* (1844), and *Sybil* (1845). A scandalous *roman-à-clef* that Disraeli regretted immediately, *Vivian Grey* is the youthful blunder that forced him briefly to embrace and then quickly to abandon the idea of sustained, gradual maturation in his own life. *Coningsby* uses intergenerational rivalry and succession to dramatize what continuous gradual progress might look like, but ultimately reveals the challenges of that project. In *Sybil*, his best and best-known novel, Disraeli moves from history to historiography, abandoning the idea of change over time and instead using the case of aristocratic inheritance to call for forms of creative anachronism that will create a better future by returning to the past.

Over the course of the three novels, Disraeli moves away from the idea of gradual continuous progress and toward embracing frenetic stasis as time's mode. All three novels are set in a present that is hyperactive with topical detail, but each novel's focus moves further backward in time, from a fictionalization of a failed business venture the previous year (*Vivian Grey*), to an engagement with eighteenth-century history (*Coningsby*), to a medievalist fantasy (*Sybil*). Disraeli illustrates a sense of frenetic stasis through figures of irregular survival. First, the novels use unexpected configurations of intergenerational tension to reflect the difficulty of reconciling the individual life's trajectory with socioeconomic, demographic, or ideological shifts. Second, vestigial objects—like superseded wills or medieval ruins—have a deceptive relationship to time in these novels, serving as carriers of complicated histories. Third, speech has a privileged relationship to its moment. Conversation reflects one's being in the present, and it becomes immediately opaque to posterity. These irregular survivors provide conservative counterprogramming to Macaulay's influential whig narrative of English history as defined by continuous, gradual improvement sparked by the 1688 Revolution. Disraeli seeks instead to imagine progress through a return to older institutions and values, but ultimately represents the past and present as the same, a closed system that renders change impossible.

As an influential formulation of the seemingly paradoxical conservative vision of historical progress, Disraeli's work warrants critical reconsideration in light of our modern post-liberal political landscape.[8] Teukolsky has recently argued that Disraeli's "novels operate within a tradition of deeply conservative aesthetics, celebrating authoritarian models" and "anticipating more virulent strains of hard-right thought and practice that would arise in the twentieth century."[9] I read Disraeli in a similar vein, turning in particular to his theorization of history. In his embrace of a medieval vision to make England great again, Disraeli is an intellectual forefather of modern right-wing historiography. Moreover, the arc of his career—in which early errors dogged his later life—prefigures modern political dynamics of ideological purity and credibility. Prefiguring urgent twenty-first-century political debates, Disraeli models ways of using history politically other than as evidence of the triumphalist march of gradual improvement.

"Lord Beaconsfield fell over a chair": *Vivian Grey* and its afterlife

The fallout from Disraeli's first novel *Vivian Grey* (1826) led him briefly to embrace and then to reject the idea of normative, gradual maturation on the level of the individual life—whether the protagonist's or the author's. Disraeli dashed off this notorious work in a matter of weeks, only to regret it for many years, during which he undertook several efforts to mitigate the damage by appealing to the idea of youthful indiscretion. The impossibility of incorporating this work into a maturational arc led Disraeli ultimately to conceive of historical time as segmented, broken into unrelated pieces. This segmented temporality shapes the text itself, which has a conspicuous yet paradoxical relationship to time. As silver-fork fiction, it showcases up-to-the-moment fashions of high-society life. As a *roman-à-clef*, it has a short but distinct delay built in, since it represents something that really happened, rather than something that could happen right now. *Vivian Grey*'s setting is thus roughly contemporary, and also a little while ago—in a near but separate past. In the years following its initial publication, Disraeli undertook various revisions and additions that worked to redeem the unscrupulous title character, initially through *Bildung*, but then by emphasizing the work's historically distant setting. These revisions ultimately reveal the difficulty of imagining past and present as separate, a political necessity for Disraeli that contributed to his theorization of progress on the stasis-and-rupture model.

Vivian Grey fictionalizes a real-life fiasco that had lasting personal and financial consequences, the 20-year-old Disraeli's close involvement in John Murray II's failed attempt to start a Tory daily newspaper. *The Representative* was perhaps doomed from the start—a lack of editorial leadership, a competitive market, and a rapid loss of capital all contributed to its demise in July 1826, six months after it began. In the process, Disraeli's and Murray's partnership was undermined by an obscure but devastating conflict: Disraeli seems to have sabotaged or perhaps botched negotiations undertaken on Murray's behalf, and possibly lied about it.[10] Capitalizing on the episode in *Vivian Grey*, however, poured salt in the wound, and the friendship between the two men and their families never recovered. Appearing anonymously from the silver-fork publisher Henry Colburn, *Vivian Grey* follows the Machiavellian schemes of the young protagonist, a figure for the author. It caused an immediate sensation—true to genre conventions, Colburn's marketing cultivated the tantalizing impression that the author drew upon personal experiences, and the novel was a hit with readers, though not with reviewers.[11] In the *Literary Gazette*, William Jerden called it "one of the things of the times, and for the times"[12]—weaponizing the novel's claim to be a window into a world of up-to-the-minute fashion. The subsequent revelation of Disraeli's authorship and middle-class Jewish identity prompted a vicious backlash that compared him to Harriette Wilson, the scandalous courtesan memoirist I discuss in Chapter 4.[13] Writing in *Blackwood's*, John Gibson Lockhart—who was involved with *The Representative* and whose fictional counterpart is murdered in *Vivian Grey*—describes the author as "an obscure person for whom nobody cares a straw."[14]

In the first of two parts, the novel retells the story of *The Representative* as an attempt to form a new political party—a transposition from the world of journalism to the world of politics that prefigures Disraeli's.[15] Murray appears as the Marquess of Carabas—"an inebriate of limited intellectual ability"[16] or "an incompetent buffoon with delusions of grandeur"[17]—who tries to spearhead the Carabas Party but is undermined by conniving advisors. A "key" to the characters appeared in the *Star Chamber*, a short-lived periodical connected with Disraeli himself.[18] With its thick descriptions of stately homes, sparkling conversations during elaborate meals, extended accounts of high-society gossip, and post-Byronic hero, part I of *Vivian Grey* conforms to the features of the popular silver-fork novel.

Yet this fashionable text had a long afterlife. As silver-fork fiction yielded to Victorian realism and Disraeli's political career advanced, *Vivian Grey* gained new notoriety as an embarrassing youthful blunder in the life of a public figure.[19] Disraeli immediately regretted the novel—he sent Murray almost thirty-five letters begging for forgiveness.[20] Part II of *Vivian Grey*, written just one year later, attempts mitigation on the level of plot: Vivian learns to leave behind his scheming and embrace idealistic principles. Whereas part I reflects what Lauren Gillingham identifies as the silver-fork's "resistance to the growing cultural authority of the *Bildungsroman*"[21] after Carlyle's 1824 translation of *Wilhelm Meisters Lehrjahre*, part II retroactively incorporates the whole novel into *Bildung*'s maturational arc. The narrator emphasizes that part I took place in the protagonist's youth. He describes Vivian as "one, whose early vices, and early follies, have been already obtruded, for no unworthy reason, on the notice of the public, in as hot and hurried a sketch as ever yet was penned; but like its subject; for what is youth but a sketch—a brief hour of principles unsettled, passions unrestrained, powers undeveloped, and purposes unexecuted!"[22] Disraeli was twenty-two years old when he wrote this passage, eager to leave last year's mistake behind him.

Appealing to the logic of the historical novel, the narrator goes on to argue that readers must understand Vivian's part I behavior as a product of his time:

> I conceived the character of a youth of great talents, whose mind had been corrupted, as the minds of many of our youth have been, by the artificial age in which he lived. The age was not less corrupted than the being it had generated .... I am blamed for the affectation, the flippancy, the arrogance, the wicked wit of this fictitious character. Yet was Vivian Grey to talk like Simon Pure, and act like Sir Charles Grandison?[23]

In claiming that "the age"—a past-tense age in which Vivian "lived" and "was"—determined Vivian's behavior, Disraeli invokes historical fiction, in which, per Lukács, historical circumstances shape characters' inner lives. Yet in the process Disraeli also emphasizes Vivian's modernity, distinguishing the character from eighteenth-century fictional paragons of virtue—from Susanna Centlivre's *A Bold Stroke for a Wife* (1718) and Samuel Richardson's *Sir Charles Grandison* (1754). Of course, Vivian differs from these figures not least because the text engages a different eighteenth-century literary tradition, the picaresque satire—Gillingham emphasizes the picaresque's major influence on the silver-fork as a sign of the way modernity is conceptualized through temporal multiplicity and doubling-back.[24] The narrator emphasizes that Vivian is a character of his time, and though only months have elapsed, that time has passed. This strategic appeal to changing mores draws upon the idea that the individual develops along with the culture at large. Insofar as cultural historians have understood the advent of an upright, middle-class "Victorian" sensibility in terms that echo Vivian's (or Disraeli's) development, the process is gradual—no culture can shift as quickly as a young protagonist. Fiction allows a character like Vivian to reify larger developments, though in this case, unlike in *Coningsby*, as we will see, the protagonist passively reflects rather than actively shapes the milieu.

Twenty-six years later, Disraeli changed strategy, attempting to redress the damage of *Vivian Grey* with a substantially revised and shortened version of the novel, edited by his sister Sarah.[25] Whereas the 1827 part II allowed Vivian to mature, the 1853 revision places the whole novel in a distant past. Consistent with other silver-fork revisions, the 1853 *Vivian* creates greater ironic distance between narrator and protagonist, consistently condemning what the original text treated with equal delight and scorn. In a new preface, Disraeli dismisses the work as juvenilia: "Books written by boys ... which pretend to give a picture of manners, and to deal in knowledge of human nature, must necessarily be founded on affectation."[26] He furthermore cuts the 1827 passage that attempted to excuse Vivian's behavior as a product of his time. This excision eliminates evidence of Disraeli's immediate regret, while at the same time the 1853 version adds new paratexts that attempt exculpatory historical contextualization. Thus, the revision collapses the perspectival distance between parts I and II, presenting the entire text as an artifact of a distant moment blithely unaware of potential critiques.

These efforts largely failed. In 1868, the novel was still used against Disraeli as prime minister; the twentieth-century biographer Robert Blake claims that *Vivian* "haunted Disraeli to the end."[27] Disraeli did choose to reprint the novel in an 1870 collected edition with a "General Preface" calling the novel "essentially a puerile work"—its reappearance reflects that it remained a marketable commodity.[28] Insofar as *Vivian*'s later revision attempts to stem the reputational damage by appealing to normative maturational expectations, its relative failure suggests the power of the idea—perhaps opportunistically adopted by Disraeli's enemies—that character is stable over the life course. As this example begins to suggest, individual development over time often confronts skepticism. As we will see more fully in *Coningsby*, in fact, progress narratives have an ironic tendency to reject the idea of personal development in favor of aggregate development.

In order to suggest that 1826 was a long time ago, the 1853 *Vivian* both aesthetically modernizes the text, bringing it closer to mid-century middle-class readerly expectations, and also, paradoxically, uses topical references strategically to demarcate its historical setting from the present. Together, these changes work to set the novel in a past that is legible but distinct. Josephine Richstad traces a similar dynamic in Catherine Gore's 1850 revision to *The Hamiltons* (1834), which involved a "sustained reworking of her book to fit a new age" by both modernizing and antiquating the text.[29] Richstad observes that Gore retained references to fashions or topics that had *not* stayed current in the intervening years and cut those that had, representing a past that is fully separate from the present.[30] Disraeli undertakes a similar project, with the changes particularly evident during the boozy dinner at which Carabas and friends hatch the plan to form a new political party. The revision carefully prunes the use of slang. In eliminating two uses of "tipsy" and one of "toper," it both de-emphasizes characters' drunkenness and removes words that were fashionable in the 1820s but whose status had since changed.[31] Although the *Oxford English Dictionary* documents "tipsy" as early as the sixteenth century, Francis Grose's *Lexicon Balatronicum: A Dictionary of Buckish Slang, University Wit, and Pickpocket Eloquence* (1811) needed to define "tipsey" as "almost drunk."[32] By the mid-century, however, "tipsy" appears to have moved into wider use, such that John Camden Hotten's *A Dictionary of Slang, Cant, and Vulgar Words* (1859) uses tipsy in the definition of other terms.[33] "Toper" seems to have had the opposite trajectory: Grose defines it as "one who loves his bottle; a soaker," but Hotten does not include it at all, suggesting that it fell out of favor.[34]

The divergent fates of "tipsy" and "toper" reveal the challenges of representing a past that is distinct from the present. The normalization of "tipsy" meant that by 1853 it no longer had the outré effect it once did. Consistent with what Richstad observes in Gore's *Hamiltons*, Disraeli's removal of "tipsy" severs this linguistic continuity to avoid making the Carabas dinner look too current. Conversely, the case of "toper" reflects that intelligibility is necessary for language to appear dated. Because the multitudinous topical details of *Vivian Grey* had variable afterlives, representing a past fashionability required a careful management of references to prioritize those elements that suggest legible difference. In the next chapter I will discuss how a similar dynamic applies to clothing: in order to be interpreted as a fashion, the fashion must be gone, but not forgotten—an irregular survivor that lives in memory but not in use.

Consistent with other silver-fork revisions, the 1853 *Vivian* blunts the original's attack on identifiable individuals, illustrating both Disraeli's regrets and the short life-cycle of satire—Murray had died a few years previously.[35] In reducing Carabas's drunkenness and clarifying his political convictions, Disraeli quietly renders the text more palatable to the 1853 readership. The revised dinner party scene dramatically curtails the original's drunken antics and animated conversations, for example, by changing verbs of quotation. "'Noble!' halloed the Marquess; who was now quite drunk" is changed to "'Noble!' said the Marquess."[36] Similarly, "bawled" and "shouted" are changed to "exclaimed"; and "burst forth" is changed to "said."[37] The subdued quotatives of the 1853 version represent a calmer and soberer gathering, reflecting an ongoing cultural shift in attitudes toward revelry. Moreover, novelistic conventions for representing speech had changed in the intervening years, and this scene's revision, like other silver-fork revisions, reduces the excessive witty dialogue characteristic of the genre.[38] As I will elaborate below, throughout Disraeli's work, long passages of sparkling and often obscure dialogue work to indicate the embeddedness of characters in their local historical moment. In tamping down on this kind of dialogue in *Vivian*'s revision, Disraeli holds the events of the novel at a remove.

I have been arguing that the push and pull of modernization and antiquation evident in the treatment of dialogue and topical references reflects the difficulties of depicting a separate past within the aesthetic and social conventions of the present. In the revision's treatment of politics, however, retroactive continuity converts the aspirations of the Carabas Party almost into a critique of pre-Reform political culture. In the 1826 version, Carabas explains his ambitions in an addled rant:

> My Lords and Gentlemen, when I take into consideration the nature of the various interests, of which the body politic of this great empire is regulated; (Lord Courtown, the bottle stops with you) when I observe, I repeat, this, I naturally ask myself what right, what claims, what, what, what,—I repeat, what right, these governing interests have to the influence which they possess? (Vivian, my boy, you'll find Champagne on the waiter behind you.) Yes, gentlemen, it is in this temper (the corkscrew's by Sir Berdmore,) it is, I repeat in this temper, and actuated by these views, that we meet together this day.[39]

Like Carabas himself, original readers of this scene were distracted by the wine, taking the mention of a corkscrew to reveal the author's unfamiliarity with how to open a bottle of champagne, raising doubts about his fashionable credentials.[40] With its interruptions and repetitions, Carabas's speech feels authentically improvisatory, and thus may be an exception that proves Patricia Howell Michaelson's rule that "representations of speech tend to clean up the spoken word."[41] In 1853, Disraeli rewrites this monologue as a longer, tempered, and fairly cogent critique of the political establishment—a rare passage where the revision adds new material rather than just removing old.[42] Carabas complains that "[t]here are few distinctions now between the two sides of the House of Commons" and alludes to instances in which well-conceived proposals were defeated by a self-interested cabal.[43] He clarifies that "I am far from wishing to witness any general change, or indeed, very wide reconstruction of the present administration .... [B]ut there are members of that administration whose claims to that distinction appear to me more than questionable."[44] Although the revised version is still vague—as elsewhere in Disraeli's novels, politics remain "fervent but misty"[45]—it moves closer to a retroactive critique of pre-Reform parliamentary politics. Whereas in the original, Carabas makes a bald grab for power, in the revision he argues, prefiguring *Coningsby*, for a personnel change that would benefit his ostensibly principled and deserving political allies.

Thus, the 1853 version enhances the ideological content of Carabas's speech, reframing it as a response to a flawed political system. It also turns Carabas's toast into a prepared speech that lacks the formal infelicities of improvised oratory that are so striking in the original. In this way, Disraeli continues to prune elements that suggest the incoherence or illegibility of the momentary, the surfeit of details whose significance is not yet known. The result is paradoxical. The management of topical references places the represented world of *Vivian Grey* squarely in an artificially distinct past, while the treatment of politics suggests the novelist's prescience, incorporating the story into a historical arc that leads to the present—the past is thus both disavowed and instrumentalized.

Additional retroactive continuities happened by accident. For example, take Lord Beaconsfield, a minor character on the periphery of the Carabas circle. At one point, "Lord Beaconsfield fell over a chair, and, extricating himself with admirable agility, got entangled in a dumb-waiter, which came tumbling down with a fearful crash of plates, bottles, knives, and decanters."[46] A town in Buckinghamshire, the county Disraeli later represented in the House of Commons, Beaconsfield was, in 1826, a plausible name for one of *Vivian Grey*'s many fictional Lords. The fact that Disraeli later became the Earl of Beaconsfield is an irony he may have appreciated. This belatedly realized connection between fact and fiction also gives the false impression that the title is hereditary, since *Vivian Grey*'s Lord Beaconsfield, had he existed, would have been a member of an earlier generation, someone closer to John Murray II's or Isaac D'Israeli's age. The case of Lord Beaconsfield is a coincidental instance of Disraeli's elsewhere deliberate strategy of self-aggrandizement through what Sophie Gilmartin has called "myths of ancestral origin," in which he "traced his pedigree back to intimates of the Queen of Sheba and the tribes of Israel," as well as, more proximately, claiming an unsubstantiated connection "with the semi-aristocratic and well-known de Lara family."[47]

Most often treated as a curiosity in Disraeli's career, *Vivian Grey* and its revision reflect his experimentation with continuous and discontinuous models of progress. Confronted with a major error in judgment, Disraeli adopted various largely unsuccessful strategies to mitigate the damage, both subsuming the text into a maturational narrative and also sealing it off from the rest of his life, severing any connection to the present. In the process, Disraeli raises questions about the extent to which the individual character or the wider culture remains stable over time. By returning to a text that once claimed to represent a fashionable present,

Vivian's revision reveals the irregular survival of topical reference. In this novel, the present is noisy and frenetic, and in hindsight, it proves difficult either to incorporate into a linear narrative or fully to disavow. Although Disraeli's fiction evolves by the 1840s, the same questions raised in *Vivian Grey* animate his later novels too, as Disraeli moves away from conceptualizing historical change on a gradualist, continual model.

Coningsby and the generation

Coningsby; or, The New Generation is a *Bildungsroman* and a *roman-à-clef* that recounts the eponymous hero's rejection of the debauchery and hypocrisy associated with his grandfather's circle, and his embrace of political sincerity, earned merit, and industrial progress. Frequent explicit references to calendar time indicate that the story unfolds between May 1832 and the spring of 1841, against the backdrop of political realignment and ideological churn that followed the passage of the Reform Act. Rachel Teukolsky reasonably calls the novel "basically Tory propaganda"[48] for the Young England movement, a short-lived parliamentary faction that advocated a paternalistic neo-feudalism. In ways that animate the novel as well, "Young England" suggests both the age of many of the movement's actors and its hearkening back to an idealized early English history—a superimposition of individual and national trajectories. Many of the novel's young men are fictional representations of Young Englanders and Disraeli himself appears as their charismatic Jewish intellectual mentor, Sidonia.[49] Coningsby's villainous grandfather Lord Monmouth—and *Vanity Fair*'s Lord Steyne, as I discuss in the next chapter—is based on the notoriously debauched aristocrat the third Marquis of Hertford,[50] and stands for the "moribund, degenerate Toryism"[51] that Young England seeks to overthrow. Although the novel appears to dramatize gradual progress though intergenerational contestation and replacement, it ultimately depicts time as characterized by periods of stasis punctuated by unseen and untheorized rupture.

Coningsby's development from a shy, sensitive boy into a self-assured Member of Parliament initially seems a microcosm for larger social progress—from a materialistic and dissipated post-Regency adolescence to a mature, modern Victorian adulthood. That is, it seems to conform to a standard reading of the early Victorian *Bildungsroman* as using individual maturation to reify bigger social changes. Andrew Elfenbein argues that Bulwer-Lytton's *Pelham* (1828) and Disraeli's *Venetia* (1837) "developed myths of historical succession in which the sexual, literary, and political shortcomings of Romanticism were corrected by ... a compromise between 'bourgeois' and 'aristocratic' systems of value."[52] Although Elfenbein's paradigm of Romanticism corrected might initially appear to describe *Coningsby* as well, on closer inspection it proves inadequate to capture the novel's segmented view of time.

Disraeli's novels are animated by the critique of Macaulay's whig historiography that Disraeli advances in *Vindication of the English Constitution* (1835). As I discussed in the previous chapter, Macaulay influentially reads the 1688 Revolution as an origin point for progress—a punctual event that inaugurated continual and ongoing improvement. Disraeli takes a dramatically more negative view of seventeenth-century British history, calling Charles I "a virtuous and able monarch martyred" and describing what Macaulay calls the "Glorious Revolution" as instead a "Dutch Invasion."[53] The year 1688 thus represents for history the same problem *Vivian Grey* represents for Disraeli's life—both are disasters that no narrative of gradual improvement can redeem. In the case of British history, Disraeli envisions forward progress by looking back further in time, imagining the restoration of crumbling medieval institutions of monarchy and church—a theme developed more fully in *Sybil*. J. W. Burrow argues that in its ancient constitutionalism Disraeli's vision of history belongs to an increasingly complex tradition of whig history, which is characterized by a central paradox in which England is both born perfect and continually improving. Whereas for Macaulay, that birth is the Glorious Revolution, for Disraeli, it is in an earlier medieval past. This distant origin allows Disraeli to relax the idea of *continual* improvement, such that the entire period from the mid-seventeenth century to the present constitutes a temporary, highly lamentable detour on the road of progress. Whereas Edmund Burke seeks to maintain and renew existing social structures, Disraeli "the radical conservative ... seeks to overturn a decadent status quo," as Teukolsky puts it.[54] Thus, Elfenbein's model of Romanticism corrected through *Bildung* does not account for how forcefully *Coningsby* rejects the recent past, imagining instead a dramatic break.

In a way, then, Coningsby *is* the glorious revolution—not just a metonym of progress but its agent. Notwithstanding *Sybil*'s medievalism, *Coningsby* arguably finds an alternative origin point for progress at end of novel, around 1845 rather than 1688. As I described in the previous chapter, nineteenth-century theorists of history debated progress's origin point—Macaulay is inconsistent on this question and differs from Acton by hundreds of years. But whenever it occurred and however it started, progress's sudden eruption set in motion future gradual progress. This is precisely how *Coningsby* ends. The story culminates as Coningsby and friends enter public life, destined to "restore the happiness of their country by believing in their own energies, and daring to be great!"[55] Although scholars observe wryly that *Coningsby*, and later *Sybil*, avoid difficult political questions by conveniently ending with action not yet taken, this promise of always starting anew is inherent to progress, whether conceived as gradual or as happening in fits and starts. As Disraeli suggests, understanding progress to have happened in the past and demanding that it happen in the future are two entirely different things. In decoupling past from future, Disraeli's argument ironically resembles that of radical thought. Cultural theorist Amy Allen, for example, advocates in the spirit of decolonization for a "much more limited forward-looking notion of moral-political progress as an imperative, one that has been disentangled from the deeply problematic notion of progress as a [historical] 'fact.'"[56]

But to focus only on Coningsby's development, whether it parallels or implicates historical progress, is to overlook the novel's emphasis on intergenerational conflict. Although Patrick Brantlinger notes that the intergenerational struggle distinguishes the novel ideologically from Burkean conservatism, this aspect of *Coningsby* is generally unremarked in the critical literature.[57] Suggested by its alternate title, "the new generation," *Coningsby* tells a story in which one cohort—Monmouth and his cronies—cedes power to another—Coningsby and his Eton classmates. As I will show, the novel's account of generational rivalry and succession proves incompatible with gradualist progress and suggests instead a segmented model.

In the previous chapter, I partially contested the influential claim that the modern concept of the generation—defined by membership in an age cohort—appeared only after the First World War, arguing that it emerged in the nineteenth century. Tom Mole has observed that "in nineteenth-century discussions of historical time ... the generation was emerging as a marker of increased importance," though its precise meaning could still be uncertain.[58] *Coningsby* is a case in point that, first, sketches the range of uses of the word "generation" in this period; second, uses the rivalry between age cohorts to dramatize historical change; and third, reveals the complexity of envisioning history as generational succession and replacement. It is the grandfather Monmouth who utters the novel's alternate title: "I fear there are evil days for the NEW GENERATION."[59] Although this sentence might seem to express concern for the welfare of young people, in context it indicates Monmouth's foreboding about the future's potential to upset existing hierarchies—he is lamenting the rise of radical sentiments and musing that his tailor might one day own Monmouth House. This does not ultimately happen in *Coningsby*, but it anticipates the ending of *Sybil*, in which property and titles dramatically change hands.

At times, *Coningsby*—like Walter Scott, as I discussed above—uses the word "generation" to refer to all current members of the reading public or political class. For example: "Now commenced that Condition of England Question, of which our generation hears so much."[60] In this passage, the topic's contemporaneity binds together individuals across a range of ages—though it doubtless excludes on grounds of gender, race, and class. This broad vision of the generation is perhaps easiest to reconcile with the idea of smoothly continuous progress, since all individuals are participating in the same ongoing conversation that—per Kant's "What is Enlightenment?" (1784)—slowly discovers new truths. Under this definition of "generation," the same individual would be part of one generation during young adulthood and a largely different generation in old age.

Yet elsewhere, Disraeli begins to suggest the more limited, modern sense of "generation." Reflecting that generational identity most strongly affixes to youth, the novel figures Coningsby and his friends as "the New Generation." For example, in a political conversation between Coningsby and an older friend, Sir Joseph Wallinger, the narrator remarks, "it was the first time that any inkling of the views of the New Generation had caught [Sir Joseph's] ear."[61] Although they both presumably hear much about the Condition of England question, Coningsby and Sir Joseph are distinguished by their respective ages in this passage. As Reinhart Koselleck suggests, this cleavage between contemporaneous individuals is an inherent element of the modern conception of progress.[62] Yet this element of progress also results in temporal reversals. That is, Sir Joseph's generation precedes Coningsby's but is late to hear about their new ideology.

This early theorization of the modern sense of generationality reflects the novel's valorization of the young—citing historical examples, Sidonia declares that "Almost everything that is great has been done by youth."[63] This utterance is ironic given Sidonia's role as a notably middle-aged mentor for Coningsby and his young friends—situated between the novel's poles of dissipated old age and feckless youth, he models the self-possession and sustained vigor ostensibly possible in middle age. Nonetheless, Sidonia's and the novel's veneration of youth poses a challenge for the narration of continuous progress. If ideology solidifies in early adulthood and then remains fixed, it becomes difficult to hold a unified contemporary conversation, across age cohorts, on the Condition of England question or another topic. In order to incorporate the non-progressing individual with social progress, one needs alternately to envision successive generational waves in which the older cohort is gradually replaced by rising youth in a seamless intergenerational turnover. This is not what happens in *Coningsby*. The novel depicts old people as successfully, and entirely inappropriately, maintaining power and privilege, reaping ongoing benefits from an outdated system of unearned merit. Rather than harmless vestiges of a libertine past, older people are actively destructive and vampiric.

Moreover, the novel largely rejects gradual individual change, whether for older or younger people. Coningsby's personal and ideological development proceeds so slowly as to be static, a protraction that results from the novel's extensive use of dialogue—I discuss more fully below the connection between speech and temporal suspension. Mary Poovey emphasizes that *Coningsby*'s "significant events are conversations (or monologues)"[64] between Coningsby and his friends and mentors. Yet while conversation does eventually earn Coningsby the confidence and power of young adulthood, there is no corresponding decline for Monmouth. When Coningsby, as a child, first meets his grandfather, Monmouth embodies established authority:

> Lord Monmouth was in height above the middle size, but somewhat portly and corpulent. His countenance was strongly marked; sagacity on the brow, sensuality in the mouth and jaw. His head was bald, but

there were remains of the rich brown locks on which he once prided himself. His large deep blue eye, madid and yet piercing, showed that the secretions of his brain were apportioned, half to voluptuousness, half to common sense. But his general mien was truly grand; full of natural nobility, of which no one was more sensible.[65]

The rich brown locks are gone, but Monmouth otherwise retains his powers. Over the course of the novel, as years pass and Coningsby grows up, Monmouth's appearance and prowess endure:

Lord Monmouth was somewhat balder than four years ago, ... and a little more portly perhaps; but otherwise unchanged. Lord Monmouth never condescended to the artifices of the toilet, and indeed notwithstanding his life of excess had little need of them. Nature had done much for him, and the slow progress of decay was carried off by his consummate bearing.[66]

Monmouth's preternaturally unchanged physical appearance represents the persistence of the past. In an early conversation, Tadpole and Taper—Tory gossips who are the Rosencrantz and Guildenstern of Disraeli's Political Trilogy—express doubts about Monmouth's ability to execute an inscrutable revanchist political scheme in the aftermath of Sir Robert Peel's reformist Tamworth Manifesto of 1834. Taper observes that "the time has gone by when a Marquess of Monmouth was Letter A. No. 1," to which Tadpole responds "Very true, ... a wise man would do well now to look to the great middle class."[67] This passage superimposes two temporalities: one charting the waning power of *the* Marquess of Monmouth under changing political circumstances, and another the waning power of *a* Marquess of Monmouth, and the aristocracy broadly, in favor of a rising middle class.

Yet in both cases, Tadpole and Taper may have spoken too soon. Monmouth's power persists, both within the fictional world, and as an agent for the plot. Discussing Dickens's early fiction, Jacob Jewusiak has argued that, "[t]ending toward digression, stasis, and senile confusion, Dickens's old men resist the progressiveness and causality of linear plotting. Yet in the process of resisting, they create the conflicts that enable developmental narrative to unfold successfully."[68] Monmouth has a similar function for Coningsby and for *Coningsby*. Consistent with the fictional trope of the wealthy elder, Monmouth's significant assets prompt intrigue among potential beneficiaries, unwillingly implicating Coningsby. In this way, his role resembles Old Martin's in *Martin Chuzzlewit*, wherein, Jewusiak explains, robust physical health and "a surfeit of resources" allow him to engage in the "protraction of plots, the creation of new ones, and the harboring of secrets" that ultimately facilitate the younger man's development.[69] Halfway through the novel, Monmouth marries Lucretia, the teenaged daughter of his longtime mistress, thus destabilizing inheritance expectations. Although the marriage ends acrimoniously, without children, the episode reflects Monmouth's ongoing vitality and virility, and participation in youthful narratives of development. Furthermore, since Lucretia was a possible match for Coningsby, her marriage helps clear the way for our hero's eventual union with the daughter of a Manchester manufacturer—a marital, economic, and ideological alliance reflecting a vision of the future that is distant from the ongoing aristocratic dissipation of the novel's present.

Monmouth's sudden death solidifies the novel's rejection of gradual progress in favor of stasis punctuated by unrepresentable rupture. After years undimmed by age, Monmouth dies nearly instantaneously, with potential witnesses realizing only after the fact. Readers learn of the death when Coningsby is told that, during a dinner party, Monmouth "suddenly found he could not lift his glass to his lips, and being extremely polite waited a few minutes before he asked Clotilde, who was singing a very sparkling drinking song, to do him that service. When in accordance with his request she reached him, it was too late."[70] Though this death is sudden, its perception is fractured through multiple stages of recognition. We extrapolate backward from the moment Clotilde reaches Monmouth, already too late; to the moment he requests her assistance, already having experienced the break in character that makes him "extremely polite"; to the moment of his own realization that a change has already occurred. Unexpected and nearly unnoticed during the evening's rollicking entertainment, Monmouth's death is an imperceptible vanishing point, an instant too brief to witness, and always in the past.

Monmouth's abrupt death departs somewhat from the 1842 demise of his alleged original, the Marquis of Hertford, about whom the memoirist Charles Greville observed, "no man ever lived more despised or died less regretted."[71] By the time of his death, Hertford was considered the last remnant of the hard-drinking, gambling, and womanizing increasingly associated with the past. In Greville's account, the gradual decline of Hertford's health parallels an intensification of his moral depravity. Greville explains with disdain and horror how Hertford maintained to the end his longstanding interest in sex workers, despite being "[b]etween sixty and seventy years old, broken with various infirmities, ... almost unintelligible from a paralysis of the tongue," and needing to be "lifted by two footmen from his carriage into the brothel."[72] Greville's ableist and ageist account of Hertford's late-life sexuality suggests that his behaviors remained consistent over time but became increasingly inappropriate as cultural attitudes shifted and Hertford aged.

As I discussed in the previous chapter, the relationship between personal development over the lifespan and historical progress writ large is remarkably complicated in nineteenth-century philosophy of history. The model of moral progress over time implied in *Coningsby* and Greville's *Memoirs* is considerably more sanguine than many influential theories of progressive history. Such theories often exclude the field of ethics, as when Ranke asserts that "The individual dies. His existence is finite.... I believe that every generation is equal in moral greatness to every other generation and that there is no higher potential for moral greatness."[73] Whereas for Ranke, one generation cannot morally exceed another, *Coningsby* assumes that it will. Whereas for Ranke, individual progress over the lifespan is probable, *Coningsby* sees individual stasis. Whereas for Ranke, death means that the wisdom of age cedes to the depravity of youth, *Coningsby* witnesses the dissipation of age ceding to the sobriety of youth. Despite all these differences, however, the models similarly reject the idea of a common conversation across age cohorts, all debating the Condition of England question together and moving gradually toward greater insight. By suggesting that contemporary individuals are siloed into generational categories with separate experiences of time, the two texts reflect the difficulty of reconciling continuous progress with the bounded temporality and normative trajectory of the individual life.

Monmouth's sustained good health right up until the end indicates that he serves as a time capsule of the ideologies and practices of an earlier moment. This is a standard fictional use of old men, from whom readers expect a high level of internal consistency of character. Jewusiak's argument about the end of *Old Curiosity Shop*—that the plot does indeed cohere if we allow that Master

Humphrey's personality changed over the life course—runs hard against the grain because readers tend to assume that such changes are implausible.[74] Yet we also demand from fictional older men a consistency with the perceived mores of an earlier time. In this way, *Coningsby* reflects a vision of history in which individuals do not change with the times—on the contrary, they become ever more like themselves, staying resolutely still as the ground shifts beneath them.

In this vision, historical change happens not through a unified continuous development in which all participate together, but rather through intergenerational succession, as unchanging older people who had old views and habits die off and younger people (also unchanging) with new views and habits replace them. This vision of progress through generational waves provides one way of reconciling the individual lifespan with larger demographic, socioeconomic, and ideological shifts. In the process, it asks us to narrate large, abstract historical changes specifically by freezing individuals in time, thus suggesting that undesirable elements of contemporary life are not truly contemporary but rather unaltered vestiges of a not-yet-overcome past, destined to disappear with generational turnover. This is the same logic that hopes for—or that fears—a future in which conservatives die off and are replaced by a younger, more diverse, and more progressive cohort.

Yet *Coningsby*'s ending—with the crushing continuity of aristocratic privilege, despite razor-thin ideological or dispositional differences between generations—reveals how difficult it is to imagine change this way. After Monmouth's death, *Coningsby* struggles to fulfill the promise that progress will result, finally, from the death of decadent elders. Monmouth's will and its codicils form a palimpsest of irregular survival in which narratives are layered incompletely over one another. The solicitor tasked with untangling the documents explains "that though Lord Monmouth had been in the habit of very frequently adding codicils to his will, the original will, however changed or modified, had never been revoked."[75] These documents vertiginously and confusingly redistribute Monmouth's assets many times. The original will and its first few codicils predate the period covered by the novel, and reflect the status of Monmouth's social relationships at the story's outset. These early documents call for a wide dispersal of assets, including several bequests to named friends, "a great number of legacies ... chiefly left to old male companions and women in various countries," and "an almost inconceivable number of small annuities to faithful servants, decayed actors, and obscure foreigners."[76] As the years go by, the reallocations of property in the later codicils become more dramatic, effectively rehearsing the novel's plot—the deepening of Monmouth's relationship with Coningsby in late 1832, his marriage to Lucretia in August 1837, their separation in June 1840, his volatile friendships with other male confidants, and his final break with Coningsby after the latter's engagement to the industrial heiress. But the codicils also reveal previously unknown narratives, including the existence of an illegitimate daughter, Flora, who unexpectedly inherits the bulk of the fortune in the end.

The will and its codicils reflect that, over time, Monmouth's property is consolidated into ever-fewer hands. As friends predecease him, the bequests become less lateral and more genealogical, and his increasing caprice in old age becomes evident. The dwindling of his social capital invests his whims with increasingly momentous consequences for the dispersal of his wealth. Yet these arabesques end up cancelling each other out. Despite dizzying ups and downs along the way, Coningsby's fortunes end exactly where they started, with the paltry £10,000 that he was promised before the novel began. Monmouth's original intent and final act is to disinherit his grandson, but the swift death of Flora allows Coningsby to assume his hereditary wealth and social position after all. As a female heiress and a misfit in the novel's intergenerational landscape (she is around Coningsby's age, but is his aunt), Flora is sacrificed to allow the restoration of patrilineal continuity that Monmouth, ironically, threatened to disrupt. Monmouth's death may represent the end of one era and the beginning of another, but it does not break the chain of aristocratic privilege.

Cotton stockings and stout woolens in *Sybil*

Whereas *Coningsby* promises and then retracts the promise of a radical break from the recent past, *Sybil* pulls the camera back in order both to reveal and to advocate for the sameness of the present and the medieval English past. As Nasser Mufti puts it, the novel figures the Norman Conquest as a "not a singular historical event but a modular and plastic 'spirit' that 'adapts' to the shifting landscape of English history."[77] In this way, *Sybil* bears comparison to the Victorian subgenre of the religious controversial historical novel studied by Miriam Elizabeth Burstein, who notes that it "explicitly calls into question [the] argument that past and present must be *different*, that the past is the necessary 'prehistory' of modernity and not identical to it."[78] Like those novels, *Sybil* reveals the long survival of the Christian typological sense of temporal simultaneity that Benedict Anderson argues is supplanted by Benjamin's homogeneous empty time around the end of the eighteenth century.[79] Thus, *Sybil* completes the trajectory this chapter has traced, in which Disraeli's novels, all set in the very recent past, are engaged with ever more distant histories, allowing the focus to become increasingly not about events themselves but about the interpretation of them, not history but historiography.

That is, *Sybil* associates different shapes of history with different attitudes toward the past. Gradual progress is associated with passivity, whereas temporal segmentation is associated with a resistant reading of the past that aims to achieve a present objective. The novel shows off creative anachronism at its most conservative, not only in its admiration for an ostensibly medieval paternalism, but also in its epistemological confidence in the knowability of historical truth. *Sybil* models the forging—in both senses, creation and fabrication—of connections across time, which invariably involves asserting that there is continuity where it seems like there has been change. Disraeli achieves this by highlighting irregular survivors of a medieval past—family lines, architectural ruins, and styles of dress. Yet in emphasizing the sameness of the past and present, he also represents individual historical moments as estranged from each other, using dialogue to suggest that the past is unknowable. This apparent paradox, in which the past is both identical and inaccessible to the present, reflects a rejection of continuous progress. Rather than events building in succession, leading in a direction, everything remains essentially the same just as it disappears from view.

Written just one year later, *Sybil; or, the Two Nations* takes place in the same fictional world as *Coningsby*, with recurring characters, and during an overlapping period, 1837 to 1844. Although *Sybil* is famous for its account of Chartism and the Condition of England debates, it remains profoundly interested in the young aristocratic protagonist's development. Like Coningsby, Charles Egremont rejects the dissipated environment of his family in favor of an earnest and reconciliatory stance toward apparent social divisions. However, as suggested by the two novels' contrasting secondary titles, "the new generation" and "the two nations," the tensions between the protagonist and his social world are more lateral than neatly genealogical in *Sybil*—*Coningsby*'s open hostility between youth and age is now muted. *Sybil* thus rejects from the outset the idea of generational succession that falters in *Coningsby*. Absent a patriarch, the aristocratic milieu is comprised by Egremont's mother, his elder brother Lord Marney, their friends the Mowbray family, and a larger circle that spans age cohorts. Yet the novel retains *Coningsby*'s narrative of aristocratic development from debauchery to sincerity. In the end, Egremont inherits his family's partially delegitimized title when his childless brother is stoned to death by an angry crowd, and the usurping Mowbrays are displaced when Sybil Gerard is restored to her rightful position. Thus, despite ironic reversals in each of their social standings, the marriage between Egremont and Sybil (unlike that between Coningsby and the industrial heiress) is entirely endogamous to the aristocracy. Although Mufti has described their union as a "recognition that the gulf between the two nations, between Sybil and Egremont, was never really there," the novel effects this resolution by elevating Sybil's class status, revitalizing rather than reforming the existing hierarchy.[80]

The character Baptist Hatton, a "heraldic antiquary" with a parasitic but powerful relationship to inherited power, centrally embodies the novel's interest in forged continuities.[81] Though his own background is obscure, Hatton uses questionable archival practices to manipulate evidence that allows certain families to claim aristocratic lineage, titles, and property. Hatton is eventually persuaded to reveal the truth and helps recover the documents he had sold to Mowbray that corroborate Walter Gerard's claim to the Mowbray title. Hatton's use of archival materials thus debunks false history with true history, though only after producing that falsity in the first place and undermining the idea of historical truth along the way. Hatton is, of course, "a figure for Disraeli the novelist"[82]—Gilmartin comments that "both have 'stories' to weave around certain historical facts."[83] The implications of Hatton's antiquarianism have long been a matter of debate, as it remains difficult to reconcile the novel's compelling picture of historical knowledge as creatively constructed with its final confidence in the truth of Sybil's pedigree. A. D. Cousins and Dani Napton even argue that Disraeli "appears to lack consciousness—or maybe, attempts to make invisible the fact" that he is engaged in a Hattonesque historiographical project.[84] Ben Moore argues along similar lines that the novel reveals the arbitrary and self-reinforcing nature of aristocratic authority in ways that are deeply subversive.[85] My reading is closer to that of Gary Handwerk, who describes the novel's "Machiavellian political dynamic" in which Hatton is a "hero of conservatism who channels and controls those forces that might otherwise rend the fabric of society."[86]

Through Hatton, the novel trains readers to recognize vectors of connection across time. The novel is littered with irregular survivors that suggest that past greatness lingers in the present, albeit in deflated and ironized forms. For example, expressing remorse for concealing evidence of Sybil's lineage, Hatton remarks that it is "Curious how, even when peasants, the good blood keeps the good old family names. The Valences were ever Sybils."[87] Here Hatton suggests that true historical continuity rests on a superficial level—not in the family name presumed to link a person to their lineage, but in the first name, through an informal tradition in which children are named after ancestors. Similarly, Sybil's dog reveals the ironic nature of true historical succession in the novel. Lamenting all that has been lost since the medieval past, Sybil's father Walter Gerard remarks, "'I cannot help wishing that Harold-----' Here the hound, hearing his name, suddenly rose and looked at Gerard, who, smiling, patted him and said, 'We were not talking of thee, good sir, but of thy great namesake; but ne'er mind, a live dog they say is worth a dead king.'"[88] Uncharacteristically slipping into a chivalric register of "thee" and "thy," Gerard reveals that the dog—an embodiment of loyalty and protection—is King Harold's true heir.

As this passage hints, the novel idealizes royal leadership but is ambivalent about its reality—a remarkable feature given Disraeli's later career. To an extent, this mixed attitude reflects *Coningsby*'s same dynamics of youth and age. Although scholarship often touches down on *Sybil*'s account of Victoria's accession, less has been written about the protracted representation of William IV's death, a dilation of *Coningsby*'s shorter version of the same event. Rumors fly about the king's declining health. Lady Marney speaks of the king in the past tense—wondering what might have happened "had he lived three months longer"—before clarifying to an alarmed Egremont that William is still alive, though "dying."[89] During this exchange a letter arrives claiming, "It is a false report;

he is ill, but not dangerously; the hay fever; he always has it," though Lady Marney disbelieves this missive.[90] The king apparently lingers in a liminal state, not dying but not recovering, for many pages of flurried speculation until "Hark! It tolls! All is over."[91] The monarch constitutes a unique case in considering the relationship between the individual life and larger historical narratives—monarchs' lives still exert a gravitational pull on historical periodization. More immediately, during this period, the death of the monarch meant a dissolution of parliament. Both *Coningsby* and *Sybil* dramatize how William's erratic decline prompts a political scramble as parties jockey for position; ultimately, the timing of the death is inopportune for the Tories. Not unlike the death of *Coningsby*'s Monmouth, the death of William is an empty center of tangled machinations, an anticlimactic end to a mediocre life.

Sybil's solemn representation of Victoria's accession, however, reflects the novel's cautious optimism in the power of the youthful monarch. Disraeli calls the eighteen-year-old Victoria a "maiden" who is "attended for a moment by her royal mother," and describes "a girl, alone, and for the first time, amid an assemblage of men."[92] Susan Zlotnick reads this account as suggesting "the 'misplacing' of authority into the hands of a girl queen," part of Disraeli's gendered rejection of industrial modernity.[93] Jennifer Sampson, by contrast, sees Disraeli targeting Victoria as a reader, offering a gently instructive guide, through the character of Sybil, for becoming a beloved leader of the people.[94] Notwithstanding the sexism of this passage, I concur with Sampson and would argue that the familiar infantilization of women in this scene works in concert with Disraeli's elevation of youth. The novel claims that at William's death, "Even the poor begin to hope; the old, wholesome superstition that the sovereign can exercise power, still lingers; and the suffering multitude are fain to believe that its remedial character may be about to be revealed in their instance."[95] Though the passage might seem ironic, the novel clearly shares this "old, wholesome superstition," hoping that its "remedial character" is reinvigorated by the young queen. The account ends with a series of hopeful rhetorical questions about what Victoria might accomplish: "Will it be her proud destiny at length to bear relief to suffering millions, and, with that soft hand which might inspire troubadours and guerdon knights, break the last links in the chain of Saxon thraldom?"[96] Reader, it will not. Yet this passage beautifully indicates the extremity of the novel's conviction that young people, even this personal representative of centuries of intergenerational continuity and inherited power, are capable of making a radical break with the past—though we never see it.

In King Harold's two descendants, dog and queen, the novel suggests that relying on passive historical continuity brings mixed results. Throughout the novel, metaphors of ripening and plucking indicate the need for a more active instrumentalization of the past. Orderly and predictable, ripening is a favorite metaphor for gradual continuous progress, one that figures change as inevitable but deferred. In "The Spirit of the Age," Mill observes that in the medieval period, "society was not yet ripe" to throw off its feudal lords or establish a new form of government.[97] A natural, passive process that unfolds on a regular timeline, ripening nonetheless implies the later act of plucking, and the question of ripeness figures frequently in *Sybil*'s heady discussions of Tory and Chartist strategy—one of many parallels between the two nations. For example, a Tory schemer asks, "but is the pear ripe?" and Marney responds, "The pear is ripe, if we have courage to pluck it."[98] Yet in neither nation does ripening seem to happen. At the beginning of Book VI, in 1842, Gerard bitterly regrets the actions taken by the Chartist movement at the end of the preceding book, three years earlier. He laments, "'affairs were not ripe. We should have waited three years.' 'Three years!' exclaimed Sybil, starting; 'are affairs riper now?'"[99] Although this exchange reflects that Sybil and her father are beginning to diverge on questions of Chartist strategy as she adopts a more accommodationist stance, it also suggests that ripening does not model the temporal trajectory of political movements.

This passage also illustrates how the novel uses topical dialogue both to orient and disorient the reader, ultimately suggesting the inscrutability of the past. Reflecting its debts to the silver-fork's heavy use of dialogue, *Sybil*'s six books begin with lengthy scene-setting conversations—many key events occur offstage between books. Secretive, gossipy, and scheming, these conversations feature unnamed characters who serve as a Greek chorus, speaking, literally, to the state of affairs. As Lauren Gillingham observes in Letitia Elizabeth Landon's *Romance and Reality* (1831), "characters come and go ... with little pretext. Many are introduced simply to espouse an opinion, style, or current customary practice, never to reappear."[100] Similarly, *Sybil*'s Book 4 begins with a

Disraeli's Frenetic Stasis 85

frenetic exchange between two previously unmentioned Members of Parliament as they walk down the street:

> "Our fellows are in a sort of fright about this Jamaica bill," said Mr. Egerton, in an undertone, as if he were afraid a passer-by might hear him. "Don't say anything about it, but there's a screw loose."
>
> "The deuce! But how do you mean?"
>
> "They say the Rads are going to throw us over."
>
> "Talk, talk. They have threatened this half-a-dozen times. Smoke, sir; it will end in smoke."
>
> "I hope it may; but I know, in great confidence mind you, that Lord John was saying something about it yesterday."
>
> "That may be; I believe our fellows are heartily sick of the business, and perhaps would be glad of an excuse to break up the government: but we must not have Peel in; nothing could prevent dissolution."
>
> "Their fellows go about and say that Peel would not dissolve if he came in."
>
> "Trust him!"
>
> "He has had enough of dissolutions they say."
>
> "Why, after all, they have not done him much harm. Even '34 was a hit."
>
> "Whoever dissolves," said Mr. Egerton, "I do not think there will be much of a majority either way in our time."
>
> "We have seen strange things," said Mr. Berners.
>
> "They never would think of breaking up the government without making their peers," said Mr. Egerton.
>
> "The queen is not over partial to making more peers; and when parties are in the present state of equality, the Sovereign is no longer a mere pageant."
>
> "They say her Majesty is more touched about these affairs of the Chartists than anything else," said Mr. Egerton.
>
> "They are rather queer; but for my part I have no serious fears of a Jacquerie."[101]

After continuing in this excited manner, the conversation is interrupted when Egerton and Berners encounter two friends, also unknown to the reader.

> "Just the fellows we wanted!" exclaimed Lord Fitz-Heron, who was leaning on the arm of Lord Milford, and who met Mr. Egerton and his friend in Pall Mall.

86   Temporality and Progress in Victorian Literature

"We want a brace of pairs," said Lord Milford. "Will you two fellows pair?"

"I must go down," said Mr. Egerton, "but I will pair from half past-seven to eleven."

"I just paired with Ormsby at White's," said Berners, "not a half an hour ago. We are both going to dine at Eskdale's and so it was arranged. Have you any news today?"

"Nothing; except thay [sic] say that Alfred Mountchesney is going to marry Lady Joan Fitz-Warene," said Lord Milford.

"She has been given to so many," said Mr. Egerton.

"It is always so with these great heiresses," said his companion. "They never marry."[102]

This vertiginously shifting conversation continues for several pages, situating the characters in a richly particularized historical context by referencing spring 1839 events, both real (Chartist agitation) and fictional (the Mountchesney/Fitz-Warene engagement). Yet the juxtaposition of registers is not only uncomfortable—the offhand reference to Jamaica typical of how Victorian fiction suppresses its awareness of colonial violence—but also confusing. Even with editorial notes, these atmospheric conversations remain somewhat obscure. In this way, they provide a kind of temporal reality effect, in which extraneous topical details give the feel of living in time. These challenging passages reflect that the exuberance of speech makes for unwieldy exposition. Through this disorientation, the novel accords to orality an intimate relationship to the present. Fleeting and opaque in hindsight, conversation is a counterpoint to the residual elements that I consider above. Whereas elderly figures like Monmouth or successive generations of Sybils in the Valance family suggest the basic sameness of past and present, conversation works to disconnect individual moments of time from each other. As we saw in the revision to *Vivian Grey*, making past conversations legible as part of a historical trajectory requires dampening the chaos. Speech thus allows the novel to represent characters embedded in their present, and by doing this, it distances and estranges that time from the reader. Past and present are thus paradoxically both the same and mutually unintelligible, undercutting the idea of linear transformation over time.

Whereas Disraeli revises *Vivian Grey*'s exuberant dialogue into sober retroactive continuity, these two modes of conversation coexist in *Sybil*. In the more linear mode, conversations are often *about* history, but also show Egremont's mind changing. Notwithstanding the novel's heavy use of gossip and chatter, Handwerk calls speech its "privileged political action."[103] Gillingham observes something similar in Landon's *Romance and Reality*, noting "the novel's seemingly endless paean to the formative influence of good conversation."[104] Like Coningsby's conversations with Sidonia, Egremont's conversations with Gerard shape his mature ideology. For example, Egremont tells Gerard, "I was reading a work the other day ... that statistically proved that the general condition of the people was much better at this moment than it had been at any known period of history."[105] Gerard responds, "Ah! yes, I know that style of speculation ... your gentleman who reminds you that a working man now has a pair of cotton stockings, and that Harry the Eighth himself was not as well off."[106] Gerard is thus suggesting that a positivistic progress narrative—in a cutting insult, he calls it "speculation"—relies on a materialistic account of lifestyle changes whose touchstone is clothing. After suggesting that the democratization of access to cotton stockings is perhaps not the best indicator of overall quality of life, Gerard attacks the argument on its face:

> I deny the premises. I deny that the condition of the main body is better now than at any other period of our history; that it is as good as it has been at several. I say, for instance, the people were better clothed, better lodged, and better fed just before the War of the Roses than they are at this moment. We know how an English peasant lived in those times: he ate fish every day, he never drank water, was well housed, and clothed in stout woolens.[107]

In contrast to Egremont's vague reference to a statistical work, Gerard cites not only Augustin Thierry's *History of the Conquest of England by the Normans* (1825), mentioned earlier in the scene, but also Thierry's primary sources, the Chronicles and the Acts of Parliament. Gerard may also have been reading *Ivanhoe* (1819), whose opening chapter features a vivid description of the clothing and habits of two peasants in a misty medieval past. Gerard's preference for stout woolens may reflect that cotton is an import that relies on enslaved labor, whereas wool is a traditional British product, perhaps better suited to the climate and to the daily activities of many workers in the medieval past and the nineteenth-century present. Similarly, fish—as more recently in regulatory negotiations with the European Union—serves as a potent metonym for an authentic, locally sourced national diet. In this eloquent rebuttal, Gerard asserts that clothing, diet, and the material articles of quotidian life *do* usefully indicate change over time, but they reveal decline or stasis rather than progress.

This scene features precisely the kind of meaningful conversation across class lines that Victorian fiction often uses to imagine rapprochement between rich and poor. As Simon During notes, the encounter is "ultimately an irreal scene—since in the real world of 1840 the son of an earl would not likely engage a worker as an equal."[108] What I want to observe here, however, is that talking about history takes the form of thoughtful dialogue, whereas living in the present is characterized by the frenetic, extemporaneous back-and-forth of the Members of Parliament. These two modes of dialogue compete and remain incommensurable in *Sybil*, reflecting that the novel theorizes the present moment as unincorporable into any larger historical narrative.

The description of the ruins of Marney Abbey illustrates the novel's rejection of gradual change and its advocacy for creative remaking under conditions of temporal stasis. Whereas the stout woolens worn by Gurth and Wamba in *Ivanhoe* would have perished long ago, medieval architecture often remains, serving as a rich metaphor for the relationship between past and present. The ruins of Marney Abbey are an architectural palimpsest, an embodiment of historical accumulation without replacement, erasure, or deterioration. Although Marney Abbey has features from various architectural periods and in various degrees of disrepair, the narrator insists that the structures are remarkably well preserved, that they stand "with a strength which had defied time."[109] A key difference between this account and Scott or Wordsworth on the ruin is that Marney Abbey is not actually a ruin, and thus does not, Disraeli suggests, reflect the leveling hand of time. Describing the central church, Egremont observes:

> On each side of the Lady's chapel rose a tower. One, which was of great antiquity, being of that style which is commonly called Norman, short, and thick, and square, did not mount much above the height of the western front; but the other tower was of a character very different. It was tall and light, and of a Gothic style most pure and graceful; the stone of which it was built, of a bright and even sparkling colour,

and looking as if it were hewn but yesterday. At first, its turreted crest seemed injured; but the truth is, it was unfinished.[110]

Disraeli's understanding of the aesthetic differences between the "Norman" and "Gothic" towers may be indebted to Thomas Rickman's popular and authoritative *Attempt to Discriminate the Styles of Architecture in England* (1819), which distinguishes a Norman style immediately following the conquest from the three subsequent "English" Gothic phases that were first outlined by John Milner's *Treatise on the Ecclesiastical Architecture of England during the Middle Ages* (1811).[111] Disraeli renders explicit the implicit patriotism of Rickman's nomenclature in the narrator's preference for the authentically English Gothic tower over that of the Norman oppressor. Although the Norman tower is actually older, it is the Gothic tower's bright and sparkling stone that inspires awe at historical survival. Like Monmouth, this Gothic tower is apparently immune from physical deterioration over time. The well-preserved condition of both towers thus facilitates a straightforward aesthetic contrast between the rude simplicity of the Norman and the sophistication of the Gothic, one that suggests a narrative of progress from foreign occupation to national flourishing.

The crest of the Gothic tower, however, sharply truncates this gradualist narrative with its witness to a sudden event. While it appears anthropomorphically "injured," as though in a violent attack, the Gothic tower was still under construction at the moment in the late 1530s when Henry VIII dissolved the monasteries and gave the abbey land to Egremont's ancestor. In this way, Marney Abbey's fate is highly atypical of real English monasteries. As the architectural historian Howard Colvin observes, "[f]or the vast majority of dissolved monasteries, ... the outcome was total or partial demolition."[112] Furthermore, surviving monasteries are often roofless, though not because they were "injured" or half-finished, but rather because the valuable lead in the roof was stripped, accelerating the structure's deterioration.[113] Were Marney Abbey's turret incomplete, this is precisely what would have happened. In its entirely unrealistic failure to deteriorate, Marney Abbey facilitates Disraeli's narrative of an incomplete project, merely paused, able to resume at any time.

Moreover, in celebrating the tower under construction at the moment the monasteries were closed, with its presumably late-Gothic aesthetic, Disraeli differs from the architectural historians Milner and Rickman, who strongly prefer the middle of the three phases and understand Gothic architecture as already in decline by the time the monasteries are dissolved.[114] Thus, although Disraeli elsewhere contests a Macaulay-style gradualist progress narrative about the eighteenth century, here he suggests a structurally similar but differently located gradualist progress narrative, albeit one that paused. As this passage indicates, durability renders the built environment interpretively challenging, in that a once-unrealized future is indistinguishable from a lost past. An attack of one kind (a decree) can look like another (a cannon), though the likeliest explanation is a third (looting). As the Gothic tower's incomplete turret is reinterpreted, the novel asserts that although architectural remnants can be misleading, when read properly, they reveal that time is static and has been for centuries, but might begin moving forward again.

Yet while *Sybil* advocates an activist presentism that remakes the past, Sybil helps clarify that the intent is *only* to reestablish or recognize what was always there. The novel clearly genders its account of time—women represent stasis whereas men enact rupture and creative anachronism. Both Sybil and Victoria are figures for linear stability, though as heirs of the past, rather than reproductive generators of the future—the novel makes no reference to future offspring for Sybil and Egremont, or to Victoria's four children. This association of women with continuity distinguishes *Sybil* from *Coningsby*, in which, as Poovey notes, "women are, for all intents and purposes, irrelevant."[115] Sybil establishes the stark limitations of the novel's creative anachronisms. She has a strong reaction to seeing Marney Abbey for the first time: "I was prepared for decay, but not for such absolute desecration. The abbey seems a quarry for materials to repair farm-houses; and the nave a cattle-gate."[116] In Sybil's distinction between decay and desecration—like that between ripening and plucking—she sharply delimits the appropriate use of agential revisionism. She viscerally rejects the agriculturally picturesque but problematically secular instances of repurposing that followed the dissolution of the monasteries, though it is this same agential remaking that the novel advocates to realize the unfinished project represented by Marney Abbey's incomplete turret. As throughout the novel, there is no decay, no decline, no ripening. The march of time has brought and will bring no meaningful change. What remains is only desecration or plucking, sudden willful acts of reinterpretation that can shift reality. In this passage, Sybil registers the danger of such sadly necessary and volatile actions. A reader could wonder whether Sybil has mixed feelings about the final revelation of her true class position and inheritance—a restoration of continuity, surely, but one that requires a violent effort. We hear little about her reaction to the news, only her sadness at her father's death.[117] Her final utterance anticipates a static future, imagined by negating the possibility of change: "'We will never part again' said Egremont. 'Never,' murmured Sybil."[118]

෨

Disraeli changed over the course of his life in ways that raised questions about both the consistency or linear development of character and the relationship between individual lives and larger historical processes. The political imperative to distance himself from youthful indiscretions and his trajectory of late-life professional success might have given Disraeli special reason to theorize models of maturation and growth into wisdom. Yet, on the contrary, Disraeli's novels valorize the vigor of youth in contrast to the lassitude and parasitism of age. Perhaps because no model of *Bildung* could redeem Disraeli's early blunders, his novels reject continuous progress in favor of a vision of segmented time. This chapter has traced the development of this outlook through three novels in which Disraeli briefly experiments with but ultimately cannot envision gradual change. The ostensibly widening perspective across the three works—from a minutely particularized 1820s and 1830s, to an eighteenth-century bureaucratic machine, to an imagined medieval idyll—reveals that the search for change over time leads Disraeli in the end to consider history as a whole, both finding and advocating for a profound sameness between past and present. This stasis is characterized by a frenetic energy in which the little details of localized time—chaotic conversations, obscure political schemes—work to estrange the past from the present, to sever historical developmental narratives. Like the theories of appositional presentism analyzed in the previous chapter, these novels suggest only structural parallels rather than genealogical relationships between disparate historical moments.

With this embrace of stasis comes a new emphasis on the power of interpretation to change reality. In these novels there is no history, only historiography—no change, only different ways of looking at time. Long before Nietzsche, they evince profound skepticism about the abuses of history, suggesting a presentist desire "to employ history for the purpose of *life!*"[119] They show that properly interpreting history's irregular survivors requires a deliberative critical practice, one that tends to undermine established narratives. Disraeli's historiography does not just prefigure post-2016 reactionary politics around the world and the faux-medievalism of white supremacy. It also anticipates critiques on the modern political left, both of liberal history, and of the adequacy of incremental progress—were it even possible—to address urgent global crises. Ongoing attempts to change the course of history in dramatically nonlinear ways—away from accelerating fascism, away from ever-increasing inequality, away from the direst climate outcomes—draw upon anachronist historical fantasies of the kind Disraeli's novels envision. As Disraeli shows us, using the past to fight for a better future is fraught, but it remains the past's best use.

Notes

1. Chase, *Victorians and Old Age*, 6.
2. Teukolsky, "Romanticism on the Right," 228.
3. Schwartz, *Disraeli's Fiction*, 1.
4. Teukolsky, "Romanticism on the Right," 216.
5. Mayer, "Prime Minister as Celebrity Novelist," 360.
6. Schwartz, "General Introduction," ix–x.
7. Teukolsky, "Romanticism on the Right," 224.
8. Strangely both central and peripheral to Victorian studies, Disraeli has received intermittent scholarly attention in the years since the great New Historicist readings analyzed his Young England Trilogy in the context of the Condition-of-England debate and the rise of nationalism (see Gallagher, *Industrial Reformation*; Poovey, *Making a Social Body*; Bodenheimer, *Politics of Story in Victorian Serial Fiction*; and Brantlinger, "Nations and Novels"). Disraeli's life remains a compelling gloss to his fiction (see O'Kell, *Disraeli*). Recent scholarship has clustered around two nodes of interest. The first considers Disraeli and theories of race. See Russell Schweller ("Mosaic Arabs"); Claire Nicolay ("Anxiety of 'Mosaic' Influence"); Jennifer Conary ("Dreaming over an Unattainable End"); and Lynn Voskuil (*Acting Naturally*). A second node of interest considers Disraeli in the interdisciplinary field of celebrity

studies and in Byronism as a cultural phenomenon (see Mayer, "Prime Minister as Celebrity Novelist," "Portraits of the Artist as Politician," and Hawkins, "Evoking Byron from Manuscript to Print").
9. Teukolsky, "Romanticism on the Right," 215.
10. See Samuel Smiles (*A Publisher and His Friends*, II:180–218), Robert Blake (*Disraeli*, 27–34), Charles Nickerson ("Disraeli"), Humphrey Carpenter (*Seven Lives of John Murray*, 151–5), and most recently Regina Akel (*Benjamin Disraeli and John Murray*). The competing accounts of *The Representative* affair take differing views on how much authority Disraeli had in conducting business for the newspaper, and the extent to which his behavior undermined it. Blake offers a tepid defense of Disraeli, noting that Murray gave him too much responsibility. By contrast, Akel is considerably more critical and observes that Disraeli's fictional version of events in *Vivian Grey* has been problematically taken to fill gaps in our limited understanding of the real-life events.
11. See Braun (*Disraeli the Novelist*), Hibbard ("Vivian Grey and the Silver-Fork Etiquette of Authorship"), and M. Sanders ("Introduction").
12. Stewart, *Disraeli's Novels Reviewed*, 115.
13. Braun, *Disraeli the Novelist*, 29–30 and 38–40; Hibbard, "Vivian Grey and the Silver-Fork Etiquette of Authorship," 256–60; M. Sanders, "Introduction," xliii–xliv; Stewart, *Disraeli's Novels Reviewed*, 116.
14. Quoted in Braun, *Disraeli the Novelist*, 39.
15. *Vivian Grey* was conceived as a two-volume novel whose success prompted a three-volume sequel (M. Sanders, "Introduction," xliv). Together they run to more than 1,500 pages.
16. M. Sanders, "Introduction," xlvii.
17. Polowetzky, *Prominent Sisters*, 110.
18. M. Sanders, "Introduction," xliii.
19. Ibid., xliv. Scholars generally read *Vivian Grey* as a sign of the young Disraeli's foolish ambition. The novel also influenced Wilde's *Picture of Dorian Grey*. In addition to the resonances between characters' names (Vivian Grey and Dorian Grey; Violet Fane and Sybil Vane), there is a similar epigrammatic wit, and a supernatural portrait in *Vivian* whose eyes mysteriously close when its subject is stabbed to death (see Nickerson, "Vivian," 909; Speare, *The Political Novel*, 2; Weintraub, *Disraeli*, 91–2).
20. Akel, *Benjamin Disraeli and John Murray*, 173.

21. Gillingham, *Fashionable Fictions*, 94.
22. Disraeli, *Vivian Grey*, 172.
23. Ibid., 173.
24. Gillingham, *Fashionable Fictions*, 95–9.
25. M. Sanders, "Introduction," xliv.
26. Quoted in Braun, *Disraeli the Novelist*, 28.
27. Braun, *Disraeli the Novelist*, 37; Blake, *Disraeli*, 49.
28. Disraeli, "General Preface," xx. *Vivian* was available in pirated European and American editions, but Disraeli clearly could have chosen to exclude it from the 1870 collection.
29. Richstad, "Genre in Amber," 550.
30. Ibid., 560.
31. Disraeli, *Vivian Grey*, 89, 90, 88.
32. *Oxford English Dictionary*, "tipsy, adj."; Grose, *Lexicon Balatronicum*.
33. Hotten, *Dictionary of Slang, Cant, and Vulgar Words*, 8, 28, 41, 59, 65.
34. Grose, *Lexicon Balatronicum*.
35. The 1840 revision of Edward Bulwer-Lytton's *Godolphin* (1833), for example, removes altogether a character who is a vicious satire of the once-prominent Lord Dudley, who died in an insane asylum shortly before the novel's publication (Cragg, "Bulwer's *Godolphin*," 678–9).
36. Disraeli, *Vivian Grey*, 89, 591.
37. Ibid., 90, 591, 89.
38. Richstad, "Genre in Amber," 561.
39. Disraeli, *Vivian Grey*, 88.
40. Akel, *Benjamin Disraeli and John Murray*, 143.
41. Michaelson, *Speaking Volumes*, 9.
42. M. Sanders, "Introduction," xxxvii.
43. Disraeli, *Vivian Grey*, 590.
44. Ibid., 591.
45. Braun, *Disraeli the Novelist*, 91.
46. Disraeli, *Vivian Grey*, 90. The 1853 revision cuts this reference to Beaconsfield, but the character is not eliminated.
47. Gilmartin, *Ancestry and Narrative*, 105.
48. Teukolsky, "Romanticism on the Right," 219.
49. Schwartz, *Disraeli's Fiction*, 81–3. Lord George Smythe appears as Coningsby, John Manners as Henry Sydney, and Alexander Baillie-Cochrane as Buckhurst. The prolific *Quarterly Review* contributor John Wilson Croker appears as the villainous Rigby.

50. Schwartz, *Disraeli's Fiction*, 90, 96; Hochstrasser, "Conway, Francis Ingram-Seymour-."
51. Teukolsky, "Romanticism on the Right," 219.
52. Elfenbein, *Byron and the Victorians*, 218.
53. Disraeli, *Sybil*, 230, 19; Schwartz, *Disraeli's Fiction*, 86–9; During, *Against Democracy*; Jupp, "Disraeli's Interpretation of History," 137–8.
54. Teukolsky, "Romanticism on the Right," 218.
55. Disraeli, *Coningsby*, 442.
56. Allen, *End of Progress*, 26.
57. Brantlinger, "Nations and Novels," 263.
58. Mole, *What the Victorians Made of Romanticism*, 39.
59. Disraeli, *Coningsby*, 57.
60. Ibid., 63.
61. Ibid., 301.
62. Koselleck, *Futures Past*, 282.
63. Disraeli, *Coningsby*, 110.
64. Poovey, *Making a Social Body*, 136.
65. Disraeli, *Coningsby*, 17.
66. Ibid., 171.
67. Ibid., 93.
68. Jewusiak, *Aging, Duration, and the English Novel*, 195.
69. Ibid., 57, 61.
70. Disraeli, *Coningsby*, 413.
71. Greville, *Memoirs*, 90.
72. Ibid., 91.
73. Ranke, *Theory and Practice of History*, 23.
74. Jewusiak, *Aging, Duration and the English Novel*, 52.
75. Disraeli, *Coningsby*, 414.
76. Ibid.
77. Mufti, *Civilizing War*, 64.
78. Burstein, *Victorian Reformations*, 6.
79. B. Anderson, *Imagined Communities*, 24.
80. Mufti, *Civilizing War*, 76.
81. Disraeli, *Sybil*, 237.
82. Bodenheimer, *Politics of Story in Victorian Serial Fiction*, 185.
83. Gilmartin, *Ancestry and Narrative*, 113–14.
84. Cousins and Napton, "Historical Romance and the Mythology of Charles I," 163.
85. Moore, "Disraeli and the Archi-Textual," 47.
86. Handwerk, "Behind Sybil's Veil," 340.

87. Disraeli, *Sybil*, 254.
88. Ibid., 168.
89. Ibid., 26.
90. Ibid., 28.
91. Ibid., 40.
92. Ibid.
93. Zlotnick, *Women, Writing, and the Industrial Revolution*, 20.
94. Sampson, "*Sybil*, or, the Two Monarchs," 98–9.
95. Disraeli, *Sybil*, 39.
96. Ibid., 41.
97. Mill, "Spirit of the Age," 70.
98. Disraeli, *Sybil*, 257.
99. Ibid., 365.
100. Gillingham, *Fashionable Fictions*, 100.
101. Disraeli, *Sybil*, 202–3.
102. Ibid., 203.
103. Handwerk, "Behind Sybil's Veil," 328.
104. Gillingham, *Fashionable Fictions*, 80.
105. Disraeli, *Sybil*, 172.
106. Ibid.
107. Ibid.
108. During, *Against Democracy*, 95.
109. Disraeli, *Sybil*, 57.
110. Ibid., 57–8.
111. Lewis, *Gothic Revival*, 48; Brooks, *Gothic Revival*, 136–7; Rickman, *An Attempt to Discriminate*, 141.
112. Colvin, *Essays in English Architectural History*, 56.
113. Ibid., 60.
114. Lewis, *Gothic Revival*, 48.
115. Poovey, *Making a Social Body*, 143.
116. Disraeli, *Sybil*, 123.
117. Ibid., 419.
118. Ibid., 417.
119. Nietzsche, "Uses and Disadvantages," 66.

3

Thackeray's Persistent Fashion

Inconsistent in the historicization of its characters' inner lives, uninterested in the implications of world-historical events like the Battle of Waterloo, and unserious in its treatment of the vagaries of life during the Napoleonic Wars, William Makepeace Thackeray's *Vanity Fair* (1847–8) seems to evince a facile or weak historicism in nearly every way. It often goes without saying that *Vanity Fair* is a far cry from, or a parody of, the historical novel in its rigorous formulation by Georg Lukács as dramatizing paradigmatic changes in the structure of society. Instead, in a typical reading, the novel uses what Harry Shaw has called "history as pastoral," wherein history provides "an ideological screen onto which" to project its critique of modern life.[1] Thackeray's narrator encourages this reading, using the example of women's clothing—a standard, sexist metaphor for superficial historical difference that belies similarity across time:

> At the time whereof we are writing, though the Great George was on the throne and ladies wore *gigots* and large combs like tortoise-shell shovels in their hair, instead of the simple sleeves and lovely wreaths which are actually in fashion, the manners of the very polite world were not, I take it, essentially different from those of the present day: and their amusements pretty similar.[2]

With references to George IV and the *gigot* or leg-of-mutton sleeve, this passage in the novel's second half confirms that the action has moved into the 1820s, while in the same breath it reassures readers of the universality of the manners and amusements depicted. This account of 1820s fashion is technical, the leg-of-mutton sleeve and the giant tortoise-shell comb providing a vivid, particularized image of the clothing of the time. By contrast, its reference to modern fashions is vague and vaguely positive—the wreaths are lovely, the sleeves simple, suggesting a minimalist rusticity that positions itself above the fray of fashion. The tongue-in-cheek contrast between the styles worn at the time and those that "*are actually* in fashion" reminds the reader that present tastes, too, are subject to fashion. As this passage begins to suggest, the novel's sheer exuberance troubles any dismissal of its historical setting as merely a screen. The novel is overstuffed with references to details of daily life that have long informed discussions of its generic indeterminacy, from Kathleen Tillotson's understanding of *Vanity Fair* as the defining example of a loosely defined category, the "[novel] about the recent past,"[3] to George Levine's observation that "circumstantial particularity ... allow[s] Thackeray to assimilate traditional literary forms into his narrative without succumbing to them."[4]

Yet to use "history as pastoral" is also to suggest that past and present are largely comparable, a vision of history as essentially static that, as I have been suggesting, is formulated alongside models of liberal progress during this period. *Vanity Fair*'s temporalities are complex and defined through negation. On the one hand, as the irony of the *gigot* sleeve passage reflects, the novel mocks the celebratory ideal of progress, whether on the sartorial, individual, or national level. Alexander Creighton reads it as an unresolved "competition between two conflicting attitudes toward time," both inconsistent with progress: "one of distraction and spontaneity" associated with cyclicality, and "the other of attentiveness and patience" associated with endless deferral.[5] On the other hand, the novel also rejects the nostalgia that would seek—with Disraeli—to recapitulate past glories or historic highs. Matthew Heitzman reads the novel through the renewed Franco–British tensions of the 1840s, arguing that it critiques "the impulse to read the present through the past."[6] In this chapter, I synthesize and build on these analyses to argue that *Vanity Fair* confronts the challenge of representing time's movement non-directionally—getting neither better nor worse, nor repeating the past. Instead, the novel understands time as constant, frenetic change that reveals a larger stasis in which history accumulates but does not evolve.

To this end, I trace the way that the novel's vision of history is both theorized and enacted as its historical backdrop shifts, from a first half that covers a two-year period culminating at Waterloo in June 1815 to a second half that sweeps the reader up through the early 1830s. David Kurnick observes that the novel's early sections are beset by a "welter of period detail" that "in the book's latter half [becomes] increasingly sporadic and half-hearted" allowing the novel to "offer a genealogy of the mid-century that understands the present as, precisely, the end of history."[7] I share Kurnick's interest in the novel's shifting sense of time, but I contest this characterization of its second half, observing that period detail persists in an altered form, reflecting the rhetorical challenge of narrating stasis. That is, as the novel goes on, its historically contextualizing references tend toward residual elements—formerly fashionable clothing reframed and reinterpreted in the present, and elderly people who have a sustained vitality and relevance to modern life. These irregular survivors simulate stasis by referencing the past with increasing insistence as time moves forward. This backward-while-forward movement shapes not only the novel's period references but also its formal style. Its first half, despite departures from Walter Scott's model for the historical novel, is nonetheless indebted to this notable generic development of the period it depicts. In the novel's comparatively critically neglected second half, its interlocutors shift to an older literary form, the *roman-à-clef*, in order to explore the continuities of aristocratic power in the long nineteenth century.

The novel's two halves are united by an interest in the world of fashion, albeit in two different senses: both the continual novelty of fashionable clothing, and the entrenched stability of fashionable high-society life. In the first half of this chapter, I analyze how the novel ironizes fashion's temporal logic. Clothing ultimately reveals that time is multiple and layered, often experienced as stasis, rupture, and cyclicality. Along the way, I challenge the critical paradigm that has long maligned conspicuous clothing in historical fiction as a kind of facile historicism. In the second half of the chapter, I take up the novel's interest in the temporal stability of aristocratic life, revealing how it undermines a fantasy of gradual liberal progress. I end the chapter by considering how the text's rejection of progress and the narration's incessant irony render *Vanity Fair* an analogue and precursor not only to modern forms of critical presentism, but also, strangely, to the amoral objectivity of positivist historical empiricism that I discussed in Chapter 1.

These readings focus on men and masculinity. Notwithstanding that an association with women informs the fashion's sexist dismissal as historiographically inconsequential, fashion is gendered male in *Vanity Fair*. As I illustrated in the Introduction through the comparison among Mill's jacketless twenty-six-year-old, Bagehot's aging man, and Dickens's Mr. Nandy, men's clothing complexly reveals historical dynamics of continuity and change. As I will demonstrate, men's clothing in *Vanity Fair* is particularly temporally vexed—simultaneously belated and anticipatory, reflecting a larger vision of layered, fractured time. Furthermore, in *Vanity Fair* as elsewhere, older men embody entrenched power as privileged subjects of genealogical succession. The novel thus uses men to reject a vision of time as smoothly and continually progressive, exploring instead the paradox of frenetic stasis—the sense that time is moving rapidly but going nowhere. Together, these readings reveal not only the resilience of class hierarchy in the face of its promised decline, but also the challenges of conceiving time outside of a directional model, whether one of progress or regress.

Jos Sedley's waistcoats

For all the novel's elaborate disavowals, including in the *gigot* sleeve passage, *Vanity Fair* remains fascinated by costume, a fraught subject in discussions of historical fiction. Nineteenth-century commentators as well as recent critics eagerly distinguish the historical novel proper—whose meaningful engagement with the past is marked by its attention to large-scale socioeconomic, demographic, and ideological shifts—from "mere costumery"— whose nominal setting in the past betrays an over-attention to material details, especially historical clothing.[8] Lukács contrasts Scott's Waverley novels favorably with predecessors that he describes as "historical only as regards their purely external choice of theme and costume," and subsequent scholarship frequently laments the drift of much historical fiction toward costumery.[9]

Yet as I have been arguing, clothing reflects temporality in complex ways and is a particularly rich example of the phenomenon of irregular survival in Victorian literature. Despite fashion's commercial logic of continual novelty, both old garments and old styles survive, experiencing diverging and unpredictable fates. Elizabeth Wilson's influential study *Adorned in Dreams: Fashion and Modernity* (1985) notes:

At "punk" secondhand fashion stalls in the small market towns of the South of France it is possible to see both trendy young holiday makers and elderly peasants buying print "granny frocks" from the 1940s; to the young they represent "retro-chic," to the older women what still seems to them a suitable style. But the granny frocks themselves are dim replicas, or sometimes caricatures, of frocks originally designed by Chanel or Lucien Lelong in the late 1930s. They began life as fashion garments and not some form of traditional peasant dress.[10]

Observing synergies of clothing across disparate cohorts, Wilson suggests that what looks classic or timeless—like a simple sleeve or lovely wreath—always originated as a fashion whose status as fashion has been forgotten. The passage also reveals the lie that clothes are a fleeting aspect of the object world. Although the phenomenon of trendy and disposable "fast fashion" has taken hold in recent decades, formerly fashionable clothes have always survived and can still today, whether on the body of the original owner, at the back of their closet, or for resale online.

Yet beyond the longevity of individual garments, the history of fashion styles indicates a multiplicity of coexisting temporalities. Characterized by periods of stasis punctuated by seismic shift, alternating phases of relative uniformity and pluralism, and unstable patterns of spatial dissemination, the apparent rapidity of fashionable time is more complicated than it seems. Timothy Campbell has argued that fashion's "production of contemporaneity" in the eighteenth century was ironically furthered by the phenomenon of the "fashionable antique," a retro style that "emphasized the peculiarly promiscuous ways in which fashionable material life crossed the boundaries between past and present."[11] Wilson sees this same self-aware doubling-back at the secondhand stalls. Campbell has traced the connection between fashion and historicism back to David Hume, whose "historiography solicited a commercial audience attuned to a dependable procession of novelty in any number of cultural domains," fashion being an exemplary case.[12] Lauren Gillingham similarly observes that "fashion invested the present age with a spirit that could be easily defined by comparison with the styles of the recent past."[13] Consequently, in the retrospective gaze, particular fashions bear the unmistakable stamp of the past—Hume describes a feeling of mild shock upon seeing "portraits of our ancestors ... [wearing] ruffs and fardingales."[14] The narrator anticipates precisely this aesthetic experience in the *gigot* sleeve passage, with two typical consequences. First, following fashion's narrative of constant change, clothing can provide the historical novel with a brute-force method for denoting the setting by pinpointing it along a rapid linear succession of styles. Second, Hume's piquant contrast suggests a critique of timeless human vanity, as past fashions often look ornamental, marked, or decorative in implicit comparison to the unmarked present of simple sleeves and lovely wreaths. Of course, in calling out the fardingale or farthingale—a hooped skirt worn in the seventeenth century, not dissimilar from that of the mid-nineteenth—Hume also unwittingly anticipates fashion's cyclicality. Moreover, as I discussed in the Introduction, modern fashions can just as soon appear to reflect a decline from the class-based paradigm of dress. In the 1867 *London Society* article "Modern Beau Brummellism," the author contrasts modern foppery unfavorably with the clothing depicted in the ruff-and-fardingale paintings of the seventeenth-century artist Anthony Van Dyck, in which unselfconscious ornamentation reflects a desirable unity between clothing and social class.[15]

As these contrasting responses to the marked alterity of historical costume begin to suggest, dress proves a site of complex temporal interactions in *Vanity Fair*. The text exposes as a fantasy the premise that the material world reflects the distinctiveness of different historical moments. In the pages that follow, I argue that *Vanity Fair* uses the temporal multiplicity and ambiguity of fashion to represent historical time as striated and multidimensional. In emphasizing the persistence of older styles, offering multiple interpretations of apparently fashionable garments, and depicting the unsynchronized life cycles of clothes, *Vanity Fair* undermines the idea that to be historically situated is to keep pace with a rapid linear narrative.

೮೨

To some degree, the increased attention historical fiction necessarily gives to clothing may result from the need to explain how that clothing contributes to what Roland Barthes calls the "characterization or atmosphere."[16] The critical intervention whereby Elaine Freedgood reveals the otherwise unseen imperial narrative suggested by *Jane Eyre*'s (1847) mahogany furniture, for example, is necessary only because the novel assumes and allows to remain implicit that the furniture straightforwardly indicates

Jane's wealth and good taste.[17] The objects of the historical novel regularly lack this transparency. They may serve as metonyms for character, but character constituted in the past; the objects themselves may be unfamiliar and their significance illegible to readers. Scott's *Ivanhoe* (1819) must, perhaps, devote sustained attention to Gurth and Wamba's clothing in its opening chapter in order to explain how their dress indicates their social position in post-Norman England. In this way, the historical novelist faces a rhetorical situation much like that of the nineteenth-century Canadian novelist Catherine Parr Traill, who must, as Freedgood puts it, "both present and represent" a foreign environment to British readers by copiously larding the narrative with expository ethnographic detail.[18]

To these ends, *Vanity Fair* introduces Joseph Sedley as follows:

A very stout, puffy man, in buckskins and hessian boots with several immense neckcloths that rose almost to his nose, with a red striped waistcoat and an apple green coat with steel buttons almost as large as crown pieces (it was the morning costume of a dandy or blood of those days,) was reading the paper by the fire when the two girls entered—and bounced off his arm-chair, and blushed excessively, and hid his entire face almost in his neckcloths at this apparition.[19]

Certainly, this passage uses Jos's relationship to clothing to sketch his character: his showy dress suggesting insecurities with his body and social position; his boots, a fanciful identification with the military; his retreat into neckcloths, an emasculated fear of women. The narrator's parenthetical aside that Jos's clothing "was the morning costume of a dandy or blood of those days," however, only begins to acknowledge that the novel's attention to clothing dramatically exceeds what would be needed to present a historicized individual character—and the meaning of Jos's clothing is considerably clearer than Gurth's and Wamba's anyway. For that matter, the clothing plainly demands greater interpretive significance than the reality effect would allow. Scholarship has interpreted this description of Jos's interest in clothing as reflecting the "artificial and performative nature of ... class personae,"[20] the "homosexualizing potential" of class pretensions,[21] or his embrace of "the perceived solaces of materialism."[22] More broadly, *Vanity Fair*'s use of clothing clearly participates in what Lisa Lowe calls a "fetishism of colonial commodities" in which "its representations of goods and commodities simultaneously recognize, *and* ingeniously suppress" their connections to colonial projects in the East and West Indies.[23]

Yet Thackeray's satire targets not only Jos personally, but also the famous male vanity of the period: accounts of his clothing include frequent reminders of the historical setting. For example,

> He never was well dressed: but he took the hugest pains to adorn his big person: and passed many hours daily at that occupation. His valet made a fortune out of his wardrobe. His toilet-table was covered with as many pomatums and essences as ever were employed by an old beauty: he had tried, in order to give himself a waist, every girth, stay, and waist-band *then invented*. Like most fat men he would have his clothes made too tight and took care they should be of the most brilliant colours and youthful cut. When dressed at length in the afternoon he would issue forth to take a drive with nobody in the park: and then would come back in order to dress again and go and dine with nobody at the Piazza Coffee House.[24]

This quietly compelling picture of loneliness and insecurity reveals not only Jos's personal vanity, but also the culture of a particular historical moment—one when, the novel suggests, men like Jos were particularly conscious of their bodies and ostentatious in their dress. The mismatch is not only bodily, between Jos's fat body and the dominant styles, but also developmental, between his age and the cuts that he chooses. Similarly, at Amelia's wedding,

> Jos Sedley was splendid. He was fatter than ever. His shirt collars were higher; his face was redder; his shirt-frill flaunted gorgeously out of his variegated waistcoat. Varnished boots were not invented *as yet*; but the Hessians on his beautiful legs shone so, that they must have been the identical pair in which the gentleman in the old picture used to shave himself.[25]

Marking the difference between men's footwear, then and now, the narrator also suggests a continuity in the desirability of a shiny boot. By "the old picture," Thackeray is probably referring to George Cruikshank's advertisement for Warren's Blacking from 1832, which depicts a man shaving in the reflection of a well-polished boot—it is "old" from the reader's perspective but had not yet appeared at the time of this fictional scene.[26] Thus, in these accounts of Jos's over-the-top clothing, we see insistent but complex references to time. Details of costume, rather than specifying the historical setting, work to muddy the waters, suggesting continuities and ironic returns.

Through prolepsis, we glimpse Jos's own understanding of his place in the history of fashion: "On returning to India, and ever after he used to talk of the pleasures of this period of his existence with great enthusiasm and give you to understand that he and Brummell were the leading bucks of the day."[27] "Buck," like "blood" earlier, denotes not only high spirits but also, specifically, fashionable clothing.[28] Moreover, as a potent, historiographically overdetermined figure for the Regency zeitgeist as constituted through fashion, Beau Brummell was renowned for his elegant dress, serving as the leading sartorial taste-maker in high society until 1816, when debts forced him abruptly to flee to France.[29] Just as Jos later claims to have been beside the Duke of Wellington at Waterloo, he places himself here with Brummell at fashion's vanguard, experiencing history through his clothing. Drawing upon the commercial logic of fashion as a rapid and unified march across a terrain of continually changing styles, Jos imagines that wearing fashionable clothing situates him in the moment. Reminiscing on this period, Jos sees in his clothing an ultimate proof of having-been-there.

Thus, the novel uses the interplay between Jos's self-interested account of his sartorial modernity and the temporal ambiguity and multiplicity of his clothing to suggest a kind of overlapping, accretive stasis. Miles Lambert demonstrates that throughout the novel, Thackeray gives Jos a wardrobe that best matches dandy fashions of the 1820s and 1830s—Disraeli's dandy period—rather than the pre-1816, Brummell-era aesthetic in which Jos claims to participate.[30] The novel's caricature of Jos and his explicit though distorting emulation of Brummell reflects and perhaps contributes to Brummell's contested legacy in the Victorian period. Although the first biographies of Brummell in the 1840s extensively documented his less-is-more aesthetic, popular articles like the widely reprinted "Modern Beau Brummellism" satirize what they construe as a highly ornamented style, reading back onto Brummell later developments in the history of men's fashion.[31] Whereas Brummell wore meticulously folded and lightly starched neckcloths, later dandies, like Jos, brought neckcloths up over their cheeks with the help of whalebone and heavy starching; whereas

Brummell wore coats and waistcoats in understated combinations of buff and blue, later dandies wore bright colors like Jos's red-striped and apple green ensemble.[32] The difference between Brummell's and Jos's clothing is one of class, certainly, but also one of time—Jos reflects a later aesthetic. Yet I believe that Eva Chen has overstated the modernity of Jos's dandy fashions in claiming that they resemble those worn in Thackeray's present.[33] Following Lambert and Ellen Moers, I understand Jos's clothing to differ from the dandy styles of the 1840s, with the looser, flowing neckcloths worn by the Count D'Orsay, or the black-and-white style first popularized by Edward Bulwer-Lytton's *Pelham* (1828).[34] Furthermore, although the dandies of the 1820s—Jos's closest match—may have self-consciously emulated Brummell, the costume historian Aileen Ribeiro has downplayed that connection, contextualizing the 1820s dandy instead within the longer tradition of the "Restoration fop and the eighteenth-century macaroni."[35]

Thus, the historicity of Jos's clothing is anything but straightforward. Within the world of the novel, and relative to his class position, Jos's clothing *is* of-the-moment. His fashion can be understood either as a belated and distorted imitation of Brummell, or as the manifestation of a longer tradition reaching back to the previous century. On the level of the connection between fictional and real fashion, the clothing is anachronistic, in that Jos wears particular styles years before they became popular. From that perspective, then, Jos reflects an extreme degree of the prescience associated with fashionability, with anticipating future trends. In this way, the novel uses the multiple temporalities of fashion thoroughly to complicate the idea of unified, continuous, linear progress from past to present, suggesting instead broad continuities and uncanny repetitions.

Clothing's temporal dilations and contractions are especially complicated in another passage and its accompanying image, which claim to clarify but ultimately muddle the novel's representational policy on historical dress. At Amelia's request, George Osborne contributes "the best hat and spencer that money could buy" to a collection of clothing for Becky to take when she leaves the Sedleys to become a governess.[36] A short jacket that ended at or above the waist, the spencer was especially popular for women at the beginning of the nineteenth century but was worn consistently through the century's end and has experienced subsequent waves of rediscovery.[37] Although this cursory account

Figure 3.1 Vignette in footnote, by William Makepeace Thackeray. *Vanity Fair*. Published at the Punch Office, 1847. Number 2, chapter 6, p. 56. Image provided by Chapin Library, Williams College.

of George's purchases supports Clair Hughes's observation that fictional clothing is "rarely described in full,"[38] Thackeray nevertheless includes the following footnote:

> It was the author's intention, faithful to history, to depict all the characters of this tale in their proper costumes, as they wore them at the commencement of the century. But when I remember the appearance of people those days, and that an officer and lady were actually habited like this—[vignette: see Fig. 3.1] I have not the heart to disfigure my heroes and heroines by costumes so hideous; and have, on the contrary, engaged a model of rank dressed according to the present fashion.[39]

But rather than establishing that characters are clothed anachronistically in modern dress, the footnote and vignette in fact raise questions about the extent to which clothing can be used to signal specific historical moments at all. George Henry Lewes and later readers have interpreted this passage as indicating Thackeray's belated realization, during the work's serial composition, of his failure to historicize the clothing in the images, a symptom of the work's larger "confusion of period," and a further sign that its satire targets the present.[40] Although Hughes similarly suggests that this passage reflects the novel's "historical confusion over dress,"[41] I would characterize it instead as productively historically ambiguous. Following the narrator, scholars have described the image as depicting "exaggerated Regency dress"[42]—a claim that assumes that a style can be exaggerated without distorting its historical denotation. Yet a closer inspection reveals that though the bonnet and hat are exaggeratedly large, the historicity of the clothing in the image is not straightforward. The woman in the vignette appears to wear a paradigmatically Regency-style dress, with a long, loose skirt without a crinoline, and perhaps also a short-sleeved spencer. Her slightly forward-bending posture and raised right arm, however, block our view of what should be a key historically distinguishing feature: the dress's empire waistline. Thus, the image does not fully exploit the potential differences between historical and contemporary fashions. Instead, it provides only an attenuated contrast with the modernized visual representations of women's clothing elsewhere in the novel—featuring tight bodices, lower waistlines, and crinolines.

A similarly mitigated contrast between old and new characterizes the man's morning or riding coat and trousers. The period between 1800 and 1830 saw the gradual decline of eighteenth-century breeches and stockings in favor, first, of pantaloons, and later, of the style of trousers still worn today.[43] Although Brent Shannon has argued that sartorial display was central to middle-class masculinity throughout the nineteenth century,[44] the period represented in *Vanity Fair* has traditionally been understood to witness what the early twentieth-century British cultural theorist John Carl Flügel called the "great masculine renunciation" of "sartorial distinctiveness."[45] This sea-change has long been a privileged development in the history of fashion, understood as meaningfully related to ideological and economic shifts. Yet this vignette downplays that transformation. By showing the man in day wear, the image features an early adoption of modern trousers. Notably, this image might plausibly have depicted the traditional knee-breeches that continued to dominate men's formal wear throughout the years represented in *Vanity Fair*, giving way to trousers only later.[46] Thus, the image understates rather than exaggerates the potential sartorial contrast between past and present. While it mocks outdated fashions, this footnote undermines any sense of clothing's historical specificity.

Furthermore, although the novel's other images generally support Thackeray's claim, and the critical consensus, that the costumes better signal the 1840s than the 1810s, such a distinction between the historical accuracy of the text and the anachronistic contemporaneity of the images is not entirely clear and is particularly uncertain in the case of menswear. As I have established, textual accounts of Jos's clothing are historically overdetermined, situating him incoherently in time, somewhere between the historical setting and the reader's present, but also in multiple places at once. The novel's images similarly feature a messy array of styles—each the prop equivalent of historical prolepsis or analepsis. In this way, Thackeray's approach to visuality starkly contrasts with that of Scott's imitators in the 1830s and 1840s, and some creators of historical film and TV today—for whom costumes and props provide a site for fastidious historical accuracy. It also differs, on the other extreme, from the approach of medieval art, in which biblical scenes are rendered in modern dress, or from theatrical productions that stage Shakespeare, say, in twenty-first-century costumes.[47] Instead, Thackeray's approach anticipates that of Christian Petzold's film *Transit* (2018), set during the Second World War, it seems, but with costumes, props, and settings that are strikingly varied in their historicity—some clearly dated to the mid-twentieth century, others clearly modern, and still others impossible to place.

For example, notwithstanding the vignette's early depiction of trousers, several images show Jos, Lord Steyne, and other male characters wearing knee-breeches. One image of the younger Sir Pitt Crawley in the "old diplomatic suit which he had worn when attaché to the Pumpernickel legion" accompanies a passage in which Becky insincerely compliments this outmoded choice: "She said that it was only the thorough-bred gentleman that could wear the Court suit [i.e. knee-breeches] with advantage: it was only your men of ancient race whom the *culotte courte* became."[48] As this passage indicates, visual depictions of knee-breeches are not simply a historically accurate representation of the survival of older garments in the wardrobes of men like Sir Pitt.

Ironically, images of knee-breeches become more frequent in the novel's second half, as the plot moves into the 1820s, during which knee-breeches continued their inexorable decline. This counterintuitive trajectory reflects the novel's retrospective pose in its latter half and the way that male sartorial distinctiveness suggests a "tentative nostalgia for anti-bourgeois values," as Moers puts it.[49] Yet this trajectory also highlights the process whereby clothing fashions become more legible *as transitory fashions* when they begin to go out of style. Sir Pitt does not realize the valence of Becky's comment—he "looked down at his legs and thought in his heart that he was killing."[50] Nevertheless, he sees his knee-breeches in a new way: not as a default choice, but rather as a mark of class distinction, reflecting his studied adherence to a traditional style in rejection of recent changes. The case of Sir Pitt's knee-breeches reflects that as particular fashions wax and wane, they are worn with variable levels of self-consciousness. And yet, even if he misjudges his ability to pull off the *culotte courte*, Sir Pitt reveals fashion's potential to disrupt a linear timeline by doubling back on itself, resignifying the old-fashioned as fashionable once again, if only under the right circumstances—to wear deliberately what had been worn by default.

As this passage suggests, the fates of formerly fashionable garments differ. Some fall permanently out of favor. Others become "timeless" or "classic" staple pieces, conforming to Raymond Williams's category of the residual, in that they were "effectively formed in the past, but [are] still active in the cultural process."[51] Still others become privileged sites of a studied retro aesthetic—these embody William's category of the archaic, in that they "are wholly recognized as an element of the past," even when revived.[52] Sir Pitt's knee-breeches traverse the border between archaic and residual, lingering in reality and in the historical imagination. Rather than seeing these elements as oppositional to an increasingly dominant paradigm of gradual liberal progress, I see them as offering a robust counterargument for the sameness of time. As I have been arguing, this line of thinking was more common in nineteenth-century literature and culture than scholarship has previously been recognized.

Jos also experiences a shift in his attitude toward his clothing, one that offers a rare and mitigated glimpse of positive personal development in this novel. Over time, Jos maintains his interest in clothes, though the meaning of that interest changes. Toward the novel's end, during a stopover in Southampton upon what proves his final return from India, Jos shops for waistcoats. He

> selected a crimson satin, embroidered with gold butterflies, and a black and red velvet tartan with white stripes and a rolling collar, with which, and a blue satin stock and a gold pin, consisting of a five-barred gate with a horseman in pink enamel jumping over it, he thought he might make his entry into London with some dignity. For Jos's former shyness and blundering blushing timidity had given way to a more candid and courageous self-assertion of his worth. "I don't care about owning it," Waterloo Sedley would say to his friends, "I am a dressy man:" and though rather uneasy if the ladies looked at him at the Government House balls, and though he blushed and turned away alarmed under their glances, it was chiefly from a dread lest they should make love to him, that he avoided them, being averse to marriage altogether. But there was no such swell in Calcutta as Waterloo Sedley, I have heard say: and he had the handsomest turn-out, gave the best bachelor dinners, and had the finest plate in the whole place.[53]

This passage—rather more critically neglected than the initial accounts of Jos's clothing—is an important follow-up that reflects his diminishing anxiety and growing self-confidence over time. With "I am a dressy man," Jos asserts that sartorial exuberance remains central to his identity, despite changing expectations for men of his age and class. Although styles have changed slightly, with the waistcoat's black-and-white elements perhaps reflecting the influence of *Pelham*, the narrator's historical contextualizing remarks are notably absent in this later description. In fact, Jos happily distinguishes himself from peers who have moved on, embracing in an active and personalized way a practice that he adopted earlier when it was more widely popular. The description of him as a "swell" rather than a "buck" and "blood" places a somewhat more positive construction on his behavior.[54] Even his avoidance of women is partially recast as a deliberate choice. Of course, this account of modest personal growth is undermined by Jos's later decline—debts, infirmities, and exploitation by Becky, leading to his suspicious death—but in this passage, we briefly trace a trajectory of non-heteronormative maturation figured through sartorial consistency.[55]

In both Jos's sustained but shifting pursuit of over-the-top waistcoats and Sir Pitt's lingering loyalty to knee-breeches, the appearance of continuity ultimately reveals change. Time is assumed to be static until the sudden apprehension of its passage. Through clothes, the novel shows how the past survives, often apparently unchanged, but in ways that remain interpretively multivalent. *Vanity Fair*'s fictional clothing is not mimetic of the actual clothing worn at any point—whether during the novel's historical setting or in Thackeray's present. Instead, it is richly metaphorical for the uneven experience of time. In *Vanity Fair*, clothing often reveals its wearer to be unfashionable, one way or another—Jos is too self-conscious while Sir Pitt not self-conscious enough. Accounts of their clothing reveal the strain among fashion's temporal logic of constant change, the uneven lived experience of time, and the representational practices of historical fiction. They make visible the considerable work involved in representing any historical moment as discrete and self-contained—when even clothing, which seems straightforwardly and superficially of its time, persistently suggests complicated and unacknowledged historical narratives. In its apparent material manifestation of the zeitgeist, clothing ironically reveals the difficulty of distinguishing past from present.

Although the broader concern over costumery in the historical novel suggests that the fascination with clothing can be a worrisome by-product of any historical gaze, *Vanity Fair* engages in an early Victorian historiographical project of finding—in Regency fashion specifically—an archaic aesthetic defined by legible illegibility. As I discussed in the previous chapter with respect to Disraeli's use of slang, elements of the past must be gone but not forgotten in order to register as the past. Yet it proves impossible in *Vanity Fair* to isolate a distinctive sartorial aesthetic that belongs squarely in the past. Ultimately, this novel's representation of clothing rejects a self-congratulatory genealogical narrative in which the materialist, time-bound past transforms into an anti-materialist, ahistorical Victorian present. In the process, it casts doubt on the very idea of meaningful change over time. Dramatizing the diverse ways that fictional clothing can undermine linear progress, *Vanity Fair* depicts history as unfolding along multiple axes, a constant interplay of old and new in which these categories themselves are deceptive. Through the Victorian interest in outmoded fashion that this novel reflects, we see in clothing's continuity and revival a metaphor for the experience of standing still in history.

Aging and succession in *Vanity Fair*'s aristocratic world

The first half of this chapter has demonstrated how *Vanity Fair* complicates fashion's commercial logic of continual novelty, depicting time as striated and multilayered. But "fashionable" has another, related meaning in the nineteenth century, referring more broadly to behavior "in accordance with prevailing usage; of the kind in vogue among *persons of the upper class*."[56] This sense of fashionable life as simply upper-class life reflects a conceptual link between the fleeting moment of fashion and the inertia of intergenerational privilege. Lauren Gillingham observes, "in an important modulation on eighteenth-century commentary, nineteenth-century critics began to identify in fashion's cyclical rhythms less the principle of novelty intrinsic to commercial modernity than the historical continuity and invariability of aristocratic life."[57] Not only are financial resources required to keep up with clothing fashions, but, as we saw with Jos and Sir Pitt, class is the substrate in which all fashion choices live. Although *Vanity Fair*'s protagonists come from the middle classes, the novel attends closely to questions of aristocratic succession, much like *Coningsby* and *Sybil*. In the second half of this chapter, I trace the aristocratic world that hovers on the periphery of the plot but anchors the novel's conceptualization of static time. The aristocracy in this novel has a temporality like that of the Victorian institution as theorized by Mary Mullen: in constant motion, it narrowly delimits futurity within its bounded horizon.[58] But whereas the Victorian institution is self-consciously modern, indeed dictating modernity's terms, the aristocracy appears, and only appears, to be a vestige of an earlier social structure. This novel uses the aristocratic world as a symbol of renewing and renewable stasis. In the process, I argue, it exposes the work involved in maintaining temporal stillness. As we saw also in Disraeli, the stability of aristocratic power relies on constant motion, unwieldy accretion, and fabricated claims of continuity.

The novel's attention to aristocratic fashionability intensifies in its second half. As the plot moves forward in time, the novel adopts representational practices from the *roman-à-clef*, a genre associated with aristocratic life and with the seventeenth and eighteenth centuries. One might take for example the Pumpernickel episode—a somewhat confounding narrative cul-de-sac near the novel's end that according to Cristina Richieri Griffin provides "an aestheticized space for belatedly rehearsing the Napoleonic wars."[59] Prior to this late point, *Vanity Fair* follows what Freedgood has called "realism's weird—although thoroughly naturalized—combination of fictionality and factuality" in which fictional characters move through factual places.[60] But then in "Pumpernickel," a thinly veiled Weimar, the novel adopts the *roman-à-clef*'s literal, yet veiled relationship to place, a shift indicative of the novel's late interest in this early representational mode.

To illustrate this shift, let's contrast the novel's early and late accounts of social scandal. In a typical early passage, the novel relays entirely fictious gossip:

> At this time as some old old readers may recollect the genteel world had been thrown into a considerable state of excitement, by two events, which as the papers say might give employment to gentlemen of the long robe. Ensign Shafton had run away with Lady Barbara Fitzurse, the Earl of Bruin's daughter and heiress, and poor Vere Vane, a gentleman who up to forty had maintained a most respectable character and reared a numerous family, suddenly and outrageously left his home for the sake of Mrs. Rougemont, the actress who was sixty five years of age.[61]

Like the conversation about the Mountchesney/Fitz-Warene engagement in *Sybil*, this passage uses fictional high-society gossip to situate the plot in a specific moment in time. Later in the novel, this uniform fictionality gives way to the *roman-à-clef*'s messy juxtaposition of references to elite society, in dashes, real names, nicknames, and oblique allusions. After describing the dreary front of Lord Steyne's mansion in Gaunt Square, the narrator continues:

> A few score of yards down New Gaunt-street, and leading into Gaunt-mews indeed, is a little modest back door, which you would not remark from that of any of the other stables. But many a little close carriage has stopped at that door, as my informant (little Tom Eaves, who knows everything, and who showed me the place) told me. "The Prince and Perdita have been in and out of that door, Sir," he has often told me; "Marianne Clarke has entered it with the Duke of ---. It conducts to the famous *petit apartements* of Lord Steyne—one, Sir, fitted up all in ivory and white satin, another in ebony and black velvet.... It was there that Egalité Orleans roasted partridges on the

night when he and the Marquis of Steyne won a hundred thousand from a great personage at Hombre. Half of the money went to the French Revolution, half to purchase Lord Gaunt's Marquisate and Garter—and the remainder—"[62]

The contrast between the two passages is striking. Whereas the earlier account discusses scandals from a more modestly "genteel" world, the later passage reviews the machinations of royals and dukes—the strikingly black-and-white rooms, perhaps reflecting *Pelham*'s influence, indicate the connection between the changefulness of fashion and the changelessness of extreme wealth. Whereas the early passage uses two apparently contemporary pieces of fictional gossip to date the setting precisely within a fictional world, the later passage references real individuals and scandals spanning the decades on either side of 1800—another way that the novel's interests move back in time and become more temporally diffuse as its plot moves forward. Whereas the early passage describes events that appear in newspapers, the later passage nervously cites Tom Eaves, Thackeray's fictional hub of gossip. Moreover, the stakes have been raised: whereas the earlier scandals might result in litigation ("employment for gentlemen of the long robe"), the gambling winnings of the later passage fund the French Revolution, a detail that evokes the tradition of secret history, in which the idiosyncrasies of powerful individuals have world-historical consequences.[63]

Early reviewers did not miss the *roman-à-clef* quality of the later parts of the novel. For a writer in *The Observer*, the description of Steyne's back door confirms that he represents the third Marquis of Hertford, the same debauched aristocrat who inspired *Coningsby*'s Lord Monmouth, as I discussed in the previous chapter.[64] Indeed, Steyne is the key figure in *Vanity Fair*'s negotiation between representational modes in its latter half. In a study of the survival of the *roman-à-clef* long after its alleged eighteenth-century death, Sean Latham has argued that the genre lingered as a "mode of reception" of Victorian realism, citing the famous example of Dickens's angry denials that *Bleak House*'s Harold Skimpole was based on Leigh Hunt.[65] Steyne is thus a figure for long continuity, not only as a fictional representative of intergenerational inherited power, but also as a generic holdover from an older literary form.

The character of Steyne reveals *Vanity Fair*'s thoroughly ironic stance toward the grand narrative of personal and cultural genealogy that falters in *Coningsby*. More like *Sybil*, *Vanity Fair* both delegitimates the historical narratives that undergird aristocratic power and also asserts that power's imperviousness to change. Treating the aristocracy as an engine of stasis allows the novels to turn from history to historiography, because if it is impossible to imagine true historical change, the question becomes how the delusion of change is created. In emphasizing the resilience of wealth and privilege, the figure of Steyne reveals the retroactive construction of historical continuity. Although the character might appear to embody the novel's critique of aristocratic excess, I read him as a neutral exploration of the mechanisms that maintain class hierarchy over the *longue durée*.

A shadowy figure who enters the story gradually and remains obscure, Steyne first appears half-way through the novel, as part of an undifferentiated "party of gentlemen ...seated around [Becky's] crackling drawing-room fire."[66] Kathleen Tillotson observes that "Thackeray's method is to make us feel that he has been there a long time."[67] Indeed, the novel's elliptical introduction of Steyne hardly suggests the important role he will play in the plot. He is named only later in the scene, when brief parallel descriptions suggest that he is an aristocratic, male foil for Becky:

> A score of candles ... lighted up Rebecca's figure to admiration, as she sate on a sofa covered with a pattern of gaudy flowers. She was in a pink dress, that looked as fresh as a rose; her dazzling white arms and shoulders were half covered with a thin hazy scarf through which they sparkled; her hair hung in curls round her neck; one of her little feet peeped out from the fresh crisp folds of the silk; the prettiest little foot in the prettiest little sandal in the finest silk stocking in the world.[68]

This blazon is immediately followed by a description of Steyne that echoes the introduction of *Coningby*'s Lord Monmouth:

> The candles lighted up Lord Steyne's shining bald head, which was fringed with red hair. He had thick bushy eyebrows, with little twinkling bloodshot eyes, surrounded by a thousand wrinkles. His jaw was underhung, and when he laughed, two white buck-teeth protruded themselves and glistened savagely in the midst of the grin. He had been dining with royal personages, and wore his garter and ribbon. A short man was his Lordship, broad-chested, and bow-legged, but proud of the fineness of his foot and ancle, and always caressing his garter-knee.[69]

This diptych, emphasizing the feet, suggests either the grotesque nature of women's formal dress or the emasculating nature of men's. The passage's accompanying illustration depicts Steyne in knee-breeches, as still befit a man of his age, class, and circumstances (dining with royals), and one "proud of the fineness of his foot and ancle."[70] The presence of Steyne contributes to the ironically increased prominence of knee-breeches in the novel's second half despite their gradual disappearance during the period, as I discussed above.

This introduction of Steyne appeared even more inconspicuous in later printings of the novel, when the illustration disappeared.[71] Although the likeliest explanation is a damaged woodblock, Peter Shillingsburg notes that "some have speculated that it was suppressed because it too closely resembled the living marquis of Hertford, but other illustrations of Lord Steyne remain, and it is disputed which marquis of Hertford the illustration resembled."[72] In fact, this confusion between the third marquis and his son, who held the title when the novel appeared, persisted as the century carried on, an error that reflects the blurring of history in the rearview mirror. In 1890, the *San Francisco Chronicle* took pains to correct the error:

> Any one who will take the trouble carefully to study the salient traits in the character of the third Marquis, as depicted in the journals and chronicles of two generations ago, will, on turning to Lord Steyne, have no difficulty in tracing a most genuine vraisemblance. Never was mordant satire more felicitously and faithfully employed than when Thackeray took in hand this singularly unique personage and gave him immortality.[73]

As we see here, the character of Steyne reveals a paradox at the heart of the novel. Steyne seems to be based on a specific individual from a particular era, but the individual and even the era are hard to pinpoint, suggesting the persistence of this character type and his debauched aristocratic milieu, despite its augured decline. Thus, the novel's claims to timelessness inhere, strangely, in vivid historical particularity that remains just indecipherable. Like the legible illegibility of Disraeli's use of slang in the revised *Vivian Grey*, the character of Steyne appears initially to contribute to an aesthetic of historical difference but ultimately reveals the persistence of the past in the present. As in the novel's treatment of clothing, Steyne seems to illustrate the adage that the more things change, the more they stay the same.

The novel waits until three numbers after the fireside introduction to present a direct exposition of Steyne's background and character. As in *Sybil*, that backstory works to delegitimize his aristocratic genealogy, despite the narrator's repeated parenthetical caveats that "(the reader must bear in mind that it is always Tom Eaves who speaks)."[74] The account focuses on the genealogy of Steyne's wife, *née* Lady Mary Caerlyon, whose family, like Sybil Gerard's, dates from a misty, dragon-beset British past. The Marchioness "was of the renowned and ancient family of the Caerlyons, Marquises of Camelot, who have preserved the old faith ever since the conversion of the venerable Druid, their first ancestor, and whose pedigree goes far beyond the date of the arrival of King Brute in these islands."[75] The family history is detailed at length from the Elizabethan period onward in an elaborate web of historical allusions. According to Eaves, Lady Mary was "married—sold, it was said—to Lord Gaunt," Steyne's name at the time, "then at Paris, who won vast sums from the lady's brother at some of Philip of Orleans's banquets."[76] Once married, "'the humiliations,' Tom used to say, 'which that woman has been made to undergo, in her own house, have been frightful.'"[77] This brief interruption of the gothic, another eighteenth-century tradition, further reflects the novel's retrograde shift in generic interlocutors. The novel thus suggests that, through marriage, Steyne usurps the true aristocracy represented by the Caerlyons, "to whom the Steynes are but lackeys, mushrooms of yesterday (for after all, they are *not* of the old Gaunts, but of a minor and doubtful branch of the house)"—that is, they are not direct descendants of John of Gaunt, father of Henry IV.[78]

Steyne is thus engaged in a higher-classed version of the same deception that George Osborne uses when asked by a General if he is related to the "L--- Osbornes," the family of the Duke of Leeds. "'We bear the same arms,' George said, as indeed was the fact; Mr. Osborne having consulted with a herald in Long Acre, and picked the L--- arms out of the peerage, when he set up his carriage fifteen years before."[79] Though years have elapsed, George is still working to suggest a conveniently vague familial relationship to the Duke of Leeds, like the centuries-long con Steyne's family attempts with respect to John of Gaunt. Notwithstanding the scalar difference in their respective temporalities of social mobility, George and Steyne share a common strategy—one of mixed success—in blurring family history in order to associate oneself with established power. Furthermore, in a more negative version of precisely what Egremont achieves in marrying Sybil Gerard, Steyne also joins a legitimately more eminent family retroactively through the lateral move of marriage. In this novel, continuity with the past is an aristocratic privilege, and though it originated in usurpation at one point or another, it remains extremely resilient in the present.

As I discussed in the previous chapter, *Sybil* also suggests that the wrong people currently hold titles and privileges—until that error is corrected at the novel's end, allowing for the aristocracy's renewed authority and leadership. *Vanity Fair* sees no such reversal, but nonetheless shares with *Sybil* a sense of the imperviousness of aristocratic power. Whereas the history preceding Lord Steyne's marriage deflates his origins, the subsequent history suggests that the promise of aristocratic decline will never be realized. The narrator claims that extreme inherited wealth is a structural strain on genealogical relationships:

> In comparing, too, the poor man's situation with that of the great, there is (always according to Mr. Eaves) another great source of comfort for the former. You who have little or no patrimony to bequeath or to inherit, may be on good terms with your father or your son, where the heir of a great prince, such as my Lord Steyne, must naturally be angry at being kept out of his kingdom.[80]

Yet despite this confidence about the natural enmity between aristocratic generations, a *Coningsby*-style rivalry and inheritance plot never emerges. When Steyne's elder son dies childless and indebted, hopes for continuity relocate to the younger, who is recalled "from Vienna, where he was engaged with waltzing and diplomacy" and promptly married off.[81] The younger son fathers several children before going insane and being secreted away on the family property. The novel presents this insanity as an overdetermined result of their lineage—"it was in the family,"[82] and both sides, apparently, have a history of mental illness, "the mysterious taint of the blood."[83] In a passage that perhaps provides the novel's only moment of sympathy for Steyne, readers learn that he is deeply affected by his younger son's fate:

> This dark presentiment also haunted Lord Steyne. He tried to lay the horrid bed-side ghost in Red Seas of wine and jollity, and lost sight of it sometimes in the crowd and rout of his pleasures. But it always came back to him when alone, and seemed to grow more threatening with years. "I have taken your son," it said, "why not you? I may shut you up in a prison some day like your son George."[84]

In contextualizing Steyne's bacchanalian lifestyle, the passage also portends the collapse of aristocratic lineage over slow time. Thinking of her descendants rather than herself, Steyne's wife similarly worries that the "awful ancestral curse"[85] will afflict her grandchildren—depicted in Thackeray's illustration with the sword of Damocles hanging over their heads.[86] Yet the sword never falls—despite the eruption of insanity in his son's generation, Steyne's numerous grandchildren are never mentioned again; the narrator explains that their "doings do not appertain to this story."[87] The apparent vulnerability of the family to devastating mental illness or destructive rivalry ultimately belies the stability of their position. The ever-present threat of degeneracy is a statement of faith about the trajectory of aristocratic power, foreshadowing a future decline that is always imminent, but always deferred.

Lord Steyne reflects that *Vanity Fair* shares *Coningsby*'s assumption that powerful older individuals remain stable rather than evolve along with changing times. Steyne's death, like that of *Coningsby*'s Monmouth, truncates this force of long consistency over time, suggesting a vision of history as stasis punctuated by untheorizable rupture:

> Everybody knows the melancholy end of that nobleman, which befell at Naples two months after the French Revolution of 1830: when the Most Honourable George Gustavus, Marquis of Steyne, Earl of Gaunt and of Gaunt Castle, in the Peerage of Ireland, Viscount Hellborough, Baron Pitchley and Grillsby, a Knight of the Most Noble Order of the Garter, of the Golden Fleece of Spain, of the Russian Order of St. Nicholas of the First Class, of the Turkish Order of the Crescent, First Lord of the Powder Closet, and Groom of the Back Stairs, Colonel of the Gaunt or Regent's Own Regiment of Militia, a Trustee of the British Museum, an elder Brother of the Trinity House, a Governor of the Whitefriars, and D. C. L.—died, after a series of fits, brought on, as the papers said, by the shock occasioned to his Lordship's sensibilities by the downfall of the ancient French monarchy.[88]

In this capsule obituary, Steyne appears as a figure for accumulation without change. Like the codicils to Monmouth's will, Steyne's titles accrue without canceling each other out, forming a palimpsest of identities, affiliations, and activities disparate in space and time. The hereditary titles early in the list reflect the consolidation of aristocratic power through generations of intermarriage. The honorary titles later in the list have a wide and implicitly contradictory range accommodated by Steyne's long life—from the diplomatic feat of being honored by both Russian and Ottoman empires, to the juggling of numerous civic, military, and court responsibilities. In the previous chapter, I observed that Monmouth's sudden death differs from the gradual decline of Hertford, arguing that this fictionalization allows the novel to suggest that progress—if possible at all—requires moments of rupture that break time's fundamental stasis. Steyne's death differs slightly in that he experiences a "series" of fits over two months, an iteration of the kind of episode that killed Monmouth. For the reader, however, that decline is collapsed and relayed only after the revelation that he has "died."

The novel offers two explanations of the shock that precipitated this turn, suggesting first, that he "never recovered" from unexpectedly encountering Becky years after their relationship ended, and then, that political events powerfully affected him.[89] The link between Steyne's demise and that of the House of Bourbon, though ironically attributed to "the papers," nonetheless suggests the possible synergy of the personal and the world-historical. The sympathetic death of an older man coinciding with a dreaded momentous change is a trope of fiction representing the years around 1830. In Bulwer-Lytton's *Godolphin* (1833), for example, a dying lord explains from his deathbed on the eve of Reform: "I am a type of a system; I expire before the system: my death is the herald of its fall."[90] This passage suggests not only the character's fantasy of a wider significance for his death, but also the way fiction uses individual death to reify cultural changes that are profound but abstract.

The death of Steyne ironizes this trope, but only to some extent. The fatal shift is displaced to France and the news reaches Steyne in Naples—a turn that associates him with pan-European counterrevolutionary politics. Putting Steyne's death in 1830, the novel neatly aligns it not only with the July Revolution but also with the death of Hertford's friend George IV—whereas the real-life

Hertford lived until the less historiographically significant year 1842. Similarly, Sir Pitt dies just after Reform revokes the Crawley family's control of two rotten boroughs and dashes their hope of a peerage, leaving him "both out of pocket and out of spirits by that catastrophe."[91] Thus, despite its somewhat ironic treatment of this trope, the novel uses the deaths of fictional old men to do the work of historical periodization.

As at the end of Disraeli's *Coningsby* and *Sybil*, death has cleared the way for change that seems inevitable but remains just beyond the horizon. Whereas Disraeli strongly considers if ultimately rejects the possibility of historical change through generational succession and replacement, Thackeray seems never to consider it. Since the faked death of Steyne's younger son, the title presumably passes to one of the grandchildren mentioned earlier, whose "doings do not appertain" to the novel.[92] In a similar passage, leaving young Georgy Osborne at school, the narrator observes, "Our business does not lie with the second generation."[93] In fact, all the novel's instances of generational succession emphasize continuity. For example, informing Sir Pitt Crawley the younger of his father's death, a servant says, "If you please, Sir Pitt, Sir Pitt died this morning, Sir Pitt."[94] Propriety requires the servant to hail the new Sir Pitt just before she tells him the news, reflecting the overlaps that continuity requires, with the final, redundant "Sir Pitt" awkwardly establishing him in this new identity. By the time that Rawdon Jr. inherits the Crawley title, furthermore, he is estranged from his mother and shares the family ideology. Becky's infiltration of the aristocracy has no appreciable effect on the institution or even the family.

Steyne's social and characterological stability in late life contrasts with the trajectory of decline experienced by the novel's middle-class men, particularly Mr. Sedley. The novel heavily foreshadows his ruin in an early passage that reveals the attenuated and distorted relationship between Sedley's financial speculation and world-historical events:

> Papa conducted his mysterious operations in the City—a stirring place in those days, when war was raging all over Europe, and Empires were being staked—when the "Courier" newspaper had tens of thousands of subscribers—when one day brought you a Battle of Vittoria, another a Burning of Moscow, or a newsman's horn blowing down Russell Square about dinner time announced such a fact as "Battle of

Leipsic, six hundred thousand men engaged, total defeat of the French, two hundred thousand killed." Old Sedley once or twice came home with a very grave face: and no wonder when such news as this was agitating all the hearts and all the Stocks of Europe.[95]

As this passage suggests, the volatility of the markets is both a consequence and a metaphor of war, which heightens financial risk and *is* a high-stakes gamble with lives and territory. Like the news business itself, Sedley's fortunes are linked to war, but counterintuitively. That is, the markets do not just abstract war's human toll, but also, apparently, reverse national interests such that two allied victories (Vittoria and Leipzig) and a pyrrhic French fiasco (the Burning of Moscow) cause Sedley's losses. Nonetheless, he is ruined ultimately by investing in French bonds, betting on the financial stability of peace, on the very day that Napoleon lands on the continent after escaping Elba.[96] Sedley interprets this turn as the result of "collusion, Sir, or that villain never would have escaped. Where was the English Commissioner who allowed him to get away? He ought to be shot, Sir—brought to a court-martial, and shot, by Jove."[97] Sedley's interpretation reflects a larger tendency among nineteenth-century historians to view Napoleon's career as evidence that history is driven by individual actors rather than structural forces—Carlyle's *On Heroes* calls Napoleon "our last Great Man!"[98]—with the escape from Elba in particular as the moment of highest and most personalized contingency.

However, narratorial comments asserting the inevitability of financial reversal undercut Sedley's theory: "All his speculations had of late gone wrong with the luckless old gentleman. Ventures had failed: merchants had broken: funds had risen when he calculated they would fall. What need to particularise? If success is rare and slow, everybody knows how quick and easy ruin is."[99] Broadening out from the one fateful incident, the narrator emphasizes that Sedley's experiences are a probable outcome of this kind of financial dealing, and the endpoint of debt's trajectory. During an early scene that contrasts age with youth, Sedley is denied a credit extension at Hulker, Bullock & Co. just as George Osborne receives a loan: "As George entered the house; old John Sedley was passing out of the banker's parlour, looking very dismal. But his Godson was much too elated to mark the worthy Stock-Broker's depression, or the dreary eyes which the kind old gentleman cast upon him. Young Bullock did not come grinning out of the parlour with [Sedley] as had been his wont in former years."[100] This juxtaposition implies a narrative in which youthful overspending leads to penurious old age, a financial rise-and-fall pattern distinct to the middle class, though one truncated for George by early death. Insofar as Sedley's financial hardships have any further explanation, it may be found in the sly winking between the two clerks, which perhaps insinuates that Sedley is being pushed out of the credit system due to the imminent marital alliance between the Bullock and Osborne families.[101] Thus, Sedley's Napoleonic delusion belies that the colluders, if they can be called that, are in his immediate social circle. Sedley's experience ironizes that of *Godolphin*'s dying lord, suggesting the appeal of a quixotic relationship to current events in which it is comforting to understand oneself as subject to the unpredictable contingencies of history rather than either one's own decisions or the inevitability of debt's narrative.

Sedley moves to the novel's background after the auction of his possessions, around the time that Steyne emerges, at a similar late point in both their lives. Sedley's attempt to import wine—reflecting a resilient confidence in international trade—suggests that he is simply too old for business success. Eager to help, Dobbin arranges a large order of "the finest and most celebrated growths of ports, sherries, and claret wines at reasonable prices, and under extraordinary advantages,"[102] only to lose money and reputation when it becomes clear that "the old gentleman's former taste in wine had gone,"[103] suggesting that the sensory losses of aging have dulled Sedley's business acumen. When he finally dies, Sedley meditates painfully on his failures, experiencing what Andrew Miller calls the optative, which "conceives of one's singularity—the sense that one has this particular life to live and no other—by contrasting it with lives one is not living."[104] The main foil for Sedley's optative regret is Mr. Osborne, whose life has seen the desirable trajectory of steadily accumulating wealth and status. Mr. Osborne tells their mutual grandson, "Look at your poor grandfather, Sedley, and his failure. And yet he was a better man than I was, this day twenty years—a better man I should say, by ten thousand pound."[105] Osborne dies a few pages later with fortune intact, though without reconciling with Amelia—that is, with one unrealized scene ahead of him.[106] Yet the novel also suggests a comparison between Sedley and Steyne that highlights the latter's stability in contrast to the former's trajectory of rise and fall. As Sedley is dying, the narrator asks, "Which, I wonder, brother reader, is the better lot, to die prosperous and famous, or poor and disappointed? To have, and to be forced to yield; or to sink out of life, having played and lost the game?"[107] This disingenuous question—of course it is better to die in prosperity—brings to mind Steyne, who is more prosperous and famous than any other character. Money cannot forestall death, but it ensures the stability of his social power right up until the end.

༄

As I have been arguing, the historical aesthetic in fiction inheres in legible illegibility—what is recognizable but still obscure. In *Vanity Fair*, this aesthetic is impossible to find because of the persistence of the past. Rather than a meaningless backdrop for the domestic plot, then, *Vanity Fair*'s historical setting proves complicatedly meaningful in revealing the unevenness of time. A sneaky, behind-the-scenes figure in the *roman-à-clef* mode, Steyne mediates between the fictional middle-class protagonists and a real, aristocratic world that is beyond their knowledge and that is characterized both by rapid change, and by total changelessness. Steyne reflects the novel's governing vision of time as stasis punctuated by rupture. Presumably, such a rupture might result in radical change, but in a way strikingly different both from the gradual progress favored by nineteenth-century theorists of history and from narratives of decline. Rather than a directional movement from one paradigm to another, history in this novel is a matter of the mechanisms of fashion that allow for stasis despite apparent change, and that allow for temporal expansions, contractions, and returns. I understand the novel's representational shifts over its long scope as part of this effort to simulate stasis within time's one-way movement, moving back as it moves forward. This disorienting stillness ultimately reveals the stability of intergenerational aristocratic power, despite its allegedly ongoing decline in the face of modern political and economic transformation.

In its rejection of the directional movement of progress or decline, *Vanity Fair* reflects the skepticism toward historical narrative seen in certain theories of appositional presentism, like Walter Benjamin's *Theses on the Philosophy of History*, Michel Foucault's "Nietzsche, Genealogy, and History," and Carlyle's "On History." I argued in Chapter 1 that these theories themselves strangely resemble positivist empiricism in eschewing narrative.

Vanity Fair, too, with its consistent irony ultimately suggests a historiographical neutrality or detachment consonant with the positivist approach. Although this method does not become prominent among historians until the twentieth century, this novel theorizes it as a form of fictional satire. And, in its paradoxical project of narrating stasis, it resonates also with Harriette Wilson's *Memoirs* (1825), which are interested, for reasons intimately connected with gender, in holding time still. When Nietzsche laments the "premature grey-beardedness of our present-day youth,"[108] he figures historical culture as both preternaturally old and distinctly male. If, as in Thackeray and Disraeli, older men represent entrenched power and its abuse, or the obstacle to progress, older women often stand oddly apart from trajectories of change over time. Yet women life-writers in the nineteenth century develop various strategies for either theorizing stasis or demanding their place in a larger narrative of progress. These approaches are the subject of my next chapter.

Notes

1. Shaw, *Forms of Historical Fiction*, 51.
2. Thackeray, *Vanity Fair*, 508.
3. Tillotson, *Novels of the Eighteen-Forties*, 93. Lukács's restrictive criteria for the historical novel can only be achieved when the historical setting is a certain distance from the present—too distant, and it can be difficult to establish a genealogical relationship between past and present, as Walker ("A False Start for the Classical-Historical Novel") demonstrates; too near, and it can be difficult to historicize at all—though Lukács himself understands the historical novel as a forerunner to the realist depiction of a historicized present (Lukács, *Historical Novel*, 83). Tillotson acknowledges that "the line between [novels of the recent past] and the historical novels may not always be easy to draw; no two readers may quite agree as to how 'historical' *Vanity Fair* is intended to be" (Tillotson, *Novels of the Eighteen-Forties*, 94). Shaw makes the same point, also citing *Vanity Fair* (Shaw, *Forms of Historical Fiction*, 38). Fleishman (*English Historical Novel*, 3), Jones (*Lost Causes*, 14), and Richstad ("Genre in Amber," 550) use Tillotson's concept as well.
4. Levine, *Realistic Imagination*, 151–2.
5. Creighton, "Tickers and Time-Keepers," 527.

6. Heitzman, "The Devil's Code of Honor," 44.
7. Kurnick, *Empty Houses*, 34, 35.
8. Lukács, *Historical Novel*, 19. The impulse to patrol the borders of historical fiction against the incursion of a superficial historicism originates in Lukács's narrow generic criteria, to which scholarship has remained largely committed. Avrom Fleishman's *The English Historical Novel* (1971), for example, is a sustained lament that the Victorian historical novel does not meet Lukács's requirements. Harry Shaw's *Forms of Historical Fiction* (1983) outlines three different ways that history functioned in Victorian historical novels—as pastoral, as a source of drama, and as subject—but nevertheless establishes an ambivalent hierarchy in which those that use history as subject are on top (Shaw, *Forms of Historical Fiction*, 53). Although Richard Maxwell's *The Historical Novel in Europe: 1650–1950* (2009) extends the Lukácsian tradition in space and time—back to the seventeenth-century French *nouvelle* and forward to twentieth-century successors in Europe and Latin America—he remains committed to similar rigorous criteria.
9. Lukács, *Historical Novel*, 19. Critical commentary on the historical novel in the 1830s and 1840s suggests that if the Waverley novels were the first to transcend costumery, they were also perhaps the last. A typical review derides the anonymous author of *Tales of the Early Ages* (1832) as belonging to "the Wardrobe School of Novelists, viz. to those writers who give the costume of the time without the life and nerve" (*Athenaeum Journal*, 251). Twentieth-century critics largely echo this response. James Simmons roundly disparages William Harrison Ainsworth and Edward Bulwer-Lytton for providing "details of costume, manners, architecture, weapons, and armor to pad out the picture" (Simmons, *Novelist as Historian*, 13). Nicholas Rance claims that these works stage modern issues "in period costume" (Rance, *Historical Novel and Popular Politics*, 8). Andrew Sanders agrees with a nineteenth-century assessment of Ainsworth as "little more than a reviver of old clothes," who "had, in fact, no real idea about history, simply a delight in being surrounded by its trappings" (A. Sanders, *Victorian Historical Novel*, 46, 33).
10. E. Wilson, *Adorned in Dreams*, 5.
11. Campbell, *Historical Style*, 15, 19.
12. Ibid., 129.
13. Gillingham, *Fashionable Fictions*, 10.
14. Quoted in Campbell, *Historical Style*, 140.

15. "Modern Beau Brummellism," 137.
16. Barthes, "The Reality Effect," 11.
17. Freedgood, *Ideas in Things*, 31.
18. Freedgood, "Fictional Settlements," 404.
19. Thackeray, *Vanity Fair*, 18.
20. Cole, "The Aristocrat in the Mirror," 139.
21. Litvak, "Kiss Me, Stupid," 224.
22. Lindner, "Thackeray's Gourmand," 571.
23. Lowe, *Intimacies of Four Continents*, 82.
24. Thackeray, *Vanity Fair*, 21–2, italics mine.
25. Ibid., 217, italics mine.
26. Thackeray (edited G. and K. Tillotson), *Vanity Fair*, 207n.
27. Thackeray, *Vanity Fair*, 21.
28. *Oxford English Dictionary*, "buck, n.1," "blood, n. (and int.)."
29. Biographies by Jesse and Barbey d'Aurevilly in the 1840s differ markedly but share an understanding of Brummell as the culmination of a specific dandy tradition that originated in the eighteenth century. This sense of Brummell as the last vestige of the past contrasts with his alternative reputation as an innovator advanced by most modern scholars (see Carter, "Brummell"; Moers, *The Dandy*; and Ribeiro, *Art of Dress*, 103). Brummell himself describes his approach as both modern and a return to ancient costumes (Brummell, *Male and Female Costume*, 127).
30. Lambert, "The Dandy in Thackeray's 'Vanity Fair' and 'Pendennis.'"
31. "Modern Beau Brummellism," 137.
32. Jesse, *Life of Beau Brummell*, 62; Moers, *The Dandy*, 62.
33. Chen, "Dobbin's Corduroys," 46.
34. Moers, *The Dandy*, 153, 82.
35. Ribeiro, *Art of Dress*, 101.
36. Thackeray, *Vanity Fair*, 63.
37. *Oxford English Dictionary*, "spencer, n.2."
38. Hughes, *Dressed in Fiction*, 3.
39. Thackeray, *Vanity Fair*, 63–4.
40. Lewes, "Review," 754; Rance, *Historical Novel and Popular Politics*, 55; Hammond, "Thackeray's Waterloo," 20.
41. Hughes, *Dressed in Fiction*, 3.
42. Leighton and Surridge, *The Plot Thickens*, 128.
43. Lambert, "The Dandy in Thackeray's 'Vanity Fair' and 'Pendennis,'" 65; Davidoff and Hall, *Family Fortunes*, 412.
44. Shannon, *The Cut of His Coat*.
45. Flügel, "The Great Masculine Renunciation and Its Causes," 103.

46. Breward, *Culture of Fashion*, 174.
47. B. Anderson, *Imagined Communities*, 22–3.
48. Thackeray, *Vanity Fair*, 455–6.
49. Moers, *The Dandy*, 14.
50. Thackeray, *Vanity Fair*, 456.
51. Williams, *Marxism and Literature*, 122.
52. Ibid.
53. Thackeray, *Vanity Fair*, 589.
54. *Oxford English Dictionary*, "swell, n."
55. Thackeray, *Vanity Fair*, 687.
56. *Oxford English Dictionary*, "fashionable, adj. and n.," italics mine.
57. Gillingham, *Fashionable Fictions*, 10–11.
58. Mullen, *Novel Institutions*, 1.
59. Griffin, "Experiencing History," 414.
60. Freedgood, "Fictional Settlements," 394.
61. Thackeray, *Vanity Fair*, 112.
62. Ibid., 464–5.
63. Maxwell, *The Historical Novel in Europe*, 12–13.
64. "Periodicals," *The Observer*, Feb. 7, 1848; "Original Lord Steyne," *San Francisco Chronicle*, Sept. 14, 1890; Hochstrasser, "Conway, Francis Ingram-Seymour-"; Stevens, "Vanity Fair and the London Skyline."
65. Latham, *Art of Scandal*, 37.
66. Thackeray, *Vanity Fair*, 376.
67. Tillotson, *Novels of the Eighteen-Forties*, 249.
68. Thackeray, *Vanity Fair*, 377.
69. Ibid., 378.
70. Ibid.
71. Ibid., 377 and note.
72. Ibid.
73. "Original Lord Steyne," *San Francisco Chronicle*, Sept. 14, 1890.
74. Thackeray, *Vanity Fair*, 467.
75. Ibid., 465.
76. Ibid., 466.
77. Ibid., 466–7.
78. Ibid., 467.
79. Ibid., 284. Thackeray might appreciate the irony that another George Osborne, though heir to a different baronetcy, served as Chancellor of the Exchequer in David Cameron's Conservative government in the early 2010s—reflecting the crushing continuity of intergenerational inherited power.

80. Thackeray, *Vanity Fair*, 467–8.
81. Ibid., 470.
82. Ibid.
83. Ibid., 471.
84. Ibid., 472.
85. Ibid.
86. Ibid., 471.
87. Ibid., 470.
88. Ibid., 651.
89. Ibid., 650.
90. Bulwer-Lytton, *Godolphin*, 273.
91. Thackeray, *Vanity Fair*, 685.
92. Ibid., 470.
93. Ibid., 521.
94. Ibid., 408.
95. Ibid., 120.
96. Ibid., 178, 201 note.
97. Ibid., 201.
98. Carlyle, *On Heroes*, 208.
99. Thackeray, *Vanity Fair*, 178.
100. Ibid., 136.
101. Ibid.
102. Ibid., 392.
103. Ibid., 393.
104. Miller, *Burdens of Perfection*, 191–2.
105. Thackeray, *Vanity Fair*, 607.
106. Ibid., 610.
107. Ibid., 605–6.
108. Nietzsche, "Uses and Disadvantages," 116.

4

Progressing in Harriette Wilson and Harriet Martineau

Harriet Martineau loves being old. Unusually for nineteenth-century women's life-writing, her *Autobiography* (1877) makes a defiant assertion of personal and professional progress over the life course. Martineau's text is exceptional because, as Mary Jean Corbett notes, "Martineau's life and her writing of it approximate the masculinist standard of significance"[1] that licenses life-writing in the marketplace, or, as Linda Peterson argues, Martineau "invokes the more modern, masculine autobiographer's privilege of focusing primarily on personal development and intellectual progress"[2] in ways that resemble John Stuart Mill or John Henry Newman. Martineau's commitment to progress constitutes one feminist response to the rhetorical dilemma presented by the patriarchal assumption that a woman's social and sexual capital declines precipitously with age. For many life-writers on the margins of social respectability in the 1820s, 1830s, and 1840s, however, the preferred strategy was different. Instead of asserting their capacity for or experience of progress, these writers rejected directional change altogether in favor of various nonlinear temporalities. For example, Harriette Wilson's *Memoirs* (1825) uses a static or cyclical conception of time to represent her encounters with famous men as occurring in a kind of de-temporalized zone. Her text embodies a distinctive literary mode that defamiliarizes the past self and the past in general, and cordons them off as separate and self-contained, resistant to genealogical narrative.

In this chapter, I juxtapose Wilson's *Memoirs* with Martineau's *Autobiography* in order to suggest surprising parallels in their representations of time. The gendered-male vision of development that scholars have identified in Martineau's *Autobiography* proves remarkably difficult to narrate, rendering her text, while perhaps less radical than Wilson's, more rhetorically fraught. For all Martineau's commitment to progress and development, she takes reluctant recourse in the nonlinear temporalities cheerfully embraced by Wilson. Ultimately, both writers share the sense that time is layered and often static until punctuated by unrepresentable paradigm shift. Thus, Martineau's *Autobiography* does not just reflect how Victorian ideologies of progress struggle to accommodate aging, particularly women's aging. It also beautifully reveals the difficulties of narrating autobiographical progress at all. That is, Martineau's text confronts not just progress's gendered exclusions but also its central representational challenges: first, that smooth gradual change seems unlikely to result in transformation and instead feels more like stasis, and second, that the past self must be both rejected and instrumentalized as a transitional stage leading to the present self. Through this analysis, I trace the stark limitations of progress as an ideological commitment and a rhetorical strategy, even in a text that seems to offer an unalloyed expression of it.

In bringing together Wilson and Martineau, I am looking past their contrasting lives, ideologies, rhetorical styles, and receptions. Wilson's infamous tell-all *Memoirs* celebrate the excesses of her career as a high-society courtesan. Despite its notoriety in popular history, it was long neglected by literary criticism.[3] Martineau's *Autobiography*, by contrast, traces an upward trajectory of intellectual and professional development and is probably the most canonical nineteenth-century autobiography by a woman.[4] Yet the two Harriet(te)s have significant similarities in the temporalities represented and embodied in their lives and texts. Although Wilson seems to belong to the Romantic period and Martineau the Victorian, Wilson's *Memoirs* and Martineau's *Autobiography* were written only thirty years apart—Daniel Cook and Amy Culley observe that British women's life-writing is especially ill-served by conventional periodization.[5] Both texts were composed at breakneck speed, without revision. In the process, they use complementary strategies to respond to the belated temporality of autobiography. Wilson's text depicts a changeless milieu, fixed in the heyday of her career and privileging the past self over the present self. Following Devoney Looser, we might understand Wilson's reliance on "the retrospective lens" as a rhetorical stance informed by a gendered experience of aging.[6] By contrast,

Martineau depicts a segmented self, a life split into distinct phases in which the present stifles the past. Nonetheless, these apparently contrasting approaches share a reluctance to draw a genealogical relationship between the selves represented at different points in the text. Thus, the texts trace opposing ways to reject linear continuity between past and present—either by emphasizing their profound sameness or their total disconnection. This is the same dual strategy toward representing time that I traced in the previous two chapters: Wilson's approach resembles the way Disraeli's revisions to *Vivian Grey* cordon off past from present, whereas Martineau's approach resonates with Thackeray's assertion of broad continuities across time. Yet both models reject linear connection between past and present.

These autobiographical texts anticipate and are illuminated by theories of women's and queer temporality. Julia Kristeva observes that under patriarchy, women are excluded from linear historical time, "time as departure, progression, and arrival,"[7] and instead associated with either repetitious cyclical time or eternal monumental time:

> On the one hand, there are cycles, gestation, the eternal recurrence of a biological rhythm which conforms to that of nature and imposes a temporality ... On the other hand ... there is the massive presence of a monumental temporality, without cleavage or escape, which has so little to do with linear time (which passes) that the very word "temporality" hardly fits: all encompassing and infinite like imaginary space.[8]

Kristeva's models of cyclical and monumental time can work together in narrative to suggest an ongoing stasis undergirded by periodic renewal that allows time to continue outside of a developmental logic. The way these two models collapse past and present may have been especially appealing to a writer like Wilson, eager to subvert the social and financial implications of aging. Wilson's and Martineau's relationships to time may be queer as well. Despite contrasting attitudes toward sexuality, both were unmarried, childless women who experienced a non-normative life trajectory disconnected from the gestational element of Kristeva's cyclical time. In Jack Halberstam's broad sense, queer temporality emerges "once one leaves the temporal frames of bourgeois reproduction and family, longevity, risk/safety, and inheritance."[9] Carolyn Dinshaw also understands queer temporality capaciously as inhering in "forms of desirous, embodied being that are out of sync with the ordinary linear measurements of everyday life, that engage heterogeneous temporalities or that precipitate out of time altogether."[10] As I'll demonstrate, both Wilson and Martineau—despite the latter's larger commitment to progress—frequently precipitate out of time in this way.

As I have argued in previous chapters, the forms of cyclical stasis, multiplicity, and temporal rupture found in modern theories of women's and queer time have analogues in nineteenth-century philosophy of history. An especially strange predecessor is Thomas Carlyle's *On Heroes, Hero-Worship, and the Heroic in History* (1840), which argues that "greatness" is an immutable, extra-temporal feature of exceptional men, one that recurs in every historical period. Changeless and impervious to contingency, Carlyle's heroism inhabits Kristeva's monumental time, despite the category being closed to women. This theory of fixed character suggests a vision of history in which time's unfolding is neither a contested interaction between multiple forces, nor a smooth development from one thing to another, but rather the imperfect expression of an immutable concept. Sharing Carlyle's commitment to understanding character as static, Wilson uses cyclical and monumental time to present her autobiographical past as detached from linear development, a period outside of directional time.

Martineau seems at first glance to understand time as a progressive developmental unfolding, but her representation of it draws frequently upon cyclical and monumental time. As I argue below, there is a monumentality to how the present self intensely shapes the account of early experiences, and a repetitive return to particular states of mind. Furthermore, Martineau's text is conspicuously reticent on key moments of ideological transformation that could offer an organic picture of personal development. In this way, she resembles Auguste Comte, whom she translated and whose theory of civilizational development sees time as segmented. Unlike Wilson, Martineau rigorously and insistently maintains the distinction between past and present; the trajectory between them remains elusive. Whereas Wilson more fully collapses time, Martineau engages in what Dinshaw describes as a "touch across time," in which discontinuous but resonant moments are layered atop each other without implying a genealogical relationship.[11] Martineau's apposition of discrete moments resembles the discontinuous presentisms I traced in Chapter 1, again reflecting that presentism is formulated and practiced in the Victorian writings.

I argue that Wilson and Martineau express these figurations of time through an aesthetics of orality. Paradigmatically fleeting, speech plays a prominent role in nineteenth-century women's life-writing. For both Wilson and Martineau, conversation is not only a representational strategy for holding time still and reveling in moments of power. It is also a symbol of the past's resistance to representation, of what is irrevocably lost. In both texts, accounts of conversation work to suggest that time is nonlinear, layered, and liable to dramatic contractions and expansions. Together, these texts reveal that the narration of individual nineteenth-century lives proves intractably resistant to linear progress. Instead, these lives and the texts they produce serve as a laboratory for the experimentation with diverse alternative visions of the shape of time.

"Ladies scorn dates!": Fast and loose with time in Harriette Wilson's *Memoirs*

A scandalous tell-all that named names, the *Memoirs of Harriette Wilson, Written by Herself* prompted an "avalanche of censorious comment" and a flurry of lawsuits upon its serialization in 1825.[12] Recent scholarship has recovered the *Memoirs* as Wilson's attempt to capitalize on her notoriety and assert control over her image, but scholars have had little to say about the text's representation of temporality, beyond occasionally defending its many chronological inaccuracies as expressions of creative license. In a frequently reprinted 1955 introduction, Lesley Blanch relishes that the *Memoirs* show "a fine disregard for exactitude, either in names, places, or dates. Incidents which most likely occurred are set wildly, some years out of date. Wellington is referred to as the Duke some years before he obtained that title. Harriette and Byron discuss Lady Caroline Lamb's roman à clef, *Glenarvon* seven years before it is published."[13] Blanch thus celebrates the audacious manipulations of temporality that for Wilson's contemporaries reflected her total lack of respectability.[14]

Yet to remark upon these purported errors is only to echo what the text acknowledges about its relationship to the events described. Wilson repeatedly admits altering the order of events to enhance narrative interest. She explains that she wrote "with little regard to dates or regularity, ... at odd times, and in very ill health";[15] that "I do not specify in what year or years, being anxious to forget all such critical matters as dates";[16] and that "everything here mentioned or told of happened within the last half century."[17] These passages lend themselves to a reading of Wilson's temporal reshufflings, whether explicitly observed or silently introduced, as a form of posturing in which her apparently slapdash persona provides opportunities for wit. Early in the account, Wilson declares:

> I will not say in what particular year of his life, the Duke of Argyle succeeded with me. Ladies scorn dates! Dates make ladies nervous, and stories dry. Be it only known then, that it was just at the end of his Lorne shifts, and his lawn shirts. It was at that critical period of his life, when his whole and sole possessions appeared to consist in three dozen of ragged lawn shirts, with embroidered collars, well fringed in his service; a threadbare suit of snuff colour, a little old hat with very little binding left, an old horse, an old groom, an old carriage, and an old chateau. It was to console himself for all this antiquity, I suppose, that he fixed upon so very young a mistress as myself.[18]

George William Campbell, Marquis of Lorne, heir to the Duke of Argyll was thirty-six years old in 1804 when he began a relationship with the eighteen-year-old Wilson, who was already several years into her career as a courtesan.[19] In this passage, however, Wilson cultivates a sense of chronological liberty that suits her authorial persona—Culley interprets it as indicating Wilson's "gendered conception of women's life writing as fragmentary and non-linear."[20] Referring to her lover alternately as Lorne, his title at the time of their affair, and Argyll, the title he later inherited, Wilson deliberately draws attention to her text's manipulations of time. The result is an overdetermination of Campbell/Lorne/Argyle/Argyll's position in time—he's both too old for Wilson and not yet in possession of his family's title.

In this passage, Wilson uses his clothes to illustrate the survival of the past in the present. Argyll's clothes date the relationship relative to his life rather than hers—Wilson remains forever young. The oldness of the clothes inheres in their worn condition rather than their style, which remains unknown. Lawn is a kind of linen and a shift an undergarment, and so, as elsewhere in the *Memoirs*, Wilson exposes her aristocratic paramours in their underwear, deflating their status. The oldness of the clothes suggests Argyll's age—he has been wearing the same garments for years—and also that he is either disinterested in fashion or cash-poor. Like Sir Pitt Crawley's knee-breeches, Argyll's threadbare suit reflects the unselfconscious comforts of class privilege: as an 1837 *Fraser's Magazine* article quips, "when a man's character is established, he may wear an old coat."[21] Along those lines, the oldness of his chateau reflects the real balance of power. Aristocratic men may be shabbily clothed, but they provide Wilson's livelihood.

The twisted chronology of Wilson's *Memoirs* is also a symptom of the conditions of its composition, a reminder that linearity is hard to reconstruct. "Written in a breathless style, … reflect[ing] the fast pace of Wilson's life, a heady cocktail of swirling parties and gay abandonment,"[22] the *Memoirs* bear evidence of a rushed writing process, as Wilson's publisher urged her to produce more volumes quickly.[23] Wilson asserts that her *Memoirs* "might have been better still—but that Mr. Stockdale won't let me, or any one else, study and correct them. The merits of such a light work as this, stupidly says he, is [*sic*], that it is written without study, and naturally, and just as you converse."[24] Bracketing to return later to the connection Stockdale draws between the *Memoirs* and orality, the text does give the impression that Wilson wrote without revision, such as when she blithely announces, "Oh, mon Dieu! it has just occurred to me, that to have told this story of Elliston and Livius, in due time, it ought not to have come in these eight years at soonest; … but what does it signify to my readers, the story will do as well, and amuse as much now, as later on."[25] Furthermore, some passages appear influenced by the latest developments in the hush-money negotiations ongoing throughout the serialization.[26] For example, Wilson interrupts the narrative about her on-again-off-again relationship with Fred Lamb to insert a story about an earlier experience with Wellington, whose response to her attempted extortion was allegedly particularly hostile.[27] As Wilson here admits, this anecdote is her revenge:

> Above all, I wanted Wellington to be exhibited, dripping with wet, standing opposite my street door, at midnight, bawling up to Argyle, who should be representing my old Abigail, from my bed-room window. Good gracious! I quite forgot to tell this adventure!! How could I be so ridiculous and negligent? Never mind, you shall have it now—But there is poor Fred Lamb waiting all this time, in my select

library! I can't help it—There's no getting on with Fred Lamb. I never could use him to any purpose in all my life.[28]

Wilson continues to relate an incident in which Wellington arrives at her apartment unannounced, just after returning from campaigns in Spain, and encounters Argyll disguised as a maid. With cavalier mockery, Wilson makes Wellington look desperate and gullible while she also uses the fact of the narrative digression to insult Fred Lamb, whose story she interrupts.

Whatever the cause of Wilson's temporal manipulations, their rhetorical effect is to present her social scene as remarkably stable. Although Wilson moves between male protectors, and those around her also change their alliances, the basic practices and concerns of this culture remain constant. Whereas Frances Wilson's biography, *The Courtesan's Revenge* (2003), traces the gradual conservative drift of sexual mores during Wilson's career,[29] the *Memoirs* recognize no such change. Despite constantly shifting loyalties, Wilson's set-piece incidents can occur in any order because they depict a stable culture of renewing and repeating affairs and rivalries that begin to resemble each other. There is a cyclicality to the progress of Wilson's relationships, from an early spark of interest, to a flowering of the connection, to its dissolution or displacement by the next relationship—which follows closely or overlaps with the previous. Representing a cyclical experience of time, if not in the reproductive sense suggested by Kristeva, the *Memoirs* place Wilson's career outside of linearity, with an indeterminate relationship to the present.

Wilson's narration at the beginning, middle, and end of her *Memoirs* suggests that her text, if not her career, could continue indefinitely. Wilson memorably begins *in medias res*, after her initial fall from propriety:

> I shall not say why and how I became, at the age of fifteen, the mistress of the Earl of Craven. Whether it was love, or the severity of my father, the depravity of my own heart, or the winning arts of the noble lord, which induced me to leave my paternal roof and place myself under his protection, does not now much signify.[30]

Lisa O'Connell reads this opening salvo as a rejection of the generic tropes Wilson hoped to transcend, observing that this passage is by far the most quoted of the *Memoirs* because of its "flaunting, flagrant expression" of writerly bravado.[31] Yet the passage also notably bypasses the period of Wilson's life before she participated in an established culture of high-society philandering. The potential trauma that led to her initiation into this lifestyle "does not now much signify."[32] Whereas her biographer catalogues that Wilson strategically launched her career by moving up the social ladder from Craven to Fred Lamb to Argyll, Wilson's *Memoirs* resist this developmental logic, presenting her career as at its apex from the first sentences of her narrative. Just paragraphs later, she attempts to solicit the future George IV as her lover. Tired of Craven's "ugly cotton nightcap," she wonders "what sort of nightcap the Prince of Wales wears"[33]—a further reminder that clothing is a metonym for the sexual intimacy that is her proof of having-been-there—and writes to him, "I am told that I am very beautiful, so, perhaps you would like to see me."[34] Just as Carlyle understands heroism as immutable, Wilson sees her own sexual capital as a precondition that is always already established.

As the *Memoirs* continue, Wilson's status in society remains stable, registering neither development nor decline. This broad stasis traced on an eventful backdrop has various parallels. As I suggested also with respect to *Vanity Fair*, Wilson's resistance to directional narrative suggests an affinity with modes of studied neutrality toward the historical record. For example, according to Hayden White, the chronicle paratactically relays events from the "unprocessed historical record" in the order of their occurrence rather than building toward a climax.[35] Her text also reflects the influence of the Epicurean hedonist tradition, which "curtails the temporal shape of the life, end-stopping the good life at the point where the right condition has been attained"[36]— though Wilson does not only end-stop but also front-stops at the point of her career's triumphant start. Frances Wilson documents that Wilson's career slowly declined during the later years of the *Memoirs*[37] and Patricia Howell Michaelson observes Wilson's "acquiescence to less and less desirable patrons."[38] In the latter half of the text, Wilson seems dimly aware that her "health and freshness are gone."[39] In particular, her toleration of the abusive behavior of Meyler, "a torment to me," whose "temper [had] become so provoking,"[40] marks a diminution of her earlier social power. Yet by the text's end, Wilson only grudgingly admits that her "habits and character became more serious and melancholy" after her mother's death, and yet in the same breath cheerily promises that a "continuation of my Memoirs[,] provided you are all grateful and civil" is forthcoming.[41] An expanded, eight-volume version of the *Memoirs* indeed appeared in 1831 including a few new anecdotes, padded out by her publisher's account of his legal travails, a reprint of Wilson's novel *Paris Lions and London Tigers* (1825), and an index. Wilson's career as a courtesan may have ended, but it could continue to yield the sort of anecdotes featured in the original *Memoirs*.

Throughout the *Memoirs*, Wilson reflects Kristeva's monumental time in that the process of getting to know other people occurs instantaneously. Just as Wilson refers to her lovers as Argyll and Wellington years before they acquired these titles, Wilson knows everything about everyone immediately, and her opinions do not change. Wilson professes always to have understood the strained nature of Beau Brummell's finances, calling him "entirely ruined" years before his debts became public.[42] Two volumes later, Wilson describes the anger among Brummell's friends when they discover that he cannot repay loans, while she herself remains completely unsurprised: "I asked Meyler how he could be so very stupid as to have been deceived, even for an instant, about Brummell."[43] Whereas others were initially under one impression and later under another, Wilson's position is prescient.

The discussion of her affair with Worcester conspicuously collapses processual change in her relationships and knowledge. In real life, Wilson seriously mishandled the affair, making it difficult for her to find another aristocratic sponsor. Believing he would eventually marry her, Wilson removed herself from high-society circulation during Worcester's military service, only to be rejected upon his return, and denied an annuity that his father promised earlier.[44] However, Wilson's account of what must have been a dramatic turn utterly lacks suspense. From the beginning, Wilson emphasizes that she is writing her *Memoirs* "because a certain duke and his son, all! all! honourable men, and with very honourable titles and ancient names, have taken such unfair advantage of my generous treatment of them, that I think they ought to be exposed."[45] Yet she emphasizes in equal measure Worcester's total devotion throughout their three-year relationship, claiming, "[i]t would be tedious to attempt relating all, or even one twentieth part, of the tender proofs of love and affection, which Worcester was in the daily, I may say, hourly habit of evincing towards me."[46]

This complex, protracted episode is difficult to follow, precisely because it only makes sense if we understand both Worcester's and Wilson's feelings to have changed over time.

To some extent, Wilson's manipulations of temporality seem motivated by the courtesan's desire to subvert the social and financial implications of aging, looking back nostalgically on earlier successes and writing in a genre, the scandalous memoir, that was itself past its prime.[47] By depicting her career as stable and her interpersonal insights as prescient, Wilson presents a flattering self-portrait that refuses to age. Yet in the process, she also produces a history of the period that emphasizes a changeless high-society culture in which individuals repeatedly shift their alliances. Although Wilson's assessments of her subjects are deeply, even confusingly mixed, her text shares with Carlyle's account of heroism a sense of personal character as static and historical time as undifferentiated, shaped by endless cycles and returns and set apart from the present moment.

Much like *Coningsby* and *Sybil*, Wilson's *Memoirs* use arabesques of sparkling conversation to represent this vision of broad stasis disconnected from the present. Consistent with the conventions of the scandalous memoir, Wilson uses extensive direct speech to imply the sexuality that undergirds the text. In this way, Wilson exploits the double meaning of "conversation." As the *Oxford English Dictionary* suggests, "conversation" could mean either oral discourse or sexual intercourse during this period, and although the latter usage was waning, the conceptual link persisted.[48] Both sex and talking, furthermore, were the courtesan's remit. *Bell's Life in London* at one point described Wilson, as "although on the wane in point of personal attractions, ... much admired for her conversational talents."[49] Since the text's initial reception, readers have shared the publisher Stockdale's appreciation for Wilson's conversational style.[50] Even Walter Scott admits that "there is some good retailing of conversations in which the stile of the speakers so far as known to me, is exactly imitated."[51] Wellington's twentieth-century biographer Elizabeth Longford concurs that Wilson "certainly has caught Arthur Wellesley's quick, peremptory speech, noted by all his friends."[52] Noting that Wilson's career is "framed largely in dialogue,"[53] Michaelson argues that while the question of verisimilitude is unanswerable, Wilson's *Memoirs* demonstrate her mastery and strategic deployment of a wide range of conversational styles, presenting her as "a supremely competent speaker," and a "master of one-upmanship, winning verbal contests through ritualized insult."[54]

Yet conversation does not just contribute to Wilson's literary self-fashioning, but also serves as a form of temporal suspension. Speech often functions as prolongation, dilating in the interstices between, and during overlap among, Wilson's otherwise serially monogamous relationships. For example, when Wilson brazenly tells her sometimes-lover Fred Lamb about her recent liaison with Argyll, she goes out of her way to assert her sexual freedom.

> You told me, he was, when he pleased, irresistible, said I.
> Yes, yes, yes, muttered Fred Lamb, between his closed teeth; but a woman who loves a man, is blind to the perfections of every other. No matter, no matter, I am glad it has happened. I wish you joy. I—
> Did I ever tell you I was in love with you? said I, interrupting him. Indeed it was your vanity deceived you, not I.[55]

In this passage, Wilson flaunts her power, taking pains to suggest that Lamb himself encouraged her attentions to Argyll. He has already relented in his half-hearted objections when Wilson interrupts forcefully to assert control over the conversation and the narrative, and to clarify precisely the terms of their relationship. Thus, speech here allows Wilson to suspend moments in which men compete for her affections. Similarly, in the confrontation between Wellington, standing outside in the rain, and Argyle, disguised as Wilson's maid, conversation both authenticates the past connection to prominent men and allows Wilson to linger in a moment of high social power:

> Endeavouring to imitate the voice of an old duenna, Argyle begged to know who was at the door?
> Come down, I say, roared this modern Blue Beard, and don't keep me here in the rain, you old blockhead.
> Sir, answered Argyle, in a shrill voice, you must please to call out your name or I don't care to come down, robberies are so frequent in London, just at this season, and all the sojers, you see, coming home from Spain, that it's quite alarming to poor lone women.
> Wellington took off his hat, and held up, toward the lamp, a visage, which late fatigue, and present vexation, had rendered no bad representation of that of the knight of the woeful figure. While the rain was

trickling down his nose, his voice, trembling with rage and impatience, cried out—You old ideot, do you know me now?

Lord, sir, answered Argyle, anxious to prolong this ridiculous scene, I can't give no guess; and, do you know, sir, the thieves have stolen a new water-butt out of our airy, not a week since, and my missis is more timbersome than ever!

The devil! vociferated Wellington, who could endure no more, and, muttering bitter imprecations, between his closed teeth, against all the duennas and old women that had ever existed, returned home to his neglected wife, and family duties.[56]

In this passage, Wilson enlists Argyll to prolong this moment in which she is at the height of power—her attentions simultaneously sought by two prominent men. Whereas with Fred Lamb, Wilson represents her own conversational dominance, here she orchestrates and then narrates the verbal sparring to a similar end.

Just as she playfully draws attention to the chronological mistakes in her account, Wilson acknowledges her cavalier representation of conversations:

As to mere harmless conversations, I do not profess more than general accuracy; I often add, a yes, a nod, or a no, or I neglect my dates and relate anecdotes together, which happened at different periods, but happen they did; and no conversation is described herein which did not take place within my own knowledge, and, for the most part, in my own hearing.[57]

Thus, like linear chronology, conversation is impossible to reconstruct. Wilson both admits the questionable accuracy and asserts the fundamental truthfulness of the *Memoirs'* represented conversations. More than simply documenting her encounters with famous men, Wilson's conversations also evince nostalgia for a particular, sparkling style of speech she associates with the past—it is the same suggestion of conversation's declining *joie de vivre* that Disraeli enacts in the revisions of *Vivian Grey*, as I discussed in Chapter 2.

The apocryphal scene in which Wilson meets Byron at Wattier's masquerade ball in 1814 takes to an extreme the text's reliance on witty, invented conversation as a technique for freezing time. *Bell's Life in London* noted immediately that the encounter was "pure invention,"[58] whereas scholars have read the scene as "informed by the life and writing of Lord Byron."[59] Intertextual analyses have identified Wilson's debts to *Don Juan* and *Glenarvon* in the early part of this passage, before the disguised figures begin speaking.[60] Yet after the initial recognition, Wilson's scene continues for many pages of florid dialogue:

> "I entreat you to gratify my curiosity. Who and what are you, who appear to me a being too bright and too severe to dwell among us?"
>
> He started violently, and reddened, while he answered rather peevishly, "You had better bestow your attention on some one more worthy of you, fair lady. I am a very stupid masquerade-companion;" and he was going away.
>
> "Listen to me," said I, seizing one of his beautiful little hands, urged on by irresistible curiosity, "whoever you are, it is clear to me, that my intrusion bores you; but it cannot be more annoying to you than your running away will be to me. Do not torment me, to secure to yourself a moment's ease. I promise to leave you at liberty in one quarter of an hour; nor will I insist on your disclosing your name, and I promise you shall not know mine... . Well, then, take out your watch. In one quarter of an hour you shall be free from all my persecution; but, give me that time, pray do!"[61]

In this passage, Wilson commandeers Byron's time, demanding fifteen minutes of conversation with the personal mascot for the zeitgeist. Like the conversations between Wilson and Fred Lamb and between Argyle and Wellington, this represented conversation enacts temporal suspension or delay. Yet it also condenses and retells through speech Wilson and Byron's real-life epistolary relationship, crystalizing in a discrete moment of encounter what had actually unfolded gradually and at a distance. Furthermore, Wilson controls the exchange, expressing passionate admiration while rejecting Byron's romantic overture. She speaks first:

> "I do not require you to like me, for you are too handsome to love in vain."
>
> "What! Then you really could not return my passion?"
>
> "No, upon my word; and yet your countenance is magnificently beautiful! ... Now would I forswear love, which has hitherto been my all, to follow you to banishment or to death, so that I could be considered your equal, worthy to be consulted by you as a friend; for, though I do not know you, yet I guess that you are on earth and that there's nothing like you."[62]

Here we see Wilson using dialogue to suggest that time is both fleeting and endless, forever in a zone of Wilson's limitless sexual power. Again, the time of her career is static, self-contained, and set apart from linear change.

Frances Wilson reads the ball scene as Wilson's attempt to place herself at the epicenter of fashionable society at a point when her career was already declining.[63] Indeed, the *Memoirs* are easily read as a self-aggrandizing fantasy, a reflection on a happier phase in the author's life, written after it ended. Yet in the process of presenting herself and her milieu as changeless, Wilson figures time as either cyclical or monumental. Fleeting and unrepresentable, conversation fittingly symbolizes this vision of time, revealing the past as just out of reach, even to survivors. Allowing Wilson to document or fabricate her privileged access to famous men, dialogue represents the ultimate ephemeral experience of having-been-there. Like Disraeli's early novels, Wilson's text contributes to an emerging historiography of the recent past in which witty dialogue is both the form and the content. Wilson isolates this past as a distinctive era, separate from the present and in an uncertain, non-genealogical relationship to it. Although her text vividly depicts the Regency, it also provides a historically portable model for representing time in a nonlinear way.

As we see in Wilson, autobiography offers an unexpectedly fruitful ground for depicting a foreign past, when even the linear continuity of the self is insufficient to ensure a genealogical relationship between past and present. In this way, Wilson's text resonates with nineteenth-century developments in philosophy of history that emphasize temporal segmentation. Because Wilson seeks to subvert her own aging, she posits forms of suspension that we see not only in Carlyle's *On Heroes*, but also in the stasis-and-rupture model of progress that lurks behind and around the gradualist accounts of Macaulay or Acton. And in its resistance to the moralizing impulse of directional narrative, Wilson's *Memoirs*, like *Vanity Fair*, reflects the detached neutrality of historical methods that do not become dominant until later in the century.

"From my youth upwards": Harriet Martineau on getting old

Martineau's *Autobiography* (1877) differs markedly from Wilson's *Memoirs* in both the life being written and the way of writing it.

In the representation of temporality, also, Wilson's cyclical and monumental models appear to contrast with the progress Martineau traces. Yet Martineau's *Autobiography* has a more complicated temporality than first appears. Although ideologically committed to progress, Martineau ultimately reveals the rhetorical difficulties of narrating it. Martineau sees the continuous, gradualist model of progress as inconsistent with real transformation. Instead, she finds a more useful conception of progress in Comte, whose theory of civilizational development—as occurring in discrete stages, punctuated by instantaneous paradigm shifts—she attempts to recapitulate in the narrative of her own life. Through the influence of Comte, she strangely shares with Wilson a vision of time as broken into separate segments whose relationships to each other remain unknowable.

The *Autobiography*'s account of its rapid composition has an opposite and complementary relationship to the text's depiction of autobiographical progress. Martineau's introduction acknowledges two early, abandoned attempts to start writing—one in 1831, when she was under thirty, and another ten years later, perhaps inspired by Charlotte Elizabeth Tonna's *Personal Recollections* (1841).[64] These false starts aside, Martineau proudly claims to have written the *Autobiography* quickly over three months in 1855, when she believed that she was imminently dying.[65] Although she lived another twenty-one years, intimations of mortality shape the work. The 1877 publication date thus belies that the *Autobiography* was not only written but also typeset and printed in the mid-1850s,[66] contributing to its sense of belatedness, like Wilson's contribution to the aging genre of the scandalous memoir. Whereas Martineau suggests that this rapid composition resulted from the temporal limitation of life itself, Linda Peterson emphasizes Martineau's ideological commitment to a composition process of careful planning followed by sustained writing—part of Martineau's effort to distinguish herself from the recursive drafting and revision she associates with female novelists and to suggest instead an affinity with male writers of serious nonfiction.[67] Thus, Martineau's processual account of her life's trajectory of improvement—"From my youth upwards," as it begins[68]—requires that the text itself is a snapshot of a single moment, a culmination of life in a discrete final burst. To acknowledge a more extended composition process would have muddied the waters.

Despite the text's larger progress narrative, from a pious and strained childhood, to an ambitious early adulthood, to a successful late-middle age, there is a radical disconnection between the selves represented at different points in the autobiography. Although the subject's transformation defines the tradition of spiritual autobiography that Martineau adapts, such texts often still reflect an underlying continuity of the self, experiencing *Bildungsroman*-like growth and development. Martineau's text, by contrast, anticipates the modernist colonial rewriting of the *Bildungsroman*, which, in Jed Esty's account, "fully excise[s] the connective tissue between youth and age" and "systematically omit[s] the process of maturation itself."[69] Martineau's dramatic loss of religious faith in the mid-1840s results in an account of her early self heavily laden with particularly harsh commentary. Martineau insistently acknowledges that later insights have radically reframed earlier experiences—she seems unable to refer even passingly to her former life without emphasizing how she now rejects her old beliefs. For example, when recounting her sweep of the Unitarian Society's three prizes for essays intended to convert Catholics, Jews, and Muslims—an early, important success—she clarifies forcefully that "I disclaim their theology *in toto*."[70]

To a similar end, the text eagerly subverts the alternative biography potentially suggested by her canon of published work or her letters. The *Autobiography* disavows the views expressed in texts as late as *Life in the Sick-Room* (1844)—"not perfectly emancipated from the *débris* of the theological"[71]—reflecting a remarkable willingness to jettison earlier selves, to the point of coopting the language of enslavement in the process. The *Autobiography*'s introduction begins with Martineau's injunction against the posthumous publication of her letters, part of a sustained effort generally understood as an assertion of control that may have contributed to her reputation's later decline. Deborah A. Logan compares the *Autobiography* unfavorably to Martineau's surviving correspondence precisely because of its diverging relationship to time, writing that the *Autobiography*, notwithstanding its rapid composition, "lacks the natural spontaneity of her letters."[72] Martineau's controlled narrative in the *Autobiography* constantly rejects potential competing narratives suggested by her previous writing.

Indeed, a deep disconnection from earlier selves suffuses the entire text. For example, Martineau is disconcertingly breezy when describing an extremely unhappy childhood in which she was "very frequently planning suicide."[73] Whereas Peterson understands this negative picture of childhood as part of Martineau's rejection of the tropes of the domestic memoir,[74] I would emphasize its privileging of later selves over earlier selves, not unlike Wilson's lighthearted dismissal of an abusive childhood that "does not now much signify."[75] Similarly, just as Wilson collapses the unfolding of the catastrophic breakup with Worcester, Martineau's brief, matter-of-fact account of the insanity and death of her fiancé bypasses what must have been an emotional episode in order to reach the blanket conclusion that she is "very thankful for not having married at all."[76] In her resistance to dwelling the contingent moments of her youth, Martineau's progressive vision of her own life contrasts markedly with Victorian progressive history itself. As I discussed in Chapter 1, whig history emphasizes an early constitutionalism, generally seeing early turning points (the Protestant Reformation, the "Glorious Revolution") as more consequential than later ones (the defeat of Napoleon, the passage of the Reform Bill). For Martineau, on the contrary, the present obliterates the past, rendering irrelevant or illusory its apparent contingencies.

Befitting this strong orientation toward the present, Martineau's account is insistently proleptic, refusing to let her earlier subjectivity stand alone. This privileging of the current self sharply contrasts with Wilson, whose *Memoirs* chaotically flash both forward and back, contributing to a sense of stasis. Whereas Wilson's narration privileges her more professionally successful younger self, Martineau's privileges her more professionally successful older self. Yet their different models of professional and personal fulfillment belie that both texts reject an organic relationship between the different selves at different life stages—an absence of continuity that suggests the challenges of linear self-narration.

The diaries, journals, and letters upon which the *Autobiography* draws, furthermore, form a disorderly archive that resists incorporation into her larger narrative. Martineau frequently cites this evidence to support a narrative about the distinct upward trajectory of her life, and vigorously to contest accusations of wavering—on the question of Abolition during her American travels, for example.[77] In this way, Martineau presents a sustained moral clarity that eschews change over time, not unlike Wilson's prescient assessment of Brummell's finances. When describing her pre-secular period in particular, Martineau's recourse to external sources confirms how completely her inner life has moved on: "I find in my Diary more and more self-exhortations and self-censures about the sufferings of that year 1838."[78] Yet this passage exposes that her thoughts and feelings are hard to conjure without the help of the diary, and indeed Martineau's diaries and letters frequently surprise her, resisting their own instrumentalization into a controlled narrative. When translating Comte, for example, she comments, "I find in my Diary some very strong expressions of rapture about my task; and I often said to myself and others, in the course of it, that I should never enjoy any thing so much again."[79] As these remarks indicate, Martineau's private source materials reveal unremembered highs and lows that troublingly exceed the text's narrative arc, presenting autobiographical progress as a retroactive reconstruction.

The text's most conspicuous episode of temporal dilation and contraction occurs with Martineau's six-year illness at Tynemouth, a vanishing point that reveals the difficulties of narrating change. Although Martineau's translation of this experience into *Life in the Sick-Room* offers a feminist representation and theorization of illness, its account in the *Autobiography* is remarkably brief. Martineau explains that her reluctance to describe the period is manifold. First, as a writer, she resolves not to repeat material discussed in earlier published work. Second, as an atheist, she rejects a Christian "worship of sorrow" in which "it is a duty and a privilege to dwell on the morbid conditions of human life."[80] Third, and most interesting for me, Martineau acknowledges that writing struggles to represent the strange temporalities of the experience. Evoking "Tintern Abbey," she remarks that "Five years seem a long time to look forward; and five years of suffering, of mind or body, seem sadly like an eternity in passing through them: but they collapse almost into nothingness, as soon as they are left behind, and another condition is fairly entered on."[81] This account of evanescence, here associated with illness, reflects that the *Autobiography*, despite running more than 900 pages, presents the past as resistant to representation and largely lost. Ultimately, Martineau concludes that "for pathological purposes, there must be study of morbid conditions,"[82] resolving to be "as brief as I can, and at the same time, as frank, in speaking of the years between 1839 and 1845."[83] Yet the account of the period remains elusive and unsatisfying as it relates to the major ideological sea-change from belief to unbelief that centrally defines Martineau's mature self.

The "Fifth Period," the section ostensibly describing the Tynemouth illness, is riddled with flashbacks, atypical of the *Autobiography* as a whole. Martineau reconsiders the experience of her childhood deafness, describes the decline of her mother's and her aunt's health, and, sounding like Wilson, digresses into unrelated anecdotes: "It reminded me of an incident which I may relate here, though it occurred three years before the time under notice."[84] In this breakdown of linear chronology, Martineau's experience of illness and her attempt to write it result in a layering of temporalities in which past, present, and future are all in play. Despite her ideological commitment to empty homogeneous time, Martineau experiences in this passage precisely what Walter Benjamin describes, in which the past is "seized only as an image which flashes up at the instant when it can be recognized and is never seen again."[85] Although Martineau eagerly distinguishes her mature ideology from that held during most of the Tynemouth period, the writing-self identifies deeply with the Tynemouth-self, because during both periods, she expects imminent death. Trev L. Broughton describes this layering of temporalities as constituting "a kind of ironic anti-narrative: a refrain, punctuating the relentless progressivism of the text,"[86] though I would argue that the passage exposes the text's progressivism as not especially relentless. The expectation of death is not only a repeated element to which Martineau returns, but a threat to truncate the narrative—the musical refrain can enact a renewal or an ending. Thus, although this identification with a former self seems to circumvent linearity, it nonetheless reminds us of the finitude of life, the ending that will come, whether in 1839, 1855, or 1876.

Martineau expresses ambivalence about Tynemouth's breakdown of linear time. Acknowledging, "I loved, as I still love, the most monotonous life possible," the *Autobiography* nonetheless makes a concerted effort to reconstruct a linear chronology of the Tynemouth period.[87] She first abandons her daily diary because she "found it becoming a burden,"[88] but maintains for several more months a journal that records her progress on *The Hour and the Man* (1840). Citing that journal, the *Autobiography* offers a precisely dated timeline of *The Hour and the Man*'s composition—from first starting to write on May 2 to correcting the last proof on November 17. Yet Martineau's sense of imminent mortality interrupts: "I find, by this record, that I wrote the concluding portion of 'The Hour and the Man' first, for the same reason that I am now writing the fifth period of this Memoir before the fourth,—lest I should not live to do the whole."[89] This acknowledgement of non-sequential writing conflicts with Martineau's other statements about her linear composition process. By the time she writes *Life in the Sick-Room* three years later, Martineau seems more fully to have lost touch with linear time, and the *Autobiography* struggles to reconstruct it. She deduces that she must have conceived *Life in the Sick-Room* on September 15, 1843: "I kept no diary at that time; but I find inserted under that date in a note-book, 'A new and imperative idea occurred to me.'"[90] The work is somehow complete six weeks later, despite Martineau having taken the entire month of October off. This rapid composition confounds even Martineau herself: "I never wrote anything so fast as that book. It went off like sleep. I was hardly conscious of the act, while writing or afterwards."[91] Thus, illness ultimately enables the nearly instantaneous composition that Martineau values.

When Martineau finally addresses her definitive shift to a secular outlook, its timing is uncertain. Having already disavowed the ideology of *Life in the Sick-Room*, she must reconcile its relatively late appearance with the idea of ongoing personal development:

> After what I have said of my Sick-room Essays, which were written only the year before my recovery, it may seem strange to say that my mind made a progress worth noting during the five heavy years from 1839 to 1844: but, small as my achievements now appear to me, there *was* achievement. A large portion of the transition from religious inconsistency and irrationality to free-thinking strength and liberty was gone over during that period.[92]

In this account, Martineau acknowledges that the mental transformation occurred slowly and was not immediately reflected in her published writing. Jane Gallop has observed that Eve Sedgwick's work leans into the twisted temporalities that result from the time-lags between the conception of a piece of writing, its later publication, and its anticipated future reading. Sedgwick "embraces the anachronism of the printed word,"[93] celebrating published writing as a technology for the non-erasure of the past. This inertia—the fact that writing cannot be updated immediately—is precisely what makes Martineau so uncomfortable, and arguably the *Autobiography*'s entire project is to manage the reception of her earlier writings by subsuming them retroactively into a temporal narrative consistent with her mature ideology. Yet despite saying in this passage that the changes were only nascent in November 1843, Martineau never fully describes the ideological shift, facilitated by mesmerism, which was apparently complete at the time of her recovery in January 1845. Martineau understands this transformation as the major turning point in her life, ushering in her fully realized self, and yet it occurs in the interstices of her narrative.

In addition to mesmerism, unrepresentable conversations also facilitate Martineau's transformation. Elsewhere, the *Autobiography* features sparkling social anecdotes like those that characterize Wilson's *Memoirs*, elaborately recreating conversations, including nonverbal cues—the pauses of slow speakers, or the panting of her asthmatic friend Jane Marcet.[94] This dialogue often indexes gradual material progress in Martineau's life. For example, when she tells Wordsworth of her decision to buy property in the Lake District, he responds, "'It is,' said Wordsworth, 'the wisest step in her life; for' ... and we supposed he was going on to speak of the respectability, comfort, and charm of such a retreat for an elderly woman; but not so. 'It is the wisest step in her life; for the value of the property will be doubled in ten years.'"[95] In this bathetic deflation, speech unfolds in fits and starts, through moments of expectation and suspense—very different from the trajectory of rising property values to which Wordsworth alludes, or the anticipation of aging that shapes Martineau's housing decision. We might also compare Martineau's use of stagey dialogue that, like Wilson's, testifies to her self-assurance and conversational prowess—for example, during hardball negotiations with the publisher Charles Fox over the *Illustrations of Political Economy*,[96] or when grilling an unidentified dinner guest who knows less about Comte than he pretends.[97] In these passages, Martineau asserts her authority through conversational dominance.

The different role of conversation in Martineau's final ideological transformation reflects that this moment is a vanishing point that is both fleeting and celestially timeless. Martineau acknowledges that the ideological shift was rooted in unrepresentable speech: "I am not going to violate any confidence here, of course, which I have considered sacred in life. I refer to these conversations with the thoughtful and the wise merely to acknowledge my obligations to them."[98] Although Martineau justifies this treatment through an appeal to propriety, it serves also to conceal the processual unfolding of her thoughts in time. Her most extended account of these conversations offers little more: "During many a summer evening, while I lay on my window-couch, and my guests of the day sat beside me, overlooking the purple sea, or watching for the moon to rise up from it, like a planet growing into a sun, *things were said*, high and deep, which are fixed into my memory now, like stars in a dark firmament."[99] This depersonalized montage, beautifully employing the passive voice, reveals conversation as consequential but ephemeral, formative but impossible to reconstruct, reflecting the ineffability of transformation itself.

Despite the only gestural representation of Martineau's ideological transformation in the "Fifth Period," the "Sixth Period" opens with triumphant rebirth enabled by the already completed anti-conversion:

> My life, it has been seen, began with winter. Then followed a season of storm and sunshine, merging in a long gloom. If I had died of that six years' illness, I should have considered my life a fair average one, as to happiness ... But the spring, summer, and autumn of life were yet to come. I have had them now, all rapidly succeeding each other, and crowded into a small space, like the Swedish summer, which bursts out of a long winter with the briefest interval of spring.[100]

This passage revises and expands on a seasonal metaphor Martineau uses earlier, to very different effect. After describing the early success of *Illustrations of Political Economy* (1832–4), Martineau observes, "And now the summer of my life was bursting forth without any interval of spring. My life began with winter, burst suddenly into summer, and is now ending with autumn,— mild and sunny."[101] In the early passage, winter bursts suddenly into summer with Martineau's critical and commercial success in the early 1830s. By contrast, in the later passage, winter continues through the mid-1840s and reflects ideological rather than professional development. Yet in both accounts, seasonal change bursts forth, with spring's transition vanishingly brief. But autumn lingers. Martineau's expectation of imminent death in 1855 was mistaken, but she never recovered from the illness and remained "largely confined to her home"[102] for the final twenty-one years of life. Martineau's text ends in triumph, and, for that matter, without acknowledging the implicit cyclicality of this seasonal metaphor. One wonders whether she entirely retained this sense of accomplishment after 1855—she continued to publish books and a staggering body of journalistic writing for several years,[103] and maintained a wide circle of correspondents,[104] but her health problems were serious. Refusing to incorporate the final period of her life into a developmental arc, Martineau perhaps anticipates the work of the philosopher Michael Slote, who, in the words of Helen Small, "puts the case for seeing old age as a stage apart from the rest of our lives ... in which many of the ethical pressures and expectations relevant in our prime are understood to be no longer appropriate."[105] This separation of old age from the rest of the life contrasts with the way the older male aristocrats of *Vanity Fair* and *Coningsby* retain the vitality and power of their social position. While autobiography must end before death, Martineau's *Autobiography* excludes an extended final period that—whatever its lived reality of illness and writerly productivity—is never incorporated into the developmental narrative that otherwise defines her life.

Martineau's recovery from the Tynemouth illness reveals a newfound joy in aging and a satisfaction with her professional, personal, and intellectual progress: "At past forty years of age, I began to relish life, without drawback; and for ten years I have been vividly conscious of its delights."[106] Although Martineau's ideological sea-change facilitates this happy shift, she also explicitly credits a growing freedom from domestic responsibilities and a female aging process of moving from the caring role to the cared-for role. These gradual changes were already palpable before her illness. A holiday in Scotland at the age of thirty-six indexes a gratifying shift in what Talia Schaffer calls the "care community":

> Another marked thing about that autumn trip was that it introduced me to that pleasant experience of middle age,—the consideration of the young. I had always been among the youngest at home in my childhood; and of late years had ministered, in the capacity of youngster, to my old ladies. Now, for the first time, I experienced the luxury of being tended as an elderly person.[107]

The passage reflects the interplay of repetition and progression. Schaffer writes, "care temporality is a fluctuating network changing over time, one that affords multiple temporal stoppages, suspensions, reanimations, and adjustments of subjective temporal experiences."[108] Yet while care itself is repetitive and nonlinear, Martineau keenly registers a shift in the care relationship that constitutes a welcome linear development. Around the time that Martineau gains the female seniority that entitles her to care from younger women, she is also relieved from caring responsibilities when her aging mother is established at Liverpool with other relatives.[109] Martineau relishes these changes. Peterson argues that when Martineau establishes a home at Ambleside in the *Autobiography*'s pastoral final sections, she is not retreating into a domestic sphere so much as proving that she has fully arrived as a professional writer who can support a household.[110] Peterson's insight begins to suggest the uneasy relationship between the text's account of Martineau's ideological development, characterized by sudden, dramatic shifts, and the more gradual material progress that subtends it. This tension is the subject of the next section.

Martineau in the middle

Martineau herself understands her life as a recapitulation in miniature of the civilizational progress theorized in Auguste Comte's *Cours de philosophie positive*, for which she was the first and long remained the standard English translator.[111] As I discussed in Chapter 1, Comte argues that civilization has unfolded in three distinct phases: the theological, the metaphysical, and finally the positive, defined by scientific fact. One paradigm replaces another, whole cloth, in a sudden and totalizing shift. Although the implications of the transformation may be realized gradually (Comte tellingly locates the present in the very moment of the shift from metaphysics to positivism), Comte's vision is profoundly segmented. In the nineteenth century, this view of progress as stasis punctuated by rupture offered a strong counterweight to the smooth, continuous progress as imagined by Macaulay or Mill. Although positivism today is associated with gradualist accumulation, in Comte's nineteenth-century formulation, gradualism begins only after two successive radical breaks.

Martineau attempts to narrate her life in a similar way. In the *Autobiography*, her life has three phases: an early period of doctrinal faith, developed in opposition to her family's Unitarianism; an ambiguous middle phase beginning around age twenty with her acceptance of Necessarianism (a form of intense determinism) as opposed to free will; and finally, her secular maturity in the years after the upheaval prompted by the Tynemouth illness. Although both Comte's civilizational and Martineau's personal narratives culminate in secularity, positivism is a totalizing ideological system whose embrace can resemble a religious conversion. Thus, as Peterson notes, the tradition of spiritual autobiography is easily reworked in positivist terms,[112] and, as Alexis Harley observes, positivism seems not just to suggest but rather to insist upon its application to the individual life.[113]

Yet this mapping of the civilizational onto the personal is more fraught than scholarship generally allows. Building upon Harley's suggestion that Comtean theory "became garbled"[114] in the "contaminated Petri dish"[115] that is the genre of autobiography, I argue that Martineau struggles to represent autobiographical rupture on a Comtean model. Despite her ideological commitment to Comte's view, and although his influence appears in the text's segmented structure, Martineau's account of stadial time must work insistently, with limited success, to eliminate evidence of gradualism in her life. In particular, the story of her writerly career reflects gradual progress, notwithstanding the breakout success of *Political Economy*. And as I suggested above, Martineau's description of her final ideological change seems eager to shortcut its long, circuitous route. Moreover, the text imagines time as not only gradual, but also multiple. Broughton reads the layering of temporalities during the Tynemouth illness as a superimposition of Comte's three phases,[116] and Harley suggests that Martineau's sustained fascination with suicide "does not allow for this neat shelving of the suicidal impulse in Martineau's theological phase."[117]

Furthermore, Martineau is conflicted on the Comtean middle stage—both for the world at large, and in her own life. This ambivalence dictates her inconsistent use of the seasonal metaphor I discussed above, in which she characterizes the period between her first professional success and her last ideological transformation alternately as either summer or winter. Martineau recounts her first transformation, the acceptance of Necessarianism in 1821 or 1822, in subdued tones. Martineau describes her big insight—that, because of the role of typology, the New Testament must assume a Necessarian outlook—as "enabling me to hold to my cherished faith,"[118] and thus as prolonging, albeit altering, her connection to religion. Although, ironically, the realization itself prompts the embrace of a determinism that suggests monumental temporality, Martineau asserts that the shift was only valuable for where it led—lamentably, much later. That is, she understands this insight as initiating a frustratingly slow transformation from piety to secularity that elapses over a period of years:

> It is clear however that a Christianity which ... is finally subjected in its doctrines, as in its letter, to the interpretation of each individual,—must cease to be a faith, and become a matter of speculation, of spiritual convenience, and of intellectual and moral taste, till it declines to the rank of a mere fact in the history of mankind. These are the gradations through which I passed. It took many years to travel through them; and I lingered long in the stages of speculation and taste, intellectual and moral.[119]

Flashing forward, Martineau jumps past what she construes as a transitional stage in her intellectual or spiritual development, despite sounding somewhat nostalgic about Christianity's "decline."

Martineau has a similar attitude toward the temporality of her advancing deafness—loving the destination but hating the journey. Martineau's deafness began in childhood, though after the acquisition of speech, and thus it conforms neither to the monumental temporality of always-having-been deaf, nor to the gradualist logic of normative aging.[120] The text is inconsistent on whether Martineau's deaf gain[121] is gradual or sudden. In the initial account of her early life, it registers fleetingly: from an early realization that she preferred to sit at the front of the schoolroom,[122] to always being the one to read aloud while sewing with her mother,[123] to the realization that she was too deaf for public worship,[124] to the shift to going out at off-hours to avoid crowds.[125] This gradual narrative is punctuated by one discrete, unspecified incident: "In 1820, my deafness was suddenly encreased by what might be called an accident, which I do not wish to describe."[126] Hundreds of pages later, during the Tynemouth illness, however, Martineau returns to the issue, discounting the gradual narrative by emphasizing the still-unexplained "accident" as the climactic event.[127] This reconsideration not only reflects how the Tynemouth illness occasions cross-temporal thinking, but also offers a new, segmented vision of her experience of disability, with a more clearly marked turning point that coincides with the theological sea-change of her early twenties.

As this coincidence of disability and religious trajectories starts to indicate, Martineau's account of deaf gain parallels her Comtean view of development, with its ambivalence toward the middle stage. That is, Martineau loves *being* deaf: "here I am now, on the borders of the grave, at the end of a busy life, confident that this same deafness is about the best thing that ever happened to me."[128] But she did not love *becoming* deaf. As in the descriptions of her childhood piety, Martineau's text frequently intercuts accounts of early shame with assertions of later satisfaction made possible by a changed outlook:

> Before we lost our money, and when I was a young lady "just introduced," my mother insisted on taking me to balls and parties, though that sort of visiting was the misery of my life. My deafness was terribly in the way, both because it made me shy, and because underbred people, like the card-players and dancers of a provincial town, are awkward in such a case. Very few people spoke to me; and I dare say I looked as if I did not wish to be spoken to. From the time when I went to London, all that was changed. People began with me as with a deaf person; and there was little more awkwardness about hearing, when they had once reconciled themselves to my trumpet.[129]

In this passage, various trajectories in Martineau's life run parallel. The parties take place before the family's financial troubles in the mid-1820s implicate their social standing, and in the period when Martineau may be expected to marry. The sonic and social environment of the ball reveals a change in Martineau's hearing—and her class consciousness—that makes it difficult or unpleasant to socialize in a loud setting among "underbred people." The move to London in November 1832 inaugurates a different phase. Around thirty years old, the point at which a single woman in the Victorian period was generally relegated to spinsterhood,[130] Martineau's unmarried status is confirmed just as her career is being established. The geographical break, with its new social contacts, means that her deafness is a premise of new relationships.

Just as Martineau laments the time it took to move through successive stages from piety to secularity, she regrets not using an ear-trumpet sooner. Regarding the 1820 accident, she writes, "I ought undoubtedly to have begun ... to use a trumpet; but no one pressed it upon me; and I do not know that, if urged, I should have yielded; for I had abundance of that false shame which hinders nine deaf people out of ten from doing their duty in that particular."[131] Broughton has observed that Martineau strategically appeals to the concept of feminine duty in order to assert her own needs,[132] and this passage is certainly open to that reading, though it also reflects the internalized ableism that pervades the text. Martineau writes, "The special duty of the deaf is, in the first place, to spare other people as much fatigue as possible; and, in the next, to preserve their own natural capacity for sound, and habit of receiving it, and true memory of it, as long as possible."[133] As Jennifer Esmail has observed, nineteenth-century medical disagreement about the use of ear-trumpets stemmed from uncertainty over whether assisted hearing was slowing or hastening the advancement of deafness, with slowing being the agreed-upon goal.[134] Martineau here contributes to that debate while at the same time succinctly expressing the ableist assumption that disability, and its undesirable social consequences, can be overcome or deferred through perseverance.

Despite figuring the ear-trumpet as preserving her residual hearing, Martineau also paradoxically frames its adoption as the final shift that reflects her full acceptance of her disability.[135] References to the ear-trumpet peter out after the Tynemouth illness, whether because Martineau's deafness has increased to the point that it no longer helps, or alternatively, because her small domestic circle has become accustomed to it. Indeed, Martineau's deafness features more prominently toward the beginning of the *Autobiography*, during its trajectory of change. Just as the knee-breeches of *Vanity Fair* are most visible when their status is most in flux, so does Martineau's deafness reflect that directional change is more narratable than stasis.

Martineau's hostility toward other deaf people reflects not just internalized ableism but also a broader discomfort with temporal lags and slow realizations. Valuing an instantaneous, synchronized, and happy shift in both one's ability and one's consciousness of that ability, Martineau criticizes deaf people who do not promptly accept their deafness. She particularly laments the scourge of discursive repetition, which she interprets as a sign that the deaf person is clinging to a category to which they no longer belong. Repetition has a complex relationship to the linearity of speech—it interrupts the stream of the conversation just as it insists upon the deaf person's access to the conversation's ebb and flow. Martineau observes that "the usual evil ... is that the sufferer is inquisitive,—*will* know every thing that is said, and becomes a bore to all the world."[136] After relating her brother's story of dining with one such woman, Martineau comes to "a resolution which I made and never broke,—never to ask what was said .... I think now, as I have thought always, that it is impossible for the deaf to divine what is worth asking for and what is not; and that one's friends may always be trusted, if left unmolested, to tell one whatever is essential, or really worth hearing."[137] Martineau here figures unprocessed conversation as fundamentally inaccessible to the deaf person, and yet she asserts the superiority of the processed conversation that deafness enables. That is, the filtering mechanism provided by hearing friends presents the deaf person with a privileged relationship to what is "really worth hearing."[138] Thus, fully accepted deafness allows a particular experience of conversation—after the fact and in digest form—that cuts out the middle stage, the unnecessarily halting process of its unfolding.

Martineau similarly worries that the world at large is stuck in a middle stage of repetition and stasis. In a series of final comments on futurity at the *Autobiography*'s end, she observes, "the civilized world is now nearly divided between gross Latin or Greek Catholicism and disbelief of Christianity in any form. Protestantism seems to be going out as fast as possible."[139] As in the account of Christianity's "decline," Martineau appears to admire the ideological totality of its early manifestations, seeing Protestantism as a detour rather than the route of progress. But it is not only the status of Protestantism at stake here. In contrast to the whig historians I discussed in Chapter 1, Martineau envisions a future not of increasing secularism (with or without a stopover at Protestantism along the way), but rather of increased polarization between religion and non-religion. That is, Martineau rejects the idea of gradual transformation on every possible scale, whether personal or civilizational. Instead of transitions, compromises, and middles, she sees—and bristles against—multiple uncoordinated temporalities. Martineau laments the forms of irregular survival I trace in this book, which reflect the persistence of the past or the temporal multiplicity of the present. Martineau's disgust at the disjunction between the body's ability and the disabled subject's self-awareness ultimately reflects this same frustration with asynchronous timelines.

Martineau remains troubled by the layered, non-universal experience of time in her final remarks. For example, America "seem[s] to be lapsing from national manliness into childhood,—retrograding from the aims and interests of the nineteenth century into those of the fifteenth and sixteenth."[140] Here Martineau suggests the real possibility of regress, and yet also imagines a stadial vision of progress in which contemporary American concerns are fundamentally those of earlier centuries. Whereas Nietzsche laments civilizational old age, "the premature grey-beardedness of our present day youth,"[141] Martineau suggests that the overall "condition of humanity appears ... as yet exceedingly infantine."[142] This civilizational youth is characterized by differences between individuals that hinder progress: "The age in which I have lived is an infant one in the history of our globe and of Man; and the consequence is, a great waste in the years and the powers of the wisest of us."[143] Echoing Rousseau, Martineau suggests that social progress fails because the group cannot—or cannot yet—benefit from the advances of individuals.

Martineau's confidence in a gently progressive British future—contrasted with her anticipations for America and for religiosity—reflects that she remains torn between stadial and gradual visions of progress. She relates that early in life, she "yet apprehended a revolution in the fearful sense in which the word was understood in my childhood, when the great French Revolution was the only pattern of that sort of enterprise."[144] Now, by contrast:

> while I see much more of human difficulty from ignorance, and from the slow working (as we weak and transitory beings consider it) of the law of Progress, I discern the working of that great law with far more clearness, and therefore with a far stronger confidence, than I ever did before. When I look at my own country, and observe the nature of the changes which have taken place even within my own time, I have far more hope than I once had that the inevitable political reconstitution of our state may take place in a peaceable and prosperous manner.[145]

Martineau observes here a shift from an old future in which change was only possible through rupture, to a new future of "peaceable and prosperous" gradualism—this imperial historiography shapes Martineau's *History of the Thirty Years' Peace: 1816–1846* (1849–50) and *Introduction to the History of the Peace: From 1800 to 1815* (1851), in which the cataclysm of the Napoleonic Wars is an "introduction" that gives way to a "Pax Britannica." This transformation of futurity reveals a central paradox of Comte, for whom the paradigm shift from metaphysics to positivism first makes possible the gradual change that was not viable in earlier phases and that accords with classical whig models. Although for Comte and for Martineau, stadial change ultimately culminates in gradualism, the vision of segmented phases sometimes provides Martineau an alternative to relentless continuous progress. It offers a way to reconcile periods or elements of non-progress—whether regress, cyclicality, stasis, or rupture—with a larger, confidently progressive model. Martineau's rhetorical negotiations between the gradual and the sudden reveal some of the many ways that progress is always contested or under erasure in Victorian texts, even those that seem to theorize it—more evidence that this ostensibly dominant ideology is not as dominant as we thought.

ಸಿ

Wilson and Martineau take what initially appear to be profoundly contrasting approaches to representing time in their life-writing. Wilson's *Memoirs* entirely conceal processual change so effectively as to make occasionally for confusing reading—in the account of her affair with Worcester, for example. Wilson's continual stasis uses cyclicality to hold time still in her desired milieu. Whereas Wilson deliberately avoids representing autobiographical change, Martineau self-consciously thematizes it, and yet the process proves difficult to capture through narrative. Martineau eagerly depicts the completion of her transformation, concealing the process. For that reason, she insistently layers temporalities such that each past moment is apprehended only through its framing by the present. This rhetoric becomes profoundly strained. Emphasizing a series of sudden transformations that fit awkwardly with the evidence of gradual change in her life, Martineau relies on aporias that elide transitional moments and recapitulations that radically rewrite incidents described earlier. Privileging retrospection, Martineau reflects a monumental temporality in which her final self is the only self.

In these two texts' shared discomfort with smooth linear change, we can see how ideologically different stances toward time run up against similar problems in the rhetorical context of life-writing. Wilson's career and her text ultimately end—she cannot suspend time—though she does vividly depict a culture of high-society philandering that preceded her and continues without her, a kind of "Vanity Fair," resilient to the turnover of personnel. Martineau, conversely, illustrates that progress is difficult to narrate even when this is the text's stated project. As in Disraeli's early work, Martineau's text must accommodate past changes that seem non-progressive. In so doing, it draws upon visions of stadial or segmented progress that reject gradual change and rely instead on unrepresentable moments of paradigm shift. In both Wilson and Martineau, narrating stasis means implying rupture elsewhere and asking readers to look away. As we see in the next chapter, Thomas Hardy is similarly interested in the temporal suspensions that shape Wilson's text and in the quiet mechanisms of change that make them possible.

Notes

1. Corbett, *Representing Femininity*, 7.
2. Peterson, *Traditions of Victorian Women's Autobiography*, 63.
3. Over the past twenty years, scholars such as Caroline Breashears, Patricia Howell Michaelson, Lisa O'Connell, Julie Peakman, Bryan Rivers, and Sharon Setzer have worked to recuperate Wilson's *Memoirs* as an example of female literary ambition. Citing its earlier critical neglect, Breashears argues that scholarship has "silenced many writers by reducing them to their transgressions rather than attending to their strategies for self-fashioning" (Breashears, "Scandalous Categories," 188). O'Connell argues that Wilson extends "into the broader public sphere of print" the same "modes of posturing for male audiences" that made her a successful courtesan (O'Connell, "Authorship and Libertine Celebrity," 175). Similarly, Peakman analyzes how Wilson's *Memoirs* highlight an alternative discourse on female sexuality, one that valued assertiveness and independence (Peakman, "Memoirs of Women," 164).
4. Corbett notes that despite its atypicality, Martineau's *Autobiography* draws more scholarly attention than its contemporaries (Corbett, *Representing Femininity*, 7).
5. Cook and Culley, "Introduction," 5.
6. Looser, *Women Writers and Old Age*, 19.
7. Kristeva, "Women's Time," 192.
8. Ibid., 191.
9. Halberstam, *In a Queer Time and Place*, 6.
10. Dinshaw, *How Soon Is Now?*, 4.
11. Dinshaw, "Got Medieval?," 203.

12. O'Connell, "Authorship and Libertine Celebrity," 167. See O'Connell for an analysis of the public response to the *Memoirs*, including their extensive coverage in print media. See Saunders ("Copyright, Obscenity, and Literary History") for an account of the legal cases brought in the wake of the *Memoirs*, including successful prosecutions for libel and the denial of copyright protection upon the work being deemed obscene. See also Colligan ("Unruly Copies of Byron's Don Juan") for a reading of these libel cases in the context of piracies of *Don Juan*. Finally, see St. Clair (*Reading Nation*, 657–8) for documentation of the text's huge sales, which K. D. Reynolds ("Wilson [née Dubouchet], Harriette") claims forced the publisher to erect a barrier to control the crowds.
13. Blanch, "Game of Hearts," 33.
14. Wilson's erstwhile friend and rival Julia Johnstone joined the chorus in harshly criticizing Wilson's tendency to refer to her lovers by titles they later acquired (Johnstone, "Confessions of Julia Johnstone," 39). In fact, Blanch's final claim is slightly inaccurate: the conversation between Wilson and Byron about *Glenarvon* is supposed to have occurred only two years before the novel's publication (F. Wilson, *Courtesan's Revenge*, 142). Wilson's *Memoirs* also discuss *Glenarvon* in a letter to her sister Fanny, supposed to have been sent in early 1812, four years before the novel's appearance.
15. H. Wilson, *Memoirs*, 90.
16. Ibid., 108.
17. Ibid., 279.
18. Ibid., 30.
19. F. Wilson, *Courtesan's Revenge*, 61.
20. Culley, *British Women's Life-Writing*, 130.
21. "Dress, Dandies, Fashion, &c," 129.
22. Peakman, "Memoirs of Harriette Wilson," 1–3.
23. F. Wilson, *Courtesan's Revenge*, 192–3.
24. H. Wilson, *Memoirs*, 162.
25. Ibid., 185.
26. F. Wilson, *Courtesan's Revenge*, 222–32.
27. Longford, *Wellington*, 166–7; Peakman, "Memoirs of Harriette Wilson," 3; Johnstone, "Confessions of Julia Johnstone," 217.
28. H. Wilson, *Memoirs*, 147.
29. F. Wilson, *Courtesan's Revenge*, 153, 215–16.
30. H. Wilson, *Memoirs*, 13.
31. O'Connell, "Authorship and Libertine Celebrity," 172.
32. H. Wilson, *Memoirs*, 13.

33. Ibid., 14.
34. Ibid.
35. White, *Metahistory*, 5.
36. Small, *The Long Life*, 92.
37. F. Wilson, *Courtesan's Revenge*.
38. Michaelson, *Speaking Volumes*, 14.
39. H. Wilson, *Memoirs*, 365.
40. Ibid.
41. Ibid., 458.
42. Ibid., 222. Wilson makes this claim in a letter whose placement suggests a date of early 1812, but whose content indicates 1816 (see also F. Wilson, *Courtesan's Revenge*, 106, 151–2).
43. H. Wilson, *Memoirs*, 434.
44. F. Wilson, *Courtesan's Revenge*, 109–35.
45. H. Wilson, *Memoirs*, 93.
46. Ibid., 244.
47. Culley, *British Women's Life-Writing*, 89.
48. *Oxford English Dictionary*, "conversation, n."
49. "Memoirs," *Bell's Life in London*, Feb. 20, 1825.
50. H. Wilson, *Memoirs*, 162.
51. Scott, *Journal*, 38.
52. Longford, *Wellington*, 166.
53. Michaelson, *Speaking Volumes*, 14.
54. Ibid., 15.
55. H. Wilson, *Memoirs*, 31.
56. Ibid., 147–8.
57. Ibid., 156.
58. "Memoirs of Wilson, &c.," *Bell's Life in London*, Sept. 4, 1825.
59. Setzer, "The Memoirs of Harriette Wilson," 150.
60. Susan Wolfson and Nicola Watson have observed that the text is indebted to the ending of Canto XVI of *Don Juan*, in which Juan encounters the Duchess of Fitz-Fulke disguised as the Black Friar. In the moment when Wilson sees Byron from across the room, she places herself in the role of Juan to Byron's Duchess Fitz-Fulke (Wolfson, "Byron's Ghosting Authority," 784; Watson, "Trans-figuring Byronic Identity," 199). Watson furthermore suggests that Wilson's portrayal of Byron in disguise may also be influenced by *Glenarvon*, in which Glenarvon/Byron first appears at a masquerade disguised as an Italian monk (Watson, "Trans-figuring Byronic Identity," 191).
61. H. Wilson, *Memoirs*, 425.
62. Ibid., 426.

63. F. Wilson, *Courtesan's Revenge*, 141–3.
64. Martineau, *Autobiography*, 34; Peterson, *Traditions of Victorian Women's Autobiography*, 59.
65. Martineau, *Autobiography*, 629.
66. Logan, *Hour and the Woman*, 31.
67. Peterson, *Traditions of Victorian Women's Autobiography*, 68.
68. Martineau, *Autobiography*, 34.
69. Esty, *Unseasonable Youth*, 3.
70. Martineau, *Autobiography*, 137.
71. Ibid., 450.
72. Logan, "Entre nous," 52–3.
73. Martineau, *Autobiography*, 45.
74. Peterson, *Traditions of Victorian Women's Autobiography*, 61.
75. H. Wilson, *Memoirs*, 13.
76. Martineau, *Autobiography*, 119.
77. Ibid., 333–4.
78. Ibid., 421–2.
79. Ibid., 600.
80. Ibid., 432.
81. Ibid.
82. Ibid.
83. Ibid., 434.
84. Ibid., 443.
85. Benjamin, "Theses," 198.
86. Broughton, "Making the Most of Martyrdom," 32.
87. Martineau, *Autobiography*, 435.
88. Ibid., 438.
89. Ibid., 439.
90. Ibid., 449.
91. Ibid.
92. Ibid., 457.
93. Gallop, "Sedgwick's Twisted Temporalities," 69.
94. Martineau, *Autobiography*, 186, 242. Although, atypical of women's life-writing in the period, Martineau places her own professional and intellectual life at the center, scholars have described Martineau's *Autobiography* as "substantially about other figures, public and private" (Amigoni, "Gendered Authorship, Literary Lionism, and the Virtues of Domesticity," 28); "lively, anecdotal, and name-dropping" (Logan, "Entre nous," 52); and "particularly fond of secretive allusions to unnamed people" (V. Sanders, "Victorian Life Writing," 11).

95. Martineau, *Autobiography*, 487.
96. Ibid., 144.
97. Ibid., 603.
98. Ibid., 461.
99. Ibid., italics mine.
100. Ibid., 472.
101. Ibid., 151.
102. Ablow, "Harriet Martineau and the Impersonality of Pain," 677.
103. Logan, *Hour and the Woman*, 33. Although Martineau herself described her late journalistic work as "the greatest literary engagement of my life," it receives scant scholarly attention (qtd. in Logan, *Hour and the Woman*, 33). Caroline Roberts justifies its exclusion from her otherwise comprehensive book-length study of Martineau's work on the grounds that it did not prompt significant controversy (Roberts, *Woman and the Hour*, 194).
104. Logan, "Entre nous," 59.
105. Small, *The Long Life*, 101.
106. Martineau, *Autobiography*, 472.
107. Ibid., 428.
108. Schaffer, *Communities of Care*, 53.
109. Ibid., 484.
110. Peterson, *Traditions of Victorian Women's Autobiography*, 76.
111. Martineau's "Freely Translated and Condensed" version of Comte's *Positive Philosophy* (1853) did considerable editorial work to streamline Comte's digressive argument and clarify his opaque prose. The abridgement was so helpful that it was translated back into French in 1871 (Harley, *Autobiologies*, 115).
112. Peterson, *Traditions of Victorian Women's Autobiography*, 64.
113. Harley, *Autobiologies*, 116.
114. Ibid., ix.
115. Ibid., x.
116. Broughton, "Making the Most of Martyrdom," 32.
117. Harley, *Autobiologies*, 122.
118. Martineau, *Autobiography*, 107.
119. Ibid., 109–10.
120. Martineau is a vexed figure in the history of disability. Esmail notes that Martineau "would have personally identified as deaf rather than Deaf"—that is, as audiologically rather than culturally deaf (Esmail, *Reading Victorian Deafness*, 71). Living between the founding of the first deaf schools in Britain in the late-eighteenth century and the movement to suppress sign language in favor of

"oralism" in the late nineteenth, Martineau certainly could have learned to sign, though she never apparently considers it (Baynton, "Deafness," 50; Esmail, *Reading Victorian Deafness*, 14).
121. Following Deaf studies scholars Dirksen Baumann and Joseph Murray, I will call it "deaf gain" rather than "hearing loss" (Baumann and Murray, "Reframing," 3).
122. Martineau, *Autobiography*, 80–1.
123. Ibid., 99.
124. Ibid., 128.
125. Ibid., 294.
126. Ibid., 114.
127. Ibid., 434.
128. Ibid., 84.
129. Ibid., 153.
130. Heath, *Aging by the Book*, 9.
131. Martineau, *Autobiography*, 114, italics mine.
132. Broughton, "Making the Most of Martyrdom," 26.
133. Martineau, *Autobiography*, 114.
134. Esmail, *Reading Victorian Deafness*, 169.
135. Esmail has emphasized Martineau's strategic use of the ear-trumpet to exert social and conversational control (*Reading Victorian Deafness*, 171). Her advocacy for its acceptance is a two-edged sword: clearly undergirded by an ableist sense of deafness as a social burden, Martineau nonetheless demands fuller deaf access to oral/aural interaction, and constantly encounters resistance from interlocutors.
136. Martineau, *Autobiography*, 81.
137. Ibid., 82.
138. Martineau's acknowledgement elsewhere that deafness has made her more of a talker than a listener hints at the way it allows her to subvert gender expectations. Sidonie Smith observes that Martineau similarly uses her deafness to downplay her agency in choosing not to marry (Smith, *Poetics of Women's Autobiography*, 138).
139. Martineau, *Autobiography*, 646.
140. Ibid., 644.
141. Nietzsche, "Uses and Disadvantages," 116.
142. Martineau, *Autobiography*, 645.
143. Ibid., 632.
144. Ibid., 638.
145. Ibid.

5

Stuck in Hardy

Whereas previous chapters have identified a reluctant or enthusiastic dissent from progressive history in Victorian realist fiction and life-writing, this chapter considers the issues raised by historical fiction—the nineteenth century's famous genre for dramatizing and theorizing historical change. *The Trumpet-Major* (1880) and *Wessex Tales* (1888) are among the more neglected texts of Thomas Hardy's large oeuvre, but they reflect his serious, lifelong interest in the Napoleonic Wars and in historical fiction: *The Trumpet-Major* culminates just after the Battle of Trafalgar, with a plot that bears comparison to *Vanity Fair*,[1] and the *Wessex Tales* take place at various points between about 1800 and the 1830s.[2] Despite signaling their participation in the genre of the historical novel as modeled by Walter Scott, these texts respond differently to its central questions about history's representability and its shape.

This chapter makes two related arguments. First, I demonstrate that *The Trumpet-Major* and *Wessex Tales* paradoxically represent the impossibility of historical representation or knowledge. Anders Engberg-Pederson has argued that the experience of the Napoleonic Wars raised epistemological questions that rendered the period a limit case for historicism, even as it receded more deeply into the past.[3] Ironically, the era that produced the historical novel proved difficult to treat in that genre. *The Trumpet-Major* and *Wessex Tales* illustrate and extend Engberg-Pedersen's thesis, meditating on the impossibility of apprehending this period in particular. Second, these texts' resistance to progress leads, I argue, to an ambivalent celebration of changelessness. As I suggested in Chapter 1 with respect to Carlyle, Nietzsche, and Foucault, deep skepticism regarding history's knowability or representability seems to necessitate the rejection not only of progress but also of directional narrative altogether. Whereas scholarship has generally dismissed *The Trumpet-Major* and *Wessex Tales* as failed historical fiction on Scott's model, I read these texts as using cyclical and monumental temporalities—like Harriette Wilson, as I discussed in the previous chapter—to theorize history as static rather than developing. Kate McLoughlin has described *The Trumpet-Major* as characterized by "suspended activity, waiting, introspection, stasis"[4] that she associates with the figure of the unwritten letter. Yet this interest in temporal suspension extends beyond the novel's treatment of epistolarity and to the *Wessex Tales* as well. And in these texts, static or uniform time dictates various rhetorical and narrative moves, some of which involve a repetitive overabundance of activity rather than its absence.

Hardy's sense of the past as unknowable and historical time as changeless is evident in how both characters and novelist attempt to situate themselves in history, only to find themselves estranged from the past, the future, and even the present. These attempts to reify or grasp history function on different thematic and narrative registers. One set of interests lies in the object world. These texts use objects that manifest a deceptively straightforward temporality—clothing, propaganda, monuments—to reveal unexpected complexities. The object world is frequently instrumentalized to index continuity over time but proves inadequate to the task. Another set of interests lies in the individuals who witness history's unfolding. Yet rather than providing continuity with the past, older people in these texts embody the contingency of having avoided an early death. In Disraeli and Thackeray, we saw a contestation between energetic or idealistic youth and decrepit or corrupt age, whereas in Martineau we caught a glimpse of young venerating old. Written decades later as the elderly were increasingly recognized as a demographic and social category, Hardy's texts reject both models, finding a reparative relationship between young and old tied to the monumental temporality of universal death. Contingency always ending in the grave, Hardy's vision of time is not only, like Thackeray's, detached from directional narrative, but also, like Martineau's, fixated on the end—less elegiac in mourning loss than completely collapsed into the inevitability of death.

The first half of the chapter analyzes *The Trumpet-Major*. I begin with the novel's theorization of a minimal historical consciousness characterized by ignorance, passivity, and vulnerability—much like Nietzsche's desirable unhistorical state. The novel celebrates this attitude for its acknowledgement of the stark limitations of individual knowledge and agency. In the novel's yawning gulf between character and reader perspectives, we see that the impossibility of cross-temporal consciousness goes both ways—readers cannot recover what characters thought or felt, just as characters remain exorbitantly ignorant about the future and even the present. I then consider the novel's attempts to imagine objects that reflect a similarly minimal historical consciousness, revealing that objects repeatedly destabilize the historical narratives they appear to support. The second half of the chapter examines the *Wessex Tales*. Through a survey of the whole collection and then readings of two stories, I argue that the tales persistently collapse moments of high narrative contingency with the inevitability of death. In their unresolvable courtship impasses, strange references to calendar time, and interest in the vanishing historicity of the landscape, the *Wessex Tales* represent time as static and repetitive but fading from view. Throughout these texts, Hardy meditates inconclusively on difficult problems: how can changelessness be narrated? And given how little we can know, what is the aesthetic or ethical value of the past?

Deaths, imagined and real

Set in "Overcombe" near "Budmouth," *The Trumpet-Major* follows the protagonist Anne Garland as she resists the aggressive advances of the villainous Festus Derriman while deliberating between two rival suitors, the worthy if uninspiring trumpet-major John Loveday and his feckless but attractive brother, Bob, who, before ultimately marrying Anne, makes and breaks an engagement with the conniving Matilda Johnson. The novel was popular and well-regarded in the nineteenth century,[5] but over the years, many readers and critics have followed Leslie Stephen in feeling that Anne marries the wrong man.[6] As Mary Rimmer suggests, Anne's final choice, a reconfirmation of her initial preference for Bob, defies the expectations of the courtship plot, in which the heroine typically grows beyond her youthful attachment to a dashing suitor in favor of a sober, mature rival[7]—one of the novel's many rejections of progressive development. Like several of the *Wessex Tales*, the novel sets this typically Hardyesque plot of romantic indecision against a historical backdrop that is paradoxically both eventful and vague. Richard Nemesvari finds that in the revisions from the manuscript to the serial to the first edition, "Hardy systematically removes any references to specific dates,"[8] turning the novel's historical setting into an indistinct temporal zone.

The Trumpet-Major takes place between the breaking of the Peace of Amiens in May 1803 and the victory at Trafalgar in October 1805, yet its plot has been called "an exercise in disappointment, at least for those who are expecting great events."[9] On the Dorset coast, this period was defined by intense fears of French invasion. The novel features a dramatic false alarm, inspired by that of May 1, 1804, when a fleet of fishing vessels was mistaken for an invading army.[10] In the novel, the rumor that "the French have landed!"[11] panics the local inhabitants. Festus's behavior during this episode is cowardly and malicious—initially terrified, he soon learns of the report's falsehood but does not spread the word, instead announcing, "The man who quails now is unworthy of the name of yeoman,"[12] and "I'll take three frog-eating Frenchmen single-handed!"[13] Like an unsympathetic historical novelist, Festus cruelly solicits others' expressions of fear that he would and did feel under the same circumstances. Then, discovering Anne hiding alone in an abandoned cottage, he opportunistically exploits her terror to further his own unwanted suit: "What do you think I am, then, that you should barricade yourself against me as I was a wild beast or a Frenchman? Open the door, or put out your head, or do something; or 'pon my soul I'll break in the door!"[14] Anne escapes on horseback, but this close call lingers on the possibility of sexual assault, whether by Festus or the invaders.

Historical fiction often uses narrative contingency (will Anne's story start to resemble Tess's?) to make immediate the historical contingency (will Napoleon invade?) that is otherwise difficult for the reader to imagine. Such a parallel tends to suggest a deterministic vision of history, since the reader may not know how the story ends but knows that the ending is already written. Furthermore, as much as readers feel for Anne, the substitution of narrative for historical contingency only highlights the impossibility of recreating the past—as Rimmer puts it, "[n]either narrator nor reader can actually see through the characters' eyes."[15] Ultimately the novel's capitalization on its characters' ignorance feels slightly mean-spirited, like Festus. In trying to make history's roads-not-taken seem like real possibilities, *The Trumpet-Major* depicts characters who are not only powerless against historical forces but also wildly mistaken about what is currently happening. The episode draws to mind Stendhal's famous ground-eye view of the Battle of Waterloo in *The Charterhouse of Parma* (1839), after which the oblivious protagonist wonders, "was what he had seen a battle, and, secondly, was that battle Waterloo?"[16] *The Trumpet-Major* similarly theorizes historical embeddedness as a profoundly restricted view, limited at best to the intensely local—the historical subject vulnerable to death or rape at any moment.

Literally and figuratively restricted perception characterizes the novel's many encounters with the royal family, figured as a deceptive vestige of the past that undercuts the idea of meaningful continuity over time. *The Trumpet-Major* is peppered with royal encounters that resemble disappointed celebrity spotting, revealing not only characters' total alienation from power but also their profound misunderstanding of it. Although Leslie Stephen cautioned Hardy against including historical characters in his novel, calling them "almost always a nuisance,"[17] the King and his family appear in repetitive distant sightings that are neither narratively nor historically meaningful. At one point, Anne travels with a family party out to the main road to see the King's procession pass by in the middle of the night.[18] After a protracted wait, the modest coaches finally appear, in a scene that presents "an *ancien regime* as not gaudy but dowdy,"[19] a shabbiness that can be read either as deflating or ironically reflecting their intergenerational inherited power:

> Anne was told to look in the first carriage—a post-chariot drawn by four horses—for the King and Queen, and was rewarded by seeing a profile reminding her of the current coin of the realm; but as the party had been travelling all night, and the spectators here gathered were few, none of the royal family looked out the carriage windows. It was said that the two elder princesses were in the same carriage, but they remained invisible.[20]

Unlike Edward Waverley's transformative encounter with Bonnie Prince Charlie, Anne's obstructed view of George III reveals both his familiarity and his inaccessibility. The aura of royal authority is completely absent, as the monarch's living body resembles the flat, motionless image on a coin, with its many circulating and interchangeable copies, a suggestion that cash is king. In this passage, historical experience is disappointingly decentralized—maybe as close as your pocket, but also out of reach or view.

Such repetitious scenes in *The Trumpet-Major* reveal characters' unfulfilled longing for meaningful access to the historical continuity that the monarchy seems to represent. At another point, villagers gather to watch the royals watch the troops be inspected—a spectatorship of spectatorship that indicates a recursive and vanishing historical agency:

> ... the King, accompanied by the Dukes of Cambridge and Cumberland, and a couple of generals, appeared on horseback, wearing a round hat turned up at the side, with a cockade and military feather. (Sensation among the crowd.) Then the Queen and three of the princesses entered the field in a great coach drawn by six beautiful cream-coloured horses. Another coach, with four horses of the same sort, brought the two remaining princesses. (Confused acclamations, "There's King Jarge!" "That's Queen Sharlett!" "Princess 'Lizabeth!" "Princess Sophiar and Meelyer!" etc., from the surrounding spectators.)[21]

From this distance, the townspeople see only the clothing and carriages of royal family members whose identities remain uncertain. Through the difficulty of getting a good look, the novel suggests characters' desire for embodied, intimate contact with history that remains distanced and intangible. Hardy's strange parenthetical narration in this passage furthermore reflects the inaccessibility of historical experience. The punctuation creates a barrier (on the page) between the crowd and the celebrities they are watching, and suggests that the crowd's responses are merely parenthetical (literally) to a spectacle of connection between past and present that is itself meaningless.

Anne's relative disinterest in these forms of contact makes her a fitting mascot for the unhistorical consciousness that the novel privileges. Watching yet another military procession, she "felt herself close to and looking into the stream of recorded history, within whose banks the littlest things are great, and outside of which she and the general bulk of the human race were content to live on as an unreckoned, unheeded superfluity."[22] This passage rewrites Scott's "Postscript, which should have been a preface," discussed in Chapter 1, in which the historical subject floats peacefully down the lazy river of history.[23] By contrast, Anne situates herself squarely outside what Helen Kingstone has called history's "social continuum"[24]—the set of individuals whose experiences count as history. Yet Anne understands her position not as an exclusion, but as contented stasis, the ground solid under her feet as the water passes by, the stream moving toward its unseen but unified end. Moreover, the modest stream magnifies "the littlest things" within its banks and is dwarfed by the "unreckoned, unheeded superfluity" that exceeds it.[25] Although the novel reveals Anne as more like a minnow in history's roiling ocean—buffeted by currents in a vast directionless expanse—the true nature of the experience is to believe oneself a spectator on the bank of a small stream, and to understand the water's movement as linear.

Anne's accidental personal encounter with the King fully deflates the idea of individual historical agency. Shortly after Bob leaves the merchant service for the navy, Anne is crying beside a spring when an inquisitive elderly man approaches. When she eventually discloses her lover's name, the King replies, "Loveday—a good name. I shall not forget it."[26] The scene bathetically rewrites Jeanie Deans's petition to Queen Caroline in Scott's *The Heart of Mid-Lothian* (1818), illustrating a different vision of royal authority and historical agency. Whereas Jeanie seeks out the Queen in a desperate attempt to save her sister from execution, Anne meets the King by coincidence. Whereas Jeanie's moving performance of plainspoken eloquence proves a turning point in the novel, Anne's encounter with the King comes to nothing. After he leaves, Anne grows excited by

> visions of Bob promoted to the rank of admiral or something equally wonderful, by the King's special command, the chief result of the promotion being, in her arrangement of the piece, that he would stay at home and go to sea no more. But she was not a girl who indulged in extravagant fancies long, and before she reached home she thought that the King had probably forgotten her by that time, and her troubles, and her lover's name.[27]

Despite the way fiction trains readers to indulge in extravagant fancies long after the characters have given them up, Anne is right—there are no consequences to this conversation. Whereas the passage easily reads as a critique of royal indifference or incompetence, Anne's conclusion reflects her confidence in and contentment with a clear separation between those in the stream of history and those (including both the King and herself) standing on the bank.

Bob's fate hinges instead on a different charismatic leader, the impressive Captain Thomas Masterman Hardy (a distant relation) who finally convinces Bob to join the navy after having resisted military service for most of the novel.[28] It is potentially a very *un*lucky break: Bob serves under Hardy on the HMS *Victory* when it sees scores of casualties at the Battle of Trafalgar. But Bob distinguishes himself by creating a barricade, carrying the dying Lord Nelson into the cockpit, and valiantly jumping aboard the enemy ship—a turn of events that occurs entirely offstage and is relayed to Bob's anxious family long after the fact. The friend who brings the news reports that "they say there's a promotion in store for'n."[29] However, by the time the promotion finally arrives, months later, any sense of royal patronage has been forgotten in favor of merit, though even that explanation is strained by the substantial delay.[30] In the meantime, Bob dallies in Portsmouth, courting another woman, one of the novel's many interludes of postponement. The flickering possibility that the King will intervene in Bob's career is undercut by a different unlikely plot twist, one that replaces the monarch with the novelist as the arbiter of fates.

His brother and now-defeated romantic rival does not fare as well—courtship and wartime fates coincide. The marriage of Bob and Anne imminent, the novel ends by revealing that John "joined his companions-in-arms, and went off to blow his trumpet till silenced for ever on one of the bloody battlefields of Spain."[31] This moment sees the culmination of a refrain throughout the novel, in the use of what Ken Ireland has identified, using Mieke Bal's term, as proleptic analepsis—moments of flash-forward within a larger flashback structure.[32] Here are three typical examples: first, a "cheerful, careless, unpremeditated half-hour" in which some off-duty soldiers pick cherries, returns "like the scent of a flower to the memories of some of those who enjoyed it, even at a distance of many years after, when they lay wounded and weak in foreign lands."[33] Second, the narrator interrupts Sergeant Stanner's satirical song about Bonaparte to reveal that "he fell at the bloody battle of Albuera a few years after this pleasantly spent summer."[34] And third, after describing the King's procession with fifteen thousand soldiers, the narrator remarks, "how entirely they have all passed and gone!—lying scattered about the world as military and other dust, some at Talavera, Albuera, Salamanca,

Vittoria, Toulouse, and Waterloo; some in home churchyards; and a few small handfuls in royal vaults."[35] Discussing this third passage, Rimmer suggests that "the ironic contrast between the 'gorgeous' review and the indiscriminate end of all participants in death suggests that to recover history is pointless as well as impossible."[36] J. M. Rignall similarly observes that "the historical past is subsumed in death."[37]

Yet the novel renders more pointedly the general observation that all life ends in death, a trope of historical fiction. As these examples reflect, *The Trumpet-Major*'s prolepses most often move not to the present, but rather to the later phases of the Napoleonic Wars, positioned between the characters' past and readers' present, though far closer to them than to us. In locating the soldiers' remains at these famous battle sites, tightly clustered between 1809 and 1814, the narrator poignantly reveals that characters' fates are sealed by what lies *just* beyond their knowledge, though deep in history's recesses for us. For John Loveday, despite the inevitability of death and the vulnerabilities of the post of trumpet-major, death in battle was not a foregone conclusion. This painful proximity between the characters and their untimely deaths does not just critique of the wasting of human life in war, but also alludes to the ruptures that render time striated and uneven. As I discuss later in this chapter, the *Wessex Tales* even more insistently incorporate these vertiginous temporal shifts, repeatedly collapsing the apparent contingency of human drama into the grave. But first, I want to return to the question of clothing in order to sketch how *The Trumpet-Major* imagines a sartorial corollary to the minimal historical consciousness that it privileges.

The days of high-waisted and muslin-gowned women

In "The Profitable Reading of Fiction" (1888), Hardy echoes an Aristotelian argument about the primacy of plot and character over incidental details by disparaging novels that are faithful to "life garniture and not life. You are fully persuaded that the personages are clothed precisely as you see them clothed in the street, in the drawing-room, at the assembly. Even the trifling accidents of their costume are rendered by the honest narrator."[38] Hardy concedes that the "attention to accessories has its virtues when the nature of its regard does not involve blindness to higher things;

still more when it conduces to the elucidation of higher things."[39] Yet his sense of precisely what accessories might elucidate seems limited to one insight only: that time conquers all. Notably switching from the nominally gender-neutral phenomenon of costume to a gendered-female example, Hardy instructs that rather than describe "a jeweled leader of society by saying baldly how much her diamonds cost at So-and-So's, what the largest of them weighed and measured, how it was cut and set,"[40] the writer should instead follow the example of Robert Herrick's "To Dianeme" in using such trifling accidents as *memento mori*:

> Be you not proud of that rich hair
> Which wantons with the love-sick air;
> Whenas that ruby which you wear,
> Sunk from the tip of your soft ear,
> Will last to be a precious stone
> When all your world of beauty's gone.[41]

In allowing material details this one meaning, Hardy suggests that "life garniture" best illustrates its own meaninglessness, that the cultural or historical particulars manifest in accessories reveal only the universal denial of the universal end in death.

Yet the unregistered shift between clothing and jewels begins to suggest the complexity of how fictional material details embed characters in time. In contrast to clothing, the pure ornamentality and durability of jewels facilitate a more straightforward illustration of Hardy's point. In Herrick, the ruby evinces what Stefanie Markovits has called "the lyric diamond's oppositional makeup,"[42] its tendency to juxtapose temporalities or frames of value. That is, the ruby embodies a striking contrast between the vast scale of geologic time, or the enduring exchange-value of the ruby, and the brief candle of human life or female beauty. Herrick's stark opposition is already complicated by Hardy's comments on jewels in the essay, which demystify Herrick's scene in acknowledging the commercial exchange that preceded their ownership and the dictates of fashion that determined how they are "cut and set." But clothing is even more difficult to stretch to Herrick's frame in that its greater practicality and shorter life-cycle fit poorly fit with the monumental temporality of jewels. Clothing suggests instead the busy movements of bourgeois life, from the street to the drawing-room and assembly—an uneven temporality of change, full of "trifling accidents"[43] that exceed the narrative that time conquers all.

Furthermore, for Herrick, as for Hardy in "Profitable Reading," the world of beauty exists in the speaker's present: Herrick admires the woman's soft ear, and Hardy recognizes the drawing-room dress. Indeed, Hardy expresses a familiar hostility to the descriptive excess of fictional representations of late-nineteenth-century bourgeois life. But historical fiction provides a different environment in which to register the leveling hand of time. As I have suggested, characters' mortality sits inherently closer to mind in historical fiction, and in this novel. Notwithstanding the different temporalities of clothing and jewelry, one might still expect the historical setting to be conducive to using clothing in the way Hardy recommends in "Profitable Reading." Yet clothing in *The Trumpet-Major* proves more complicatedly meaningful than the essay allows. Although scholars frequently cite the novel's attention to clothing as evidence of its facile historicism,[44] its satire of early nineteenth-century fashion ultimately uses "life garniture" to suggest multiple alternative relationships to contemporaneity. That is, it establishes a contrast between, on the one hand, a self-conscious high-fashionability of striking, impractical dress that puts the wearer out of sync with seasonal and diurnal time and, on the other hand, an unconscious and understated mode that reflects a privileged, passive relationship to time.

The novel's descriptions of fashionable clothing often highlight its contextual inappropriateness. For example, Bob goes to the theater dressed as follows:

> As finished off by this dashing and really fashionable attire, he was the perfection of a beau in the dog-days; pantaloons and boots of the newest make; yards and yards of muslin wound round his neck, forming a sort of asylum for the lower part of his face; two fancy waistcoats, and coat-buttons like circular shaving glasses. The absurd extreme of female fashion, which was to wear muslin dresses in January, was at this time equalled by that of men, who wore clothes enough in August to melt them.[45]

This exuberant passage echoes the description of *Vanity Fair*'s Jos Sedley that I discussed in Chapter 3—with the encased neck and extra-large waistcoat buttons. As with Jos, scholarly interpretations of the passage have drawn on gender, sexuality, and class—for example, Rimmer observes that Bob's "conscious manipulation of costume is conventionally coded feminine."[46] But as with Jos, the passage both asserts that contemporary practices condition Bob's clothing and also muddles his clothing's historicity. That is, while the clothes are usually interpreted as an exaggeration of the male fashions popular at Bob's moment, they also constitute a non-exaggerated account of the clothing worn a few decades later. Thus, the novel's illustration of its historical setting ultimately reveals the temporal contractions and dilations of historical fiction. And in observing the studied defiance of seasonal cycles, this passage also reveals fashion's inherently complicated relationship to time.

I will return below to the female style of diaphanous muslin, whose climatological inappropriateness was the subject of misogynist satire and also feminist advocacy for dress reform.[47] For the moment, allow me to emphasize that the novel's account of women's fashion at the beginning of the nineteenth century suggests competing representational paradigms that reveal the multiplicity of time. The most fashionable female character, Anne's duplicitous romantic rival Matilda, is described in terms that highlight the bright colors and striking cuts of her clothing, rather than the materials. When Matilda belatedly arrives in Overcombe, Bob is surprised at the contrast between her garments and her conveyance:

> In dress, Miss Johnson passed his expectations—a green and white gown, with long, tight sleeves, a green silk handkerchief round her neck and crossed in front, a green parasol, and green gloves. It was strange enough to see this verdant caterpillar turn out of a road-waggon, and gracefully shake herself free from the bits of straw and fluff which would usually gather on the raiment of the grandest travellers by that vehicle.[48]

Delayed by the need to take an economical mode of transportation after overspending on clothing, Matilda also appears literally immature, as a "verdant caterpillar" rather than a beautiful butterfly. Aesthetically, Matilda's striking, monochromatic green ensemble departs conspicuously from the trope of white muslin (understated, though nonetheless differently impractical) that dominates Victorian representations of early nineteenth-century women's clothing. Temporally, it differs too. Whereas white muslin is a basic paradigm sustained over decades, Matilda's dress is a high-resolution snapshot of a specific point in time. The detailed account reflects the arabesques of the fashion moment while it also figures the outfit as a developmental stage leading to a dramatic transformation—from caterpillar to butterfly.

As Hardy's "Trumpet-Major Notebook" documents, the novel's critique of this clothing does not depend on historical distance. Simon Gatrell observes that Hardy has lifted not only the features of Matilda's green ensemble and Bob's theater outfit but also the condescension toward them from dueling letters to the *St. James Chronicle* for 1804, in which a male and a female correspondent each ridicule the other's fashions.[49] Thus, despite how the novel's structure parallels Hume's encounter with the ugly "ruffs and fardingdales" worn in seventeenth-century portraiture (discussed in Chapter 3), this critique of Regency fashion is entirely contemporary with the setting. Whereas in "To Dianeme," Herrick sees in beauty the inevitability of death, Hardy makes it impossible to entertain that Matilda's and Bob's clothing is simply attractive. Their clothing is neither beautiful, nor fully dictated by the time. That is, whereas fashionable clothing may appear a pure, spontaneous reflection of contemporaneity, these accounts of Matilda and Bob demonstrate instead that a heightened self-consciousness results ironically in a rejection of clothing tailored to its temporal contexts. Clothing thus reveals not Matilda's and Bob's embeddedness but rather their forceful and thus estranging embrace of the historical moment.

The novel's account of Anne's ostensibly less fashionable clothing reflects that her lower self-consciousness results in an uncomplicated identity with her time and place. The novel opens: "In the days of high-waisted and muslin-gowned women ... there lived in a village near the Wessex coast two ladies of good report, though unfortunately of limited means."[50] Here, the narrator does not necessarily indicate that Anne and her mother themselves wore muslin gowns with high waists, but rather references this sartorial paradigm to situate the novel broadly in time. Elsewhere, however, Anne frequently wears muslin, a gauzy cotton fabric quintessential of women's clothing in the period. Absent references to any specific style, Anne is called a "muslin apparition,"[51] a "white muslin figure,"[52] and, as she escapes from Festus on horseback, a "bundle of drapery"[53]—visions of disembodied fabric that contrast with Matilda's green, earthy physicality. Although muslin places Anne around the turn of the nineteenth century, it is a relatively blunt historical marker due to its long popularity.

In fact, the novel's few descriptions of the style of Anne's clothing undermine any close correspondence between specific fashions and the historical moment. During a trip to see the royal family, Anne "had a very nice appearance in her best clothes as she walked along—the sarcanet hat, muslin shawl, and tight-sleeved gown being of the newest Overcombe fashion, that was only about a year old in the adjoining town, and in London three or four."[54] Again, the description focuses on textiles—muslin and sarcanet, a delicate silk used in the diaphanous garments of the period—rather than colors or styles. The passage also typifies the novel's insistent undercutting of characters' individual agency by revealing their subjection to larger unseen forces. As with Becky Sharp's hat and spencer, as I discussed in Chapter 3, this account of Anne's clothing lacks particularizing details but nonetheless prompts narratorial comment on the historicity of these fashions. That comment may reveal Anne as unfashionable—wearing a sleeve popular four years ago—but it also figures belatedness as time's fundamental mode. That is, notwithstanding its gentle mockery, this passage demystifies fashion's apparent immediacy—we are apprised that the outfit belatedly imitates metropolitan trends but also assured that Anne, like Jos Sedley, is indeed fashionable relative to her local context. Thus, as in the repeated prolepsis to death in battle, the novel charts a fundamental perspectival distinction between the historically embedded subject, for whom this striation of time remains imperceptible, and the narrator and reader, for whom it is impossible not to see.

If muslin serves as a synecdoche for women's clothing in this era generally, Anne's association with muslin noticeably contrasts with the bright colors and fashionable cuts worn by other female characters. Even the most detailed accounts of Anne's clothing still emphasize fabrics and materials, such as the occasion on which she "wore her celebrated celestial blue pelisse, her Leghorn [straw] hat, and her muslin dress with the waist under the arms; the latter being decorated with excellent Honiton lace."[55] From the perspective of fashion, Anne's Honiton lace is both belated and early. Although, as Elaine Freedgood notes, "the historical vicissitudes of lace are difficult to discern from the vantage of the present,"[56] it nonetheless "seems reasonably clear that for most of the nineteenth century lace was less central as an object of fashionable dress than it had been in the preceding two, and that the demand for it tended to spike for brief periods only,"[57] such as after Queen Victoria wore Honiton lace on her wedding dress in 1840. Thus, Anne wears lace during an unfashionable period. It connects her to a local tradition—Honiton is in Devonshire—and yet also, in combination with her presumably white dress, anticipates the later revival prompted by Victoria's wedding.

By contrast, when Anne's mother remarries, she wears a bold color combination, "her best plum-coloured gown, beneath which peeped out her shoes with red rosettes."[58] In another scene, Matilda is "fashionably dressed in a green spencer, with 'Mameluke' sleeves"[59]—a style in which puffed sleeves are gathered in by a series of tight bands at intervals down the length of the arm. As Elsie Michie has noted, references to historical clothing elsewhere in Hardy sometimes track the disappearance of the traditional sartorial distinctions between social classes.[60] Yet this novel imagines a past in which class already has only subtle consequences for clothes. Anne's tenuous claim to genteel status registers in her comparatively less deliberate and less effortful fashionability. As in the case of Sir Pitt's knee-breeches in *Vanity Fair* or Harriette Wilson's aristocratic lover's threadbare shirts, this unselfconscious mode can tip over into the unfashionable, depending on the viewer's perspective.

The novel establishes early on the distinction between Anne and other women, for instance when Hardy characterizes a group of soldiers' wives as "very brilliantly dressed, with more regard for colour than for material. Purple, red, and blue bonnets were numerous, with bunches of cocks' feathers; and one had on an Arcadian hat of green sarcenet, turned up in front to show her cap underneath."[61] As Hardy instructs in "Profitable Reading," this lively description of the soldiers' wives' clothing draws to mind their impending widowhood, with its somber sartorial consequences. The novel treats similarly the spectacular weaponry and uniforms of their husbands, the "bright and attractive" York Hussars.[62] At one point, Anne observes a procession in which "the burnished chains, buckles, and plates of their trappings shone like little looking-glasses, and the blue, red, and white about them was unsubdued by weather or wear."[63] Gatrell observes that "such a dazzle of costume tends to blind the spectator to the fact that in pursuit of their essential function these men's uniforms will not just be weather-worn but torn apart, spattered with blood, and perhaps will in the end cover their corpses."[64] Though, per "Profitable Reading," the dazzle arguably draws the reader's attention to that eventuality.

Although the distinction between the wives' colorful, attention-grabbing headwear and Anne's Leghorn hat certainly reflects differences of class, ideology, and marital status, it also indicates alternative relationships to contemporaneity. Insofar as styles and colors appear to change more quickly, the passage privileges a passive mode of being-in-time, buffeted by fashion's winds, rather than chasing them. These different ways of relating to fashion take strange form in the novel's retrospective gaze. Although the soldiers' wives are more fashionable than Anne, her muslin is more legible as a historicizing detail, more evocative of the period for the reader. Muslin is memorable, whereas the green Mameluke sleeve is the flash in the pan. In order to register as transitory in historical fiction's hindsight, the fashion needed, paradoxically, to have endured. As I suggested above, all the novel's characters—and, by extension, its readers—are deeply powerless and profoundly vulnerable to history's whims. Anne's passivity to fashion, as to history, reflects an acknowledgement of the impossibility of seeing beyond one's immediate context, of somehow cannily gaining insights that could shape one's fate. Like Nietzsche's account of the desirable unhistorical state, enclosed within a bounded horizon, Anne teaches us that our best strategy in light of history's cruel determinism is to ignore it altogether.

Imagining the occasional object

I have been arguing that Hardy underscores a sharp perspectival contrast between characters and readers and presents their perspectives as epistemologically equivalent. In characters' diverging relationships to clothing, the novel privileges a historical unselfconsciousness that does not aspire to impact the outcome or to contextualize the self in the present. I turn now to the novel's varied experiments in imagining the occasional object—the object that is time-stamped with an intimate relationship to the present. These experiments attempt to find a corollary in the object world to Anne's minimal historical consciousness. In these passages, the temporalities of objects prove misleading: those that appear to capture, preserve, or channel a point in time ultimately signal a more extended temporality, whereas those that appear to represent continuity prove short-lived. In their deceptive material manifestation of the present moment, occasional objects ironically reveal the difficulty of imagining the past or the future.

For example, the novel's treatment of print propaganda reflects the temporal expansions and contractions of what might appear ephemeral. Like fashionable clothing, war propaganda seems spontaneous: "We punned on Buonaparte and his gunboats, chalked his effigy on stage-coaches, and published the same in prints."[65] Yet *The Trumpet-Major* reveals that these prints have a complicated relationship to historical time. At one point, Bob shows Anne a piece of paper, "something to make us brave and patriotic":[66]

> It was a hieroglyphic profile of Napoleon. The hat represented a maimed French eagle; the face was ingeniously made up of human carcases [sic], knotted and writhing together in such directions as to form a physiognomy; a band, or stock, shaped to resemble the English Channel, encircled his throat, and seemed to choke him; his epaulette was a hand tearing a cobweb that represented the treaty of peace with England; and his ear was a woman crouching over a dying child.[67]

Hardy based this description on a real image, Rudolf Ackermann's British adaptation of a famous German print, Johann Michael Voltz's "Triumph des Jahres 1813," which caricatured an 1806 bust portrait by Heinrich Anton Dähling.[68] In Voltz's caricature, each element of Napoleon's head, shoulders, and hat is composed of a smaller image representing his brutality; Ackermann's adaptation altered these images slightly to fit the British national context (see Fig. 5.1).[69] In a Walter Scott-esque preface in 1895, Hardy claims to have found this print "in an old woman's cottage near 'Overcombe'"[70]—though the differences between Ackermann's version and the fictional print are likely Hardy's own invention.

Hardy's fiction collapses the longer historical narrative told by the real-life print. In so doing, it reveals the novel's investment in the fantasy that the historical moment can be crystallized in a physical form that can be preserved unaltered in a rustic cottage. The novel's description is indebted to the text that accompanied the original prints, but Hardy changes the details: first, emphasizing Napoleon's threat to England specifically and second, giving the image a different and narrower set of historical referents. In a way, Hardy does precisely what Walter Benjamin advocates,

Figure 5.1 Napoleon caricature by Johann Michael Voltz, adapted by Rudolf Ackermann, 1814. Image provided by Cornell University, PJ Mode Collection of Persuasive Cartography.

capturing a still image of a point in time as it flares up. Yet to do this, he must artificially excise the real image's broader historical consciousness. We might take for example the epaulette, which both Voltz and Ackermann describe as a hand leading and tearing apart the Confederation of the Rhine, a group of German client states that existed between 1806 and 1813.[71] To fit the novel's setting a few years earlier, Hardy describes the epaulette as tearing apart the Treaty of Amiens, a reminder of the seemingly imminent and immanent threat of French invasion.

Yet Hardy's changes do not just remove anachronistic elements, but rather manifest the historical and cultural limitations of characters' consciousness. In Voltz's original caricature the red collar represents "the great stream of blood so long outpoured for his ambition,"[72] and in Ackermann "the *Red Sea*, in allusion to his Drowned Hosts,"[73] a reference to the 1799 Battle of Aboukir, in which thousands of Ottoman troops drowned. Although Bob and Anne could have known of Aboukir, Hardy describes the collar—color unspecified—as the English Channel, a yet-further, redundant reminder of the apparent threat of invasion. When Voltz's and Ackermann's caricatures appeared in 1813, they referenced Napoleon's aggression over a wide temporal and geographical scope, and in fact, the many adaptations of the image helped unify Napoleon's disparate enemies at a late stage in the war.[74] Whereas the real caricatures were international and cumulative, Hardy's fictional caricature is local and temporally restricted. In both changing and narrowing the image's references, the novel imagines an identity between the object and its moment, a more direct connection than existed in reality. In its hyper-specificity, it imagines total historical immersion in the immediate time and place—like Anne, unaware of wider contexts.

Recent scholarship has explored Hardy's interest in the material remains of the past, situating his historicism in the context of late nineteenth-century developments in anthropology, archaeology, and history. Adam Grener highlights Hardy's use of the distinctive narrative structure of the relic—preserved and excavated accidentally, lingering without being repurposed.[75] According to Grener, the "relics attest to the persistence of a vanishing past and bring it into contact with … the present, pointing to discontinuity, fragmentation, and loss."[76] Yet whereas the 1895 preface suggests that the print was accidentally preserved and excavated, the novel's fictionalization of the image reveals the imaginative work of finding a connection to history in lingering objects. That is, although the preface to *The Trumpet-Major* mentions the persistence of "casual relics"[77] of the Napoleonic period, the novel itself reveals material connections to history as misleading or fabricated, whether within the world of the novel, or as part of the novelist's art.

Like the hieroglyphic portrait, the novel's effigy to George III differs from its real-life prototype in its discrete point of origin and limited broader consciousness. Directly after the victory at Trafalgar, local men begin "cutting out a huge picture of the king on horseback in the earth of the hill. The king's head is to be as big as our mill-pond and his body as big as this garden; he and the horse will cover more than an acre."[78] In *The White Horses of the West of England* (1885), William C. Plenderleath describes the phenomenon of hillside carvings of horses, created by cutting deep grooves in the soil and refilling them with crushed chalk.[79] The novel's fictional hill carving resembles the Osmington White Horse, whose relationship to historical time is more diffuse: dating from 1808, it commemorates the King's regular visits to the area.[80] Thus, although the real carving honored the King's repeated practice of many years, the novel's version commemorates a specific event, immediately thereafter—and moreover, an event in which he had no involvement. Like *The Trumpet-Major* itself, most existing British monuments to the Napoleonic Wars are belated Victorian projects. In manipulating the timeline to suggest an effigy created in the first glow of victory, the novel imagines the instantaneous material solidification of the fleeting moment—concealing the work involved in using objects to this end.

Moreover, departing dramatically from the trajectory of real horse carvings, the novel imagines its fictional horse carving to survive permanently in unchanged form. Andrew Radford has identified Hardy's debts elsewhere to the Victorian anthropologist Edward Burnett Tylor's concept of "survivals," "primitive or ancient forms of thought and practice, which ... lingered into later culture, thus revealing the continuity between early and more developed forms of civilization."[81] While some of the real-life white horses allegedly have ancient origins, they require frequent, substantial upkeep—for example, the Westbury Horse, thought to commemorate the victory of King Alfred over the Danes in the 870s CE, was entirely redesigned in 1778.[82] Ongoing preservation efforts at the Osmington Horse attest that although these horse carvings give an impression of timeless antiquity, they are nothing like survivals in Tylor's sense. In this way, the fictional effigy captures the uncertain afterlife of victory; Trafalgar did not end Napoleon's career, but it remains a point of British national pride. Yet it also begins to suggest how Hardy's landscapes reflect the persistence of the past. As I discuss below with respect to the *Wessex Tales*, Hardy imagines human manipulations of the landscape that remain in place, nature strangely inert to the erasures of time.

Notwithstanding the self-conscious modernity of the York Hussars' gleaming arms as they hurtle toward imminent death, weaponry in this novel also reveals complex temporalities.

The ceremonial pikes in the village church, for example, initially seem pregnant with future violence that hearkens back to ancient warfare. As Anne and Bob sit in the church, the narrator relates:

> The religion of the country had, in fact, changed from love of God to hatred of Napoleon Buonaparte; and, as if to remind the devout of this alteration, the pikes for the pikemen (all those accepted men who were not otherwise armed) were kept in the church of each parish. There, against the wall, they always stood—a whole sheaf of them, formed of new ash stems, with a spike driven in at one end, the stick being preserved from splitting by a ferule. And there they remained, year after year, in the corner of the aisle, till they were removed and placed under the gallery stairs, and thence ultimately to the belfry, where they grew black, rusty, and worm-eaten, and were gradually stolen and carried off by sextons, parish clerks, whitewashers, window-menders, and other church servants for use at home as rake-stems, benefit-club staves and pick-handles, in which degraded situations they may still occasionally be found.
>
> But in their new and shining state they had a terror for Anne whose eyes were involuntarily drawn toward them as she sat at Bob's side during the service, filling her with bloody visions of their possible use not far from the very spot on which they were now assembled.[83]

These pikes bear witness to time in two ways. First, they highlight the contrast between Anne's fanciful vision of guerilla resistance to French invaders and the more mundane future reality. This passage is one of many satirizing frantic local preparation for a future that never arrives—such as when volunteers practice paramilitary drills holding denuded stalks of Brussels sprouts in place of firearms.[84] These pikes thus serve as a false *memento mori* that reminds Anne of deaths that will not come to pass—the pikes will be used in the future, but not in the way Anne expects. Relatedly, the repurposing and deterioration of the pikes over a matter of decades imbues the world of modest objects with the close calls and roads-not-taken of capital-H History. Imagining the moldering rake or pickaxe currently languishing in a closet as the afterlife of the shiny new pike, Hardy suggests that never-actualized futures live on, domesticated into everyday life. As a metonym for the historical counterfactual, the pikes embody, on the level of history, the optative speculations that shape Hardy's characters' inner lives.

Second, the passage ironizes liberal narratives of secularization and declining violence. Anne sees the pikes as combat-ready, connecting past, present, and future with the universality of violence. As I discussed in Chapter 1, Henry Thomas Buckle or Steven Pinker might see them as the last vestiges of a bellicose past. The narrator, though, undercuts both Anne's vision of stasis and Buckle's progress narrative, emphasizing that these traditional weapons were already long obsolete when they were installed in the early nineteenth century—they are not, in fact, a survival of an ancient past. Their final, belated removal and repurposing offers a bathetic deflation of Buckle's historical narrative of progress through declining violence. The passage treats secularization with similar irony. Like Martineau, the passage suggests that religion is initially degraded through transformation—in this case as anti-French sentiment—and later mined as a repository of useful materials. We might contrast this passage with the way Sybil laments the creative misuse of religious infrastructure in the ruins of Marney Abbey (discussed in Chapter 2). In *Sybil* and *The Trumpet-Major*, objects follow the same trajectory—from sacred to profane, from symbolic to use-value, from unity to diversity of purpose—and yet what *Sybil* mourns, *The Trumpet-Major* treats with a shrug, reflecting the later novel's disinterest in grand historical narratives of transformation. The multiple trajectories of the pikes ultimately undermine the idea that material objects can embody long continuities, revealing instead the challenges of registering time in the fictional object world.

The Napoleon caricature, the horse carving, and the pikes initially suggest a straightforward linear temporality: an instantaneous moment of creation followed by unchanged persistence, indexing continuity between past and present. Yet in each case, these objects embody complicated temporalties that disrupt linear narrative. As the pikes reflect, the object's trajectory tends toward decline, degradation, or ironic descent—whereas the human life, at least in theory, though not really in this novel, holds the potential for growth and development over time. As I have suggested, *The Trumpet-Major* uses fashionable clothing and other time-stamped objects to highlight a stark contrast between character and reader perspectives, undermining larger historical narratives and illustrating the value of an un-historical consciousness. In the *Wessex Tales*, as I argue in the remainder of the chapter, this disjunction between character and reader perspectives becomes so insistent as almost to preclude narrative altogether. Everyone remains stuck in time, unable to see beyond their own immediate situation and living in the aftermath of their decisions.

The uppermost sod

Hardy's *Wessex Tales* is a retro-retroactive construction whose complex publication history mirrors the diffuse and layered temporalities of the tales themselves. The individual short stories that ultimately comprise the *Tales* were originally published in various magazines and newspapers between 1879 and 1890. The 1888 volume *Wessex Tales: Strange, Lively, and Commonplace* drew together five of these stories. For an 1896 edition, Hardy added a sixth tale and a preface. In 1912, when the *Wessex Tales* appeared in their final form as volume IX of the Macmillan Wessex Edition, Hardy expanded the preface, removed one story, and added two others—tinkering with the grouping of his short stories to sort them by their historical settings. The resulting collection, as David Grylls observes, is "united temporally, being set largely in the decades immediately preceding Hardy's birth."[85] This accretive and piecemeal composition followed by reiterative reorganization has meant that despite strong thematic unities across the collection, scholars most often treat the tales individually for their respective connections to Hardy's full-length novels.[86] Along those lines, the two stories set during the Napoleonic Wars, "A Tradition of Eighteen Hundred and Four" and "The Melancholy Hussar of the German Legion," are often read alongside *The Trumpet-Major* as different expressions of Hardy's sustained interest in the Napoleonic period, and indeed the three texts draw upon the same research.

But the connection between *The Trumpet-Major* and the *Wessex Tales* as a whole far exceeds this content overlap with two of the stories. Following Kristin Brady, critics generally read the *Tales* in the pastoral tradition,[87] drawing a parallel between the economic hardships of the period depicted—the stories' "encryption, or even deflection from, the extremely harsh realities of agricultural poverty and injustice in Dorset"[88]—and the "the background of the contemporary agricultural crisis"[89] against which they were written. Yet such readings overlook how the passage of time itself is the subject of the tales, which extend and intensify *The Trumpet-Major*'s suggestion of the inaccessibility of the past. Whereas in

The Trumpet-Major, historical distance renders the past unknowable to readers, in the *Wessex Tales*, characters themselves live in the aftermath of past decisions that are inescapably present and yet impossible to reconsider. As in the autobiographies I analyzed in the previous chapter, characters' lives in the *Wessex Tales* unfold in radically non-normative, anti-progressive, and nonlinear ways. The stories picture the misfires of courtship and the failures of reproductive futurity, while individual aging is uneven and takes strange forms. Instead, the tales depict stasis overshadowed by the inevitability of death and contingency collapsing into a sense that time is all the same.

In these tales, the land robustly indicates the identity of past and present. The stories often emphasize an intense topographical continuity sustained between the historical setting and the moment of reading—the narrator regularly directs the reader toward the still-existing locations in and on which the narrative takes place. The stories furthermore de-naturalize and instead historicize the land: features that look natural are revealed as the result of earlier human action, albeit modest and interpersonal rather than structural. Whereas *Sybil* depicts Marney Abbey as preternaturally unchanged despite the passage of time, the *Wessex Tales* extends static historicity not only to the built environment but also to the land itself. For example, the deictic opening passage of the "Melancholy Hussar of the German Legion" describes an area on which there once was a German encampment: "Here stretch the downs, high and breezy and green, absolutely unchanged since those eventful days. A plough has never disturbed the turf, and the sod that was uppermost then is uppermost now. Here stood the camp; here are distinct traces of the banks thrown up for the horses of the cavalry, and spots where the midden-heaps lay are still to be observed."[90] Although Sophie Gilmartin and Rod Mengham call this passage a "characteristic attempt to defeat time with intense sensory perceptions,"[91] I would observe that it invites a layered imagination, as the reader imagines perceiving a real landscape on which is superimposed a further-imagined history. How, precisely, are the midden or refuse heaps "still to be observed"? A heap of partially decomposed matter? A lack of sod? The built environment of the camp seems to have disappeared, but the manipulations of the earth remain rigorously consistent with the past. Although this continuity hints at a lack of agricultural productivity (a plough has never disturbed the turf), it also provides a striking image of the non-erasure of the past. The sod, even, is still distinct as sod, having neither fused with the underlying soil, nor been displaced by other foliage. Though these human manipulations of the landscape are subtle, they linger undisturbed by further human activity or natural processes.

"The Distracted Preacher" similarly ends by explaining the origin of a modest but still perceptible feature of the local landscape. The tale culminates in the discovery and destruction of an underground storehouse of smuggled liquor, concealed underneath what appears to be an apple orchard. During an invasive village-wide search, the authorities determine that an apple tree is actually growing in a shallow box:

> As soon as the tubs were taken out, they began tearing up the turf, pulling out the timbers, and breaking in the sides, till the cellar was wholly dismantled and shapeless, the apple-tree lying with its roots high to the air. But the hole which had in its time held so much contraband merchandise was never completely filled up, either then or afterward, a depression in the greensward marking the spot to this day.[92]

As in the other passage, this unremarkable and seemingly natural depression, its shape "shapeless," proves to be the aftermath of human drama. In drawing the reader's attention to these origins, the *Wessex Tales* repeatedly undoes the process through which history disappears into a textured landscape—the cellar is dismantled, the upside-down tree removed, and the contraband seized, but the hole remains, again undisturbed by the self-erasing cycles of agricultural productivity or natural processes. These stories offer a way of looking at landscape in which every tiny hill or valley, verdant or barren patch, potentially reflects a human narrative—the natural world an infinite resource, not of commodifiable raw material, but rather of small human histories, situated at the limits of memory and perceptibility. What the *Wessex Tales* depict as a real, if modest connection between the land and its history contrasts with the conspicuous but deceptive historicity of *The Trumpet-Major*'s giant horse carving or *Sybil*'s Marney Abbey. The *Wessex Tales* suggest that true continuity between past and present is quiet, local, and unchanging, but bound to be forgotten.

Whereas the *Wessex Tales*' frequent prolepses remind the reader of the distance between the historical setting and the moment of reading, the tales themselves also incorporate temporal distance into their narrative structure. Just as the land continues to bear traces of fictional events, characters too remain marked by the past. Time heals no wounds, but instead only exacerbates existing indecisions or problems, as characters experience divergent emotional lives, often around thwarted or frustrated courtship. "The Distracted Preacher" features a denouement that showcases time's failure to effect change. After the climactic raid on the apple-orchard storehouse, the preacher Stockdale leaves town without Lizzy, the unrepentant smuggler he has repeatedly failed to woo. Typical of the *Tales*, rather than ending here, the story continues: Stockdale returns two years later having established himself professionally only to discover that Lizzy's life has changed for the worse.[93] Atypical of the *Tales*, she finally repents, and they marry. But Hardy's 1912 note partially reverses this tidy conclusion to resolve the story in a way more consistent with the other *Tales*: "The ending of the story with the marriage of Lizzy and the minister was almost *de rigueur* in an English magazine at the time of writing. But at this late date, thirty years after, it may not be amiss to give the ending that would have been preferred by the writer to the convention used above."[94] As in the similar note appended to *The Return of the Native*, "the demands of magazine publication are blamed for the lapse into happiness," as Grylls puts it.[95] Describing an alternative ending in which Lizzy emigrates with her smuggler beau, Hardy extends to the writing process itself the reconfirmatory indecision experienced by the characters—Jacob Jewusiak has also noted this parallel between the novelist's work and Hardy's characters' consciousness of counterfactual possibilities in their lives.[96] This fluidity between text and paratext reveals the temporal logic of the collection itself—in which, once a decision is taken, it becomes impossible to undo (Hardy could have revised, rather than merely describe a revised ending). As with Disraeli's *Vivian Grey*, post-publication revisions and new paratexts can only do so much to alter the original—republication itself is a model of temporal layering without erasure. Although the romantic failures of the other *Tales* attest to the viability, in the 1880s periodical context, of the ending that Hardy later claims to prefer, this note adds an additional trajectory of changing fictional conventions atop the history traced by the story itself.

Just as *The Trumpet-Major* ends with reference to John Loveday's later death, the *Wessex Tales* often begin or end with explicit confirmation that all parties are now dead. Almost everybody dies, whether within the story itself or as prolepsis between the story and the present. As I suggested above, this trope of historical fiction is particularly pronounced in *The Trumpet-Major* and *Wessex Tales*, which constitute a departure from Gillian Beer's observation that Hardy's fiction typically "pays homage to human scale by ceasing as the hero or heroine dies."[97] For example, rather than ending with the daring, climactic escape of the condemned prisoner, the final paragraph of "The Three Strangers" reveals the fates of the minor *dramatis personae*, the hosts and guests of the party disrupted by the unexpected arrival of the strangers: "The grass has long been green on the graves of Shepherd Fennel and his frugal wife; the guests who made up the christening-party have mainly followed their entertainers to the tomb; the baby in whose honour they all had met is a matron in the sere and yellow leaf."[98] These references to the regenerative and cyclical temporalities of the landscape are juxtaposed with the universal human trajectory toward death to suggest a monumental stasis.

As this contrast between the prisoner's escape from the gallows and the characters' graves suggests, several tales culminate in death narrowly avoided, immediately followed by a reminder that death is never avoided. "A Tradition of Eighteen Hundred and Four" is framed by a scene of storytelling in which the narrator listens to "old Solomon Selby's story"[99] of being a young boy overhearing or dreaming of two French scouts planning Napoleon's invasion (the same rumor about French scouts circulates in *The Trumpet-Major*). Selby's framed narrative ends, "We coast-folk should have been cut down one and all, and I should not have sat here to tell this tale."[100] This moment reflects that the Napoleonic Wars prompted the development of counterfactual thinking that later found its way into literature, as Anders Engberg-Pedersen and Catherine Gallagher have explored.[101] The contingency of Napoleon's possible invasion is represented in the survival of an oral tradition that would have been destroyed or overshadowed if the invasion had happened. The passage also reflects the paradox that mass violence registers on the historical record just as it erases the experiences of the victims, such that becoming a historical subject in one way means losing the opportunity to become a historical subject in another.

This passage and indeed the *Wessex Tales* as a whole offer a particular variant of Andrew Miller's concept of "lives unled"[102] or Michael Tondre's counterfactual "ensemble effects," "moments that break the diegetic frame of a plot to suggest other possible distributions of characters, actions, and setting, and that revise what happens as a multiplicity of alternatives."[103] In the *Wessex Tales*, the alternative to the lived past is never a different life, but rather, always death, allowing the road-not-taken and the road-taken to reconverge. In this way, counterfactualism briefly appears to open up alternative possible worlds only immediately to reconfirm the inevitable trajectory toward the grave. We cut from Selby's utterance directly to the tale's final paragraph, in which the frame narrator observes: "We who listened to old Selby that night have been familiar with his simple grave-stone for these ten years past."[104] Thus, despite capitalizing on the disjunction between Selby's perspective and that of the frame narrator and reader, the story ends by emphasizing that with respect to Selby's mortality, Napoleon's possible invasion is inconsequential.

"The Melancholy Hussar of the German Legion" similarly uses intergenerational oral storytelling to reveal growing old as a contingent rather than an inevitable experience and the past as incommunicable.[105] The story opens by establishing the contrasting life stages and future trajectories of the storyteller and her audience: Phyllis "was then an old lady of seventy-five, and her auditor a lad of fifteen … . Her life was prolonged twelve years after the day of her narration, and she has now been dead nearly twenty."[106] Phyllis's story reflects on a youthful romance with a handsome German soldier stationed at the encampment where midden-heaps are "still to be observed." At the last moment, she decides not to elope as he deserts his regiment; he is then caught and executed along with another soldier. Like "The Three Strangers" and the "Tradition of Eighteen Hundred and Four," "The Melancholy Hussar of the German Legion" ends with a description of a burial place:

> Their graves were dug at the back of the little church, near the wall. There is no memorial to mark the spot, but Phyllis pointed it out to me. While she lived she used to keep their mounds neat; but now they are over-grown with nettles, and sunk nearly flat. The older villagers, however, who know of the episode from their parents, still recollect the place where the soldiers lie. Phyllis lies near.[107]

Despite this reference to nature's reclamation of the land, notably absent in the account of the former German encampment, this ending exemplifies that the *Tales* persistently collapse moments of high narrative contingency with the determinism of death. What does the reader make of this glimpse of Phyllis's emotional aftermath? It seems harsh to observe the uncertainty of the road-not-taken—Phyllis could have died during their flight; she might not have been happy in his hometown of Saarbrucken. The story's final word skips past the years that Phyllis survived her lover to repeat what has already been established and would have been implicit anyway: that this previously old person has now died. Although this moment might be read as a *memento mori*, it also coldly turns away from Phyllis's feelings toward a universal point about the end of all human drama. In the same way, the story casts doubt on Phyllis's and its own impulse to preserve the past. As with the disused smuggling storehouse, the subtle evidence of Phyllis's story on the landscape is perceptible only with the assistance of imminently disappearing human knowledge. Despite telling Phyllis's story, the text dramatizes the process in which it ceases to matter. That is, the "The Melancholy Hussar" figures itself not as preserving and transmitting something important that is slipping from memory, but rather as disinterestedly exploring the mechanism by which the slip occurs.

Cyclical stasis in "Fellow-Townsmen" and "Interlopers at the Knap"

"Fellow-Townsmen" weaves together two plots that reflect the *Wessex Tales*' vision of time as cyclical stasis: its marriage plot remains stuck, depicting the forever-lingering effects of past decisions, while its business plot depicts a predictable rise-and-fall pattern. The tale traces the intersecting and diverging lives of Mr. Barnet and Mr. Downe, "fellow-burgesses of the town."[108] At the story's outset, Mr. Barnet is unhappily married. His wife insists upon the construction of the opulent "Chateau Ringdale" to lend an impression of pedigree commensurate to their new industrial wealth. Barnet envies the loving relationship of Mr. and Mrs. Downe, and imagines being happier had he married Lucy Saville, whom he courted but lost to miscommunication and indecision. After Mrs. Downe's unexpected death, Lucy Saville enters the Downe home as a governess, only to marry the widower a few years later, just around the time that Mrs. Barnet's death would have allowed a match between the former lovers. Anticipating the plots of *The Mayor of Casterbridge* and *Jude the Obscure*, the story's "intricate character geometry"[109] maps the long, painful aftermath of decisions about marriage.

Yet the love plot unfolds upon a backdrop that charts the fortunes of the Barnet family flax business. Walking around town at the beginning of the story, Barnet observes visual evidence of his family's history in this industry:

> Here, though his family had no more to do with the flax manufacture, his own name occasionally greeted him on gates and warehouses, being used allusively by small rising tradesmen as a recommendation, in such words as "Smith, from Barnet and Co."—"Robinson, late manager at Barnet's." The sight led him to reflect upon his father's busy life, and he questioned if it had not been far happier than his own.[110]

Gilmartin and Mengham describe Barnet as one of a type in Hardy's fiction, "those raised to a higher social class by an ambitious parent or through marriage, and they are mostly childless and somehow disappointed or unsuccessful in life."[111] By the time the story begins, the family has already translated industrial wealth into social capital, allowing Barnet to step away from the work that occupied his father. Thus, although the allusions to the Barnet flax business are vestiges of an earlier business configuration, the story begins at the height of the marketing value of the Barnet name—the original business has birthed not only Barnet's prominent position but also small rising tradesmen. In this way, the Barnet flax business is residual in Raymond Williams's sense—a product of the past, but insistently present.

The story's central gap of twenty-one-and-a-half years has contrasting implications for its romantic and business plots. Crestfallen at Lucy's marriage to Downe, Barnet undertakes what Gilmartin and Mengham call "self-obliteration,"[112] selling his property and disappearing to travel the world. When he returns two decades later, he marvels at time's erasure of the evidence of his father's business: "His chief interest at present seemed to lie in the names painted over the shop-fronts and on doorways, as far as they were visible; these now differed to an ominous extent from what they had been one-and-twenty-years before."[113] Despite having actively shed his inherited social position, Barnet strangely finds "ominous," portending an unpleasant future, something that has already happened: the fade of the family name in a town he left twenty years ago, and in a business his family had left even earlier. A young bookshop clerk confirms the impression given by the town shop-fronts. Barnet asks:

> "And is the firm of Barnet, Browse, and Company still in existence? They used to be large flax-merchants and twine-spinners here?"
> "The firm is still going on, sir, but they have dropped the name of Barnet. I believe that was a sort of fancy name—at least, I never knew of any living Barnet. 'Tis now Browse and Co."[114]

The story presents this natural business life cycle with poignancy. As the idea of a "fancy name" suggests, the branding value of a name eventually dies, though sometime after the death of the businessperson bearing it—another instance of the belated death of memory that we see in the other *Tales*. Notwithstanding that what Ranke calls "the realm of material interests"[115] sometimes appears in the nineteenth century to index relentless growth, this story uses the workings of business to suggest a cyclical rhythm lagging behind but related to the human life.

Whereas the Barnet flax business experiences a corporate trajectory of rise, reproduction, and fading away, the love story of Barnet and Lucy remains frustratingly static, revealing the inertia of romantic disappointment. In the conversation at the bookshop, Barnet learns that most of his former acquaintances have died, with the exception of the widowed Lucy, that is, Mrs. Downe. She lives at Chateau Ringdale, which Mr. Downe purchased after Barnet's abrupt departure—and the clerk believes that the home has been in Lucy's family for generations. Thus, as with *Sybil*'s Marney Abbey, current ownership appears to extend backward, indicating intergenerational inheritance. Chateau Ringdale succeeds in Mrs. Barnet's original intention of indicating family lineage, though it is conferred on someone else, the woman who might have been Mrs. Barnet under different circumstances.[116] The establishment of Lucy at Chateau Ringdale thus mirrors the replacement, in the flax industry, of the name Barnet name with Browse and others.

Chateau Ringdale itself reflects the story's logic of change over time as non-genealogical substitution. Whereas *Sybil*'s Marney Abbey is authentically old and simply in the wrong hands, Chateau Ringdale fabricates a connection between past and present. Barnet's initial resistance to building it stems from loyalty to his actual family home: "It is my own freehold; it was built by my grandfather and is stout enough for a castle. My father was born there, lived there, and died there."[117] His wife's proposed name for the residence does not just signal her rejection of a "stout" English freehold in favor of a French *château*—we might compare Walter Gerard's nationalist preference for "stout woolens" over imported cotton in *Sybil*. It also indicates her own romantic disappointments, at least according to Barnet, who claims that she "once had a fancy"[118] for Lord Ringdale. Thus, the building and its occupancy reflect a series of romantic substitutions and disappointments that, from the young bookshop clerk's perspective, look like continuity over time.

The recapitulated courtship plot ends just like the original, reflecting the failure of time to resolve what had been irresolveable. Excited that his former flame is single again, Barnet prepares to visit. After dinner at the hotel, "he made some change in his dress, shaved back his beard to the fashion that had prevailed twenty years earlier, when he was young and interesting."[119] The current longer beard may indicate that he has returned to town as something of a wild man after many years abroad, or it may reflect his sense of romantic defeat, or it may be a popular choice among men of his age and status. In Sir Pitt Crawley's lingering loyalty to knee-breeches in *Vanity Fair*, we saw a vision of men's aging as unselfconsciously continuing to wear the clothes of one's youth. Prompted by the prospect of courtship, Barnet actively returns to the fashions of his youth—within the contemporary fashion landscape, the implications of shaving the beard are unclear. Hair, its color and cut, figures centrally in the story's suggestion that the appearance of change belies the reality of changelessness. Lucy's maid describes the unknown visitor as "a staidish gentleman, with grey hair."[120] Lucy has aged too:

> The round cheek of that formerly young lady had, of course, alarmingly flattened its curve in her modern representative; a pervasive greyness over-spread her once dark brown hair, like morning rime on heather. The parting down the middle was wide and jagged; once it had been a thin white line, a narrow crevice between two high banks of shade. But there was still enough to form a handsome knob behind, and some curls beneath inwrought with a few hairs like silver wires were very becoming. In her eyes the only modification was that their originally mild rectitude of expression had become a little more

stringent than heretofore. Yet she was still girlish—a girl who had been gratuitously weighed by destiny with a burden of five-and-forty years instead of her proper twenty.[121]

Lucy is thus both prematurely weighed by the years and yet girlish in attitude. Though the hair itself has changed, she still wears a similar hairstyle. Indeed, Lucy's stasis parallels that the second courtship fails just like the first. Early in the story, we learn elliptically that some kind of misunderstanding doomed the original match—Barnet blames Lucy for not sending him a note to clarify where things stood.[122] In this much later scene, Barnet proposes, Lucy declines, she regrets, and she sends him a note, but he never comes back. Thus, despite Lucy having learned the value of follow-up communication, her original decision remains irrevocable, and the plot finally resolves through its permanent non-resolution.

In "Interlopers at the Knap," frustrated and misdirected courtship similarly contrasts with a business backdrop to further illustrate the *Wessex Tales*' cyclical static temporality. The tale begins on the night that should see the engagement of Sally Hall and Charles Darton. Like the similarly named Barnet, Darton is the beneficiary of his father's material successes in building up the family farm into a large and profitable business, but he lacks his father's entrepreneurial spirit: "up to his present age of thirty-two, he had neither advanced nor receded as a capitalist—a stationary result which did not agitate one of his unambitious unstrategic nature, since he had all he desired."[123] Of course, this trajectory reflects that capitalist accumulation is the exception rather than the rule and that wealth tends to stay with those who have it. Nonetheless, his social and financial situation renders him an advantageous match for the humble Sally, Darton having sworn off "superior women."[124] As Darton wanders lost on his way to Sally's house, her brother unexpectedly returns from Australia, a "tramp,"[125] ill, and with a wife, Helena, and children. Although Sally and her mother initially fear that the embarrassing appearance of this poor relation will threaten her marriage prospects, the arrival of the brother and his wife prevents Sally's engagement for other reasons. As her brother lies dying upstairs, Sally notices a connection between Darton and Helena, revealed to be former lovers, and announces, "I will never marry him, and she will."[126] More a prediction than a statement of desire, this seemingly impetuous utterance proves true.

As in "Fellow-Townsmen," this initial courtship is separated from its recapitulation by a five-year period that proves both eventful and static: Darton marries Helena, who has a child and then dies. For Sally and her mother, as for Harriet Martineau at Tynemouth, "Time passed, and the household on the Knap became again serene under the composing influences of daily routine."[127] Despite this temporality of repetition, subtle clues indicate that unlike Darton's farm, their dairy business grows in the interval between the story's two halves. Meanwhile, Darton's feelings change again—seeking a stepmother for his children, he plans finally to propose to Sally. On the evening of his return to Sally's house, the narrator establishes the sameness of past and present by locating the passage of time on the level of the built environment and fashion:

> Upon the whole there was little change in the household economy, and not much in its appearance, beyond such minor particulars as that the crack over the window, which had been a hundred years coming, was a trifle wider; that the beams were shade blacker; that the influence of modernism has supplanted the open chimney corner by a grate; that Rebekah, who had worn a cap when she had plenty of hair, had left it off now she had scarce any, because it was reported that caps were not fashionable; and that Sally's face had naturally assumed a more womanly and experienced cast.[128]

In the physical space, criss-crossing trajectories of deterioration and modernization suggest a fundamental stasis. For Rebekah too, changes in fashion and changes in her own hair conspire to effect a persistent mismatch between the dominant style—as belatedly "reported"—and the state of the aging body.

A strange combination of specificity and vagueness governs the tale's references to calendar time in its second act, as in the other stories. "The Three Strangers," for example, begins on "the night of the twenty eighth of March 182-,"[129] and "The Distracted Preacher" arrives in town on "the thirteenth of January 183-."[130] Indicating the day and month but leaving the year unspecified within the decade, Hardy suggests a conception of time attuned to annual cyclicality rather than the linear count of years. In "Interlopers at the Knap" especially, cyclicality and an emphasis on the self-reinforcement of decisions work together to suggest a monumental temporality of imperviousness to events or change.

Sally's mother, remembering the dramatic evening on which the story began, observes that it happened, "Five years ago this very night, if I am not mistaken" / "Not this very night—though 'twas one night this week,' said the correct Sally."[131] The mother's remark reflects that in an anniversary, the date will fall on a different day, and the day on a different date, whereas Sally's correction emphasizes that there is no true repetition, only return with difference. Yet Sally's utterance also reveals her deep connection to that memory, despite the five-year period having only reconfirmed the feelings she then discovered.

Although the initial rejection of Darton was an impulsive act that allowed Sally to defy expectations for her gender and class, she does not experience the "powerful counterfactual ache"[132] that Jewusiak associates with Hardy's characters' impulsive decisions. Five years later, Sally rejects Darton's proposal, disappointing everyone—Sally's mother calls her "a very ungrateful girl."[133] Darton then reiterates the proposal by letter, to which Sally responds "my answer is just the same as before."[134] Months later, Darton begins to suspect that her rejection was influenced by a false rumor that his business was ruined—apparently another "farmer named Darton had lost heavily,"[135] causing some temporary confusion. And yet the sense of alternative possibility raised by a doppelgänger immediately closes down. Darton's name cleared, he proposes a third time: "Anniversaries having been unpropitious, he waited on till a bright day late in May."[136] But Sally rejects him again, forcefully: "I will never, never marry you, Mr. Darton. I would have done it once; but now I never can."[137] A short afterward confirms that Sally, "notwithstanding the solicitations her attractions drew upon her, had refused several offers of marriage, and steadily adhered to her purpose of leading a single life."[138] Her motivations remain frustratingly unclear to Darton and are never explained to the reader—scholars even sometimes take Darton's side.[139] Once her decision is made, in a vanishingly brief moment, it becomes impossible to reconsider.

૪૭

In *The Trumpet-Major* and *Wessex Tales*, nothing ever really changes. These texts test strategies for narrating a lack of development over time. On the register of courtship, never reconsidered romantic choices and reiterative rejected proposals reveal the individual as unable or unwilling to change their life. On the register of mortality, the inevitability of death insistently undercuts narrative contingency. On the register of clothing and the object, what seems to crystallize a specific moment ultimately reveals a longer narrative that suggests both the sameness of time and the impossibility of transcending one's limited perspective. Whether using rhetorical cyclicality, repetition, or a monumental temporality, *The Trumpet-Major* and *Wessex Tales* allow for non-progressive narrative unfolding. Such narratives sometimes prove frustrating for the characters—Darton frustrated with Sally's self-possessed unwillingness to reconsider, and Sally frustrated with his refusal to accept her answer.

The Trumpet-Major and *Wessex Tales* depict individual moments as cordoned off from each other. Readers in the present cannot fully understand or sympathize with characters in the past. Similarly, the characters remain intensely ignorant of their future and even present, and alienated from their own past, situated always outside or after the contingent moment. These siloed historical moments work also to suggest the fundamental insignificance of the passage of time. As we have seen throughout this book, the recognition that change is unlikely or impossible prompts a shift from history to historiography—to epistemological and ethical questions about studying the past. These texts emphasize the total erasure of the past's meaning over time. Although they aestheticize that process in fiction, they evince uncertainty about what warrants preserving and why. These texts present the stasis of time ambivalently. Certainly, they negate the possibility of celebrating changelessness as tradition or meaningful continuity. And yet their vivid pictures of suffering resist any narrative of decline from a better, more humane, or simpler past. Instead, human drama, uncertainty, or indecision remains entirely inert to change over time, and is ended only in death. This more neutral, mixed, or detached picture of stasis reflects the broader movement that this book has traced, from considering progress as a viable shape for history, to mapping history's other shapes, to doubting whether shapes can be traced at all.

Notes

1. Michael Millgate and Barbara Hardy have noted the influence of *Vanity Fair* on *The Trumpet-Major*, observing the novels' parallel off-stage treatments of Waterloo and Trafalgar, connections

between the characters of Becky Sharp and the scheming Matilda Johnson, and correspondences between the Dobbin-George-Amelia love triangle and that of John Loveday, Bob Loveday, and the guileless Anne Garland (Millgate, *Thomas Hardy*, 160; B. Hardy, "Introduction," 17–18). T. R. Wright identifies a number of other literary influences on the novel, including *Persuasion* and *Tom Jones* (Wright, *Hardy and His Readers*, 125).

2. This chapter will not discuss Hardy's *The Dynasts* because doing that text justice would have required more space than I could devote. In addition to being a verse epic—a genre I do not consider—*The Dynasts* is unfamiliar even to dedicated Hardy scholars. Although it had a long composition process, the work did not come together until at least 1910, and thus it would have extended by twenty years the historical scope of this book.
3. Engberg-Pedersen, *Empire of Chance*, 3.
4. McLoughlin, "Missing Letters," 1235.
5. Wright, *Hardy and His Readers*, 115.
6. Ibid., 119.
7. Rimmer, "History and the Bogus Heroine," 74. See also Mistichelli for a review of the way scholars have preferred John, understanding Anne's "frankly sexual" preference for Bob to reflect "Hardy's distrust of women" (Mistichelli, "The Trumpet-Major's Signal," 48).
8. Nemesvari, "Anti-Comedy of *The Trumpet-Major*," 10.
9. Wright, *Hardy and His Readers*, 123.
10. Clammer, "The Corsican Mischief," 48.
11. Hardy, *The Trumpet Major*, 155.
12. Ibid., 161.
13. Ibid.
14. Ibid., 166–7.
15. Rimmer, "History and the Bogus Heroine," 72.
16. Stendhal, *Charterhouse of Parma*, 80.
17. Quoted in Wright, *Hardy and His Readers*, 116.
18. Hardy, *The Trumpet-Major*, 67–8.
19. Neill, "Mixed Modes in *The Trumpet-Major*," 364.
20. Hardy, *The Trumpet-Major*, 71.
21. Ibid., 73.
22. Ibid., 77.
23. See Grener ("Hardy's Relics," 123–4) for a different reading of Hardy's adaptation of Scott's river metaphor.
24. Kingstone, *Victorian Narratives*, 56.
25. Hardy, *The Trumpet-Major*, 77.

26. Ibid., 215.
27. Ibid., 216.
28. Ibid., 203–6.
29. Ibid., 219.
30. Ibid., 240.
31. Ibid., 256.
32. Ireland, *Thomas Hardy, Time, and Narrative*, 87.
33. Hardy, *The Trumpet-Major*, 17.
34. Ibid., 26.
35. Ibid., 76.
36. Rimmer, "History and the Bogus Heroine," 73.
37. Rignall, "The Historical Double," 28.
38. Hardy, "Profitable Reading," 82.
39. Ibid., 83.
40. Ibid.
41. Quoted in Hardy, "Profitable Reading," 83.
42. Markovits, "Form Things," 602.
43. Hardy, "Profitable Reading," 82.
44. Millgate writes, "although the characters … are authentically dressed and housed, [and] their lives impinged upon by the great events of the day, little in them as thinking and acting individuals could be said to mark them as belonging quintessentially to their period" (Millgate, *Thomas Hardy*, 162). Nemesvari similarly comments that "the accurate descriptions of period clothing" are insufficient to classify *The Trumpet-Major* as a historical novel in the rigorous sense (Nemesvari, "Anti-Comedy of *The Trumpet-Major*," 9). As Allingham relates, the novel's illustrations, even, "spared no pains in fleshing out the period piece with accurate costumes and accessories" to the point that they "occasionally neglected continuity of form and physiognomy for the more significant characters" (Allingham, "John Collier's Pre-Raphaelite Illustrations," 52–3). Reilly comments that the "narrative itself it half in love with the lost glamour of military/historical appearances" and places the novel within "the costumed subgenre of romantic light fiction" (Reilly, *Shadowtime*, 3).
45. Hardy, *The Trumpet-Major*, 181–2.
46. Rimmer, "History and the Bogus Heroine," 76.
47. See Pomeroy, "Rational Dress Reform," 80.
48. Hardy, *The Trumpet-Major*, 98.
49. Gatrell, *Thomas Hardy Writing Dress*, 177.
50. Hardy, *The Trumpet-Major*, 3.

51. Ibid., 20.
52. Ibid., 30.
53. Ibid., 170.
54. Ibid., 79.
55. Ibid., 182.
56. Freedgood, "Fine Fingers," 626.
57. Ibid., 626–7.
58. Hardy, *The Trumpet-Major*, 123.
59. Ibid., 148.
60. Michie, "Dressing Up," 316.
61. Hardy, *The Trumpet-Major*, 14.
62. Ibid., 7.
63. Ibid., 5–6.
64. Gatrell, *Thomas Hardy Writing Dress*, 173–4.
65. Ibid., 153.
66. Ibid., 151.
67. Ibid., 151–2.
68. Ashton, *English Caricature and Satire on Napoleon I*, 358; Broadley, *Napoleon in Caricature*, II:246–7; Trezise, "Thomas Hardy and the Hieroglyphic Napoleon," 62.
69. Broadley, *Napoleon in Caricature*, II:244–5; Trezise, "Thomas Hardy and the Hieroglyphic Napoleon," 62.
70. Hardy, "Preface," xxv–xxvi.
71. Broadley, *Napoleon in Caricature*, II:245, II:247.
72. Ibid., II:244.
73. Ibid., II:247.
74. Ibid., II:256.
75. Grener, "Hardy's Relics," 111–13.
76. Ibid., 118.
77. Hardy, *The Trumpet-Major*, xxv.
78. Ibid., 232.
79. Plenderleath, *White Horses*, 12.
80. Ibid., 33.
81. Radford, *Thomas Hardy and the Survivals of Time*, 22.
82. Plenderleath, *White Horses*, 24.
83. Hardy, *The Trumpet-Major*, 142.
84. Ibid., 141.
85. Grylls, "Thomas Hardy," 140.
86. Book-length studies of Hardy's short fiction by Kristin Brady (*The Short Stories of Thomas Hardy*) and by Sophie Gilmartin and Rod Mengham (*Thomas Hardy's Shorter Fiction*) each devote a chapter

to *Wessex Tales*, yet even here, synthetic commentary is relatively limited. Nathalie Oussaid describes the tales as united by "Hardy's vision of man as a tragic hero facing the silence of a world he cannot fathom although he thinks he can" (Oussaid, "A Reading of *Wessex Tales*," 25).

87. Brady, *The Short Stories of Thomas Hardy*, 2.
88. Gilmartin and Mengham, *Thomas Hardy's Shorter Fiction*, 17.
89. King, "Introduction," xii.
90. Hardy, *Wessex Tales*, 39.
91. Gilmartin and Mengham, *Thomas Hardy's Shorter Fiction*, 30.
92. Hardy, *Wessex Tales*, 211.
93. Ibid., 222.
94. Ibid., 223.
95. Grylls, "Thomas Hardy," 142.
96. Jewusiak, "Hardy's Impulse," 462.
97. Beer, *Darwin's Plots*, 239.
98. Hardy, *Wessex Tales*, 30.
99. Ibid., 32.
100. Ibid., 38.
101. Engberg-Pedersen, *Empire of Chance*; Gallagher, *Telling It Like It Wasn't*.
102. Miller, *Burdens of Perfection*.
103. Tondre, *Physics of Possibility*, 11.
104. Hardy, *Wessex Tales*, 38.
105. The element of oral storytelling is more fully thematized in *Wessex Tales*, but the narrator of *The Trumpet-Major* briefly suggests that he has learned the story from "members of the Loveday family and other aged people now passed away" (Hardy, *The Trumpet-Major*, 29).
106. Hardy, *Wessex Tales*, 40.
107. Ibid., 56.
108. Ibid., 86.
109. Herzog, "Hardy's 'Fellow-Townsmen,'" 231.
110. Hardy, *Wessex Tales*, 91.
111. Gilmartin and Mengham, *Thomas Hardy's Shorter Fiction*, 40.
112. Ibid., 39.
113. Hardy, *Wessex Tales*, 127.
114. Ibid., 128.
115. Ranke, *Theory and Practice of History*, 22.
116. Hardy, *Wessex Tales*, 128.
117. Ibid., 88–9.

118. Ibid., 89.
119. Ibid., 129.
120. Ibid., 130.
121. Ibid., 130–1.
122. Ibid., 95.
123. Ibid., 137.
124. Ibid., 138.
125. Ibid., 142.
126. Ibid., 155.
127. Ibid.
128. Ibid., 160.
129. Ibid., 10.
130. Ibid., 167.
131. Ibid., 160.
132. Jewusiak, "Hardy's Impulse," 463.
133. Hardy, *Wessex Tales*, 161.
134. Ibid., 163.
135. Ibid., 164.
136. Ibid.
137. Ibid., 165.
138. Ibid., 166.
139. See, for example, Brady, *The Short Stories of Thomas Hardy*, 36.

Conclusion
Fashionable Aging in Margaret Oliphant's *Kirsteen*

In 1995, I felt a thrill of recognition when bellbottom jeans came roaring back into style at my grade school, having seen my mother wear them in an old photograph. I was gravely disappointed to learn that that pair had not survived the 1970s. The clothes that my mother did keep from that period and that roughly fit my growing body—a rust-colored polyester double-knit jacket, a diaphanous blue-gray peasant top—differed in small but troubling ways from the neo-hippie aesthetic I was after. My mother helped me cut a slit up the inseam of my own straight-legged jeans to mimic, imperfectly, the bellbottom shape. Although she assured me that this was a historically authentic practice, it did not look quite right. As a child, I did not recognize that I was living through a reimagination rather than a straightforward return of the fashions of the late 1960s. More recently, I observed with mild alarm one of my students wearing a floral print, tea-length, faux silk dress eerily reminiscent of one I loved in 1997. I wore it for only a year or two after buying it at *The Limited Too*—a girls' clothing store and suburban mall fixture whose name reflected its generational posteriority to the women's apparel parent company *The Limited*. But the dress has a longer history—my late grandmother Ruth, a midwestern Lutheran pastor's wife, apparently hated that style because it was popular among an older cohort of Midwestern Lutheran pastors' wives. Unsure what to make of my student's re-resurrection of the floral-print, tea length dress—admittedly with the modern addition of a high slit up the leg—I remembered my mother's wry observation, while guiding my scissors along the length of the jeans, "If you wore it the first time, you can't wear it the second time." Whereas I fantasized about a direct inheritance, a pair of jeans passed from mother to daughter, she recognized that at most, we creatively remake fashion's pasts with unfashionable materials.

At one point in Margaret Oliphant's *Kirsteen* (1890), a historical novel set in the 1810s, Mary Douglas feels something similar. As her sisters prepare for an upcoming ball, Mary wishes that she had some of her mother's old gowns. It has been many years, and fourteen children, since Mrs. Douglas's favorite spangled muslin was ripped by the spurs of a clumsy dancing partner—a young officer himself vulnerable to violent destruction in the military conflicts of the early 1780s. Mary may be mistaken about the modern fashionable currency of her mother's old dress. In a rare moment of animation and insight, Mrs. Douglas rightly observes, "it would be clean out of the fashion if ye had it,"[1] describing the garment as "one of the last of the old mode before those awfu' doings at the French Revolution that changed everything,"[2] ushering in an era of plain white, neoclassical gowns. Here, Mrs. Douglas expresses a widespread understanding of this paradigm shift in women's fashion as stemming from the rupture of foreign revolution. The fashion theorist Daniel Leonhard Purdy describes this development instead as "the quiet spread of" distinctly "English preferences,"[3] a gradualist narrative that differs from Mrs. Douglas's in both its temporality and its national origins. As a proud Scottish Highlander, Mrs. Douglas might be equally horrified—as at the guillotine—at the encroachment of English preferences on Highland life.

Yet Mrs. Douglas's reminiscence on the big hoop skirts, flounces, and ruffles of an eighteenth-century youth reflects not only fashion's logic of change, but also its ironic continuities and cycles. Mrs. Douglas's mildly negative attitude toward Regency fashion, a perspective forged in the preceding era, essentially prefigures the Victorian retrospective assessment. Echoing Thackeray and Hardy, Oliphant's narrator remarks, "I do not myself think that dress was pretty in those days—but every fashion is beautiful to its time."[4] Although the spangled muslin dress was destroyed—a reminder that garments often predecease their aesthetic obsolescence—Mary's longing reflects that formal gowns remain the required uniform for a ritual that still launches young women into marital futurity. Mrs. Douglas's dress, furthermore, anticipates modern fashions more than she realizes—in the 1780s, the non-universal choice of muslin may have reflected her family's limited budget or her early youth. By the 1810s, however, muslin has become the default fabric for gowns. Moreover, had it survived, the outfit might have provided raw materials for further sartorial transformation. Mrs. Douglas remarks, "there was enough muslin in my petticoat to have made three of these bit skimpit things,"[5] referring to the Regency gowns preferred by her daughters. The dress could be, like Mrs. Douglas herself, a mother many times over. Yet this passing down and remaking are elusive. Mrs. Douglas's petticoats, like my mother's old bellbottoms, are long gone. As Oliphant suggests, fashion's cycles rarely benefit the individual. As we saw with the maid Rebekah in Hardy's "Interlopers at the Knap," urged by changing styles to remove her cap only after her hair has lost its color and sheen, the trajectories of the life and the fashion are inconveniently out of sync.

Nonetheless, the Douglas sisters arguably have great timing with respect to fashion history. As Mrs. Douglas's comment about the petticoat suggests, the minimalist aesthetic of Regency fashion—the need for only one piece of plain muslin per daughter, and not the all the crinolines, ribbons, fans, jewels, or hairpieces of the eras before and after—allows the Douglas sisters to justify the expense of the ball to their tight-fisted father. That this sartorial paradigm, associated with the imperative of equality, should allow the family access to an elite social space is one of the novel's many ironies. The Douglases descend from Scottish Highland lairds long dispossessed of their ancestral land, a family whose declining wealth and influence cratered after their support for the 1745 Jacobite Rebellion. The heroine Kirsteen shares her despotic father's intense pride in a family pedigree that jars with their current social status.

Generically and temporally overdetermined, *Kirsteen* is a fitting end to this book, drawing together the themes I have explored about the non-progressive temporalities of objects and the individual life. Between the 1810s setting and the 1890 moment of writing, *Kirsteen* encompasses this book's historical scope and both formally and thematically reflects the multiplicity of time that characterizes the period. As a historical novel set initially in the Scottish Highlands, it rewrites Walter Scott's work and, like *Vanity Fair*, depicts the period of the genre's emergence. Yet as a New Woman novel, it engages modern questions of the 1890s. *Kirsteen* charts women's varied struggles for fulfilment within a limited range of marital and professional options. A successful career in dressmaking ultimately facilitates the heroine's personal growth and material advancement. The novel thus reflects the paradox that although the *fin-de-siècle* is often associated with decadence and decline, the period also sees some of the most confident assertions of historical progress from Lord Acton and others, as we saw in Chapter 1.

Having secretly pledged love to her neighbor Ronald Drummond just before he goes to India, Kirsteen refuses an advantageous match with a much older man, Glendochart, and must flee her father's violent recrimination, finding work as a dressmaker in London. This rupture radically reshapes Kirsteen's life, enacting a shift from fashion consumer to producer that allows the novel to engage not only fashion's continual novelty but also the continuity of dressmaking as a feminized, pre-industrial craft. Although lukewarm on the stylistic elements of Kirsteen's creations, the narrator asserts that their materials have a still-legible appeal. As in *The Trumpet-Major*'s treatment of Anne, *Kirsteen*'s narrator describes reverently the fine textiles and meticulous tailoring of Kirsteen's dresses: "The fashions of 1814 look like simplicity itself; the long, straight, narrow skirt, the short waist, the infantile sleeves, would seem to demand little material and less trouble for their simple arrangement. But no doubt this was more in appearance than in reality."[6] Indeed, in preparation for the ball, the village seamstress spends hours measuring and fitting the Douglas sisters. This protracted visit figures dressmaking as a process unfolding in time, and a metaphor for the trajectory of the life. The seamstress explains to Kirsteen, inexperienced in dressmaking at this point in the novel, "'If ye dinna get the skirt to fall straight from the waist, ye will never mend it at the foot ... A careless start means double vexation in the finish. And that ye'll find to apply ... to life itsel'."[7] This vision of the human life as rapidly declining potentiality parallels a normative female trajectory toward marriage, and in fact Kirsteen's early love for Ronald, with its foreclosure of other marital prospects, sets her on a separate path that allows for progressively accumulating power. Thus, as in nineteenth-century progressive history itself, rupture in one arena precedes and enables gradual progress in another.

When she learns of Ronald's death a few years later, Kirsteen vows to remain unmarried and devotes herself fully to professional development—employment intended as temporary becomes, eventually, a distinguished career. Although Kirsteen's apparent privilege initially separates her from the other young women workers, her ambiguous class status proves an asset. Eventually a co-partner in the business, Kirsteen has the insight that by publicly refusing custom from commoners, the dressmaking shop will become wildly in-demand with aristocratic clients. Thus, like *Sybil*'s Baptist Hatton, Kirsteen advances materially by cannily bolstering traditional hierarchies. Yet while her proximity to high-society life facilitates the business's success, her professional identity solidifies over time, reinforcing what seemed initially a permeable barrier between Kirsteen and the aristocratic world. She remains to the end profoundly torn between her pride in her work and her pride in her family pedigree, to the point that she remains known professionally as "Miss Kirsteen," because it would besmirch her family's name to add it to the business.

Like Harriet Martineau's *Autobiography*, *Kirsteen* traces a woman's gradual, hard-won success over time, a narrative of growth afforded by an unmarried, childless life. This growth is also enabled by her survival in a world surrounded by death. The large age gaps between the remaining Douglas siblings—which render them emotionally distant from one another—are the result of childhood mortality. On her deathbed, Mrs. Douglas observes, "Jeanie's my youngest and Alison my firstborn, and yet Jeanie's a woman and Alison a little playing bairn at heaven's gate. Isna that strange?"[8] As in the *Wessex Tales*, growing older is both inevitable and contingent, an experience both universal and exclusive to those who avoided early death.

Kirsteen's female progress narrative, though painful and ambivalent, contrasts with the novel's vision of male stasis. While the novel's gendered experience of time—women age, men don't—might appear a form of exclusion, it ultimately allows women to experience growth or progress unavailable to men. The rage of Kirsteen's father, Drumcarro, eventually escalates to the murder of a different daughter's suitor, in a scene that defies expectations about the male life-course. The suitor, Lord John, is "young but not strong,"[9] while Drumcarro is "old, but not beyond the strength of his prime."[10] Even at the novel's end, despite overwhelming evidence, no one suspects the truth—they "could not imagine indeed how in any circumstances Drumcarro, an old man, could have had anything to do with the death of Lord John, a young one."[11] As in *Coningsby* and *Vanity Fair*, the vitality of male old age may contravene normative heterotemporal expectations, but violently.

Conclusion: Fashionable Aging in Oliphant's *Kirsteen*

Glendochart suggests a more benignly inept form of late-life male inertia. When Kirsteen finally recognizes Glendochart's courtship, his advanced age is only a cover story for rejecting the suit—her true motivations are her love for Ronald. Glendochart remains a loyal if toothless ally to Kirsteen even after he makes a companionate and mutually socially beneficial marriage to her younger sister Mary. Although Glendochart's age anxiety reflects the growing concern Kay Heath identifies in the period among "midlife men about whether aging makes them lose masculinity and marriageability,"[12] the novel suggests that this anxiety is misplaced, figuring male adulthood as resilient changelessness. As elsewhere in *Temporality and Progress*, glimpses of personal progress—Jos Sedley's self-actualized dressiness in his maturity, Martineau's late-life pastoral retreat, Sally and her mother's expanding dairy in "Interlopers as the Knap," and Kirsteen's accumulating wealth—have centered on women and queer figures.

Kirsteen reflects the yearning for and enduring appeal of progress that we have seen throughout this book. I began by analyzing historians' confident attempts to theorize progress, attempts that ultimately take recourse in stasis, cyclicality, and rupture. As in Macaulay, Mill, Buckle, and Acton, mapping the space of gradual progress means delimiting it, often within remarkably narrow bounds. From the first, these writers acknowledge progress to be an ideological commitment that frames the analysis of evidence, as in Mill's aside that the doctrine of universal improvement is "not a question of the method of the social science, but a theorem of the science itself."[13] The subsequent chapters considered novelists and life-writers who either revel in the joys of temporal suspension and cyclicality (like Wilson's never-ending party), or who imagine progress that incorporates or inheres in those seemingly non-progressive structures (like Martineau's stasis-and-rupture model of personal development). In many cases, a recognition that progress has not occurred in the past and seems unlikely in the future moves the writer to consider epistemological questions about history and its shape—as in Disraeli's fiction, in which progress becomes possible only by recognizing the basic stasis of time, or in Hardy's, wherein the past is both identical to and inaccessible from the present. As we have seen, narratives of progress are troubled by the strange and unpredictable ways that individuals, garments, and other objects either linger or perish over time, like Mrs. Douglas's old petticoats or my refashioned jeans.

The end of *Kirsteen* figures fashion not only as a metonym for continuity amid apparent change, but also as the source of that continuity. Absurdly improbably, Kirsteen eventually buys back the family's long-lost ancestral property with her dressmaking earnings—fashion enables the restoration of the past. Meanwhile, her siblings each rise to prominence in their respective arenas, the brothers through merit and the sisters through marriage, thus completing the family's trifecta of social status, wealth, and pedigree. Reminiscent of the ending of *Sybil*, the Douglases are reinstated with the full benefits of an ancestral social status that they had lost for more than one hundred years. As throughout *Temporality and Progress*, continuity across time is constructed effortlessly and retroactively. Yet the agent of this construction, Kirsteen herself, remains "a rare and not very welcome visitor at the house she had redeemed."[14] The family who benefits from her money never reconciles to its origins—Kirsteen's exclusion reflects the incomplete erasure of the creative work involved in this genealogical restoration.

But the novel's final paragraphs leave the Douglases at their Highland estate and flash forward to Kirsteen's retirement in Edinburgh in the 1850s. She has consolidated her personal wealth and social position to become a society hostess and benefactor, "the best dressed woman in Edinburgh, always clothed in rich dark-coloured silks and satins, with lace which a queen might have envied."[15] Sartorially, times have changed, moving to the darker color palate that Kirsteen adopted earlier in the novel as a professional uniform and perhaps also a presciently fashionable choice. As with Wilson and Martineau, this final phase of Kirsteen's life has an appositional, discontinuous relationship to the earlier chapters that enabled it, a sign of the way that personal development over time remains incompletely domesticated into a linear narrative. Despite her career trajectory of steadily accumulating wealth and power, her retirement is set apart from it—she successfully uses incremental progress to effect radical change. Like her family, Kirsteen seems chagrined to have secured social status through her craft. In retirement, she finally retakes the name "Miss Douglas." Although her relationship to the Highland family is now public, their long interlude of financial hardship and the origin of their new wealth have been forgotten by those outside the family. Acquaintances wonder "as to how it was that she had never gotten a man—a question more than usually mysterious, seeing how well off she was."[16] Society has a short memory, reflecting that change over time, whether progressive or otherwise, tends to erase itself, becoming normalized just as soon as we glance away. The present moment never registers as simply a moment, but instead extrapolates forward and backward, usually misleadingly. In the end, Kirsteen breaks from both her family's Highland heritage and the London scene of her professional success, establishing herself in a metropolitan society that splits the difference between, or synthesizes, these two contrasting pasts. In the new environment of Edinburgh, Kirsteen can reap the benefits of the life she has made for herself. In the 1850s, still squarely in Oliphant's past, and ours, we catch a last glimpse of Kirsteen living out her future, not the one she originally wanted, but the one she fashioned with what she had.

Notes

1. Oliphant, *Kirsteen*, 68.
2. Ibid.
3. Purdy, *Rise of Fashion*, 4.
4. Oliphant, *Kirsteen*, 197.
5. Ibid., 68.
6. Ibid., 76.
7. Ibid., 78.
8. Ibid., 299.
9. Ibid., 361.
10. Ibid.
11. Ibid., 370.
12. Heath, *Aging by the Book*, 14.
13. Mill, *System of Logic*, 914 (VI.x.3).
14. Oliphant, *Kirsteen*, 385.
15. Ibid., 386.
16. Ibid.

Bibliography

Abel, Elizabeth, Marianne Hirsch, and Elizabeth Langland, eds. *The Voyage In: Fictions of Female Development*. Lebanon, NH: University Press of New England, 1983.

Ablow, Rachel. "Harriet Martineau and the Impersonality of Pain." *Victorian Studies* 56, no. 4 (2014): 675–97.

Acton, John Emerich Edward Dalberg-. "The Study of History." In *Selected Writings of Lord Acton*, edited by J. Rufus Fears, vol. II, 504–52. Indianapolis, IN: Liberty Classics, 1985.

Adams, Edward. *Liberal Epic: The Victorian Practice of History from Gibbon to Churchill*. Charlottesville: University of Virginia Press, 2011.

Akel, Regina. *Benjamin Disraeli and John Murray: The Politician, the Publisher, and the Representative*. Liverpool: Liverpool University Press, 2016.

Allen, Amy. *The End of Progress: Decolonizing the Normative Foundations of Critical Theory*. New York: Columbia University Press, 2016.

Allingham, Philip V. "John Collier's Pre-Raphaelite Illustrations to *The Trumpet-Major*." *Hardy Review* 16, no. 2 (2014): 50–91.

Amigoni, David. "Gendered Authorship, Literary Lionism, and the Virtues of Domesticity: Contesting Wordsworth's Fame in the Life and Writings of Harriet Martineau and Thomas Carlyle." *Critical Survey* 13, no. 2 (2001): 26–41.

Anderson, Amanda. *Bleak Liberalism*. Chicago: University of Chicago Press, 2016.

Anderson, Benedict. *Imagined Communities: Reflections on the Origin and Spread of Nationalism*. Revised edition. New York: Verso, 2006.

Arata, Stephen. *Fictions of Loss in the Victorian Fin de Siecle*. Cambridge: Cambridge University Press, 1996.

Ashton, John. *English Caricature and Satire on Napoleon I*. London: Benjamin Blom, 1968.

Athenaeum Journal of English and Foreign Literature, Science, and the Fine Arts. "Tales of the early ages. By the Author of 'Brambletye House.'" Apr. 21, 1832. Google Books.

Augustine of Hippo. *The City of God against the Pagans*, edited and translated by R. W. Dyson. Cambridge: Cambridge University Press, 1998.

Bagehot, Walter. *The English Constitution*. Edited by Miles Taylor. Oxford: Oxford University Press, 2001.

Barbey d'Aurevilly, Jules Amédée. "The Anatomy of Dandyism with Some Observations on Beau Brummell (1845)." In *The Rise of Fashion, a Reader*, edited by Daniel Leonhard Purdy, translated by D. B. Wyndham Lewis, 174–91. Minneapolis: University of Minnesota Press, 2004.

Barthes, Roland. "The Reality Effect." In *French Literary Theory Today, A Reader*, edited by Tzvetan Todorov, translated by R. Carter, 11–17. Cambridge: Cambridge University Press, 1982.

Baumann, H-Dirksen L., and Joseph J. Murray. "Reframing: From Hearing Loss to Deaf Gain." *Deaf Studies Digital Journal* 1 (2009): 1–10.

Baynton, Douglas C. "Deafness." *Keywords for Disability Studies*, edited by Rachel Adams, Benjamin Reiss, and David Serlin, 48–51. New York: New York University Press, 2015.

Beauvoir, Simone de. *The Coming of Age*. Translated by Patrick O'Brian. New York: Norton, 1996.

Beer, Gillian. *Darwin's Plots: Evolutionary Narrative in Darwin, George Eliot, and Nineteenth-Century Fiction*. Boston: Routledge and Kegan Paul, 1983.

Bell, Duncan. "Empire." In *Historicism and the Human Sciences in Victorian Britain*, edited by Mark Bevir, 211–36. Cambridge: Cambridge University Press, 2017.

Bell's Life in London and Sporting Chronicle. "Memoirs of Harriette Wilson and Others." Feb. 20, 1825. *British Newspaper Archive*, www.britishnewspaperarchive.co.uk.

Bell's Life in London and Sporting Chronicle. "Memoirs of Harriette Wilson, &c." Sept. 4, 1825. *British Newspaper Archive*, www.britishnewspaperarchive.co.uk.

Benjamin, Walter. "Theses on the Philosophy of History." In *Illuminations*, translated by Harry Zohn, edited by Hannah Arendt, 196–209. New York: Houghton Mifflin Harcourt, 2019.

Bentley, Michael. *Modernizing England's Past: English Historiography in the Age of Modernism, 1870–1970.* Cambridge: Cambridge University Press, 2005.

Bentley, Michael. "Shape and Pattern in British Historical Writing, 1815–1945." In *The Oxford History of Historical Writing. Vol. IV, 1800–1945,* edited by Stuart Macintyre, Juan Maiguashca, and Attila Pók, 204–24. Oxford: Oxford University Press, 2011.

Bevir, Mark, editor. *Historicism and the Human Sciences in Victorian Britain.* Cambridge: Cambridge University Press, 2017.

Blake, Robert. *Disraeli.* London: Eyre and Spottiswoode, 1966.

Blanch, Lesley, ed. "The Game of Hearts." In *The Game of Hearts: Harriette Wilson's Memoirs, Interspersed with Excerpts from The Confessions of Julia Johnstone, Her Rival,* 3–60. New York: Simon and Shuster, 1955.

"blood, n. (and int.)" def. 15b. *Oxford English Dictionary Online,* Oxford University Press. doi: 10.1093/OED/4196790062. Accessed Sept. 1, 2023.

Bodenheimer, Rosemarie. *The Politics of Story in Victorian Serial Fiction.* Ithaca: Cornell University Press, 1988.

Bourdeau, Michel. "Auguste Comte." *The Stanford Encyclopedia of Philosophy* (Spring 2023 Edition), edited by Edward N. Zalta and Uri Nodelman, Accessed Aug. 31, 2023. https://plato.stanford.edu/archives/spr2023/entries/comte/.

Bowler, Peter J. *The Invention of Progress: The Victorians and the Past.* Cambridge: Basil Blackwell, 1989.

Brady, Kristin. *The Short Stories of Thomas Hardy.* London: Macmillan Press, 1984.

Brantlinger, Patrick. "Nations and Novels: Disraeli, George Eliot, and Orientalism." *Victorian Studies* 35, no. 3 (1992): 255–75.

Braun, Thom. *Disraeli the Novelist.* Boston: Allen and Ulwin, 1981.

Breashears, Caroline. "Scandalous Categories: Classifying the Memoirs of Unconventional Women." *Philological Quarterly* 82, no. 2 (2003): 187–212.

Breward, Christopher. *The Culture of Fashion: A New History of Fashionable Dress.* Manchester: Manchester University Press, 1995.

Bristow, Joseph. "Why 'Victorian'? A Period and its Problems." *Literature Compass* 1, no. 1 (2004): 1–16. doi: 10.1111/j.1741-4113.2004.00055.x.

Broadley, Alexander Meyrick. *Napoleon in Caricature, 1795–1821.* New York: John Lane Co., 1911.

Brooks, Chris. *The Gothic Revival.* New York: Phaidon, 1999.

Broughton, Trev Lynn. "Making the Most of Martyrdom: Harriet Martineau, Autobiography and Death." *Literature and History* 2, no. 2 (1992): 24–45.

Brummell, Beau. *Male and Female Costume: Grecian and Roman Costume, British Costume from the Roman Invasion until 1822, and the Principles of Costume Applied to the Improved Dress of the Present Day*, edited by Eleanor Parker. New York: Doubleday, Doran and Company, 1932.

"buck, n.1." def. 2b. *Oxford English Dictionary Online*, Oxford University Press. doi: 10.1093/OED/7741129197. Accessed Sept. 1, 2023.

Buckle, Henry Thomas. *History of Civilization in England*. New York: D. Appleton and Co., 1862. HathiTrust Digital Library.

Buckley, Jerome Hamilton. *The Triumph of Time: A Study of Victorian Concepts of Time, History, Progress, and Decadence*. Cambridge, MA: Harvard University Press, 1966.

Bulwer Lytton, Edward. *Godolphin*. New York: R. Worthington, 1884.

Burke, Edmund. *Reflections on the French Revolution*. London: J. M. Dent and Sons Ltd, 1953.

Burn, W. L. *The Age of Equipoise: A Study of the Mid-Victorian Generation*. New York: W. W. Norton and Co., 1964.

Burns, Robert M., and Hugh Rayment-Pickard. *Philosophies of History: From Enlightenment to Postmodernity*. Oxford: Blackwell Publishing, 2000.

Burstein, Miriam Elizabeth. *Victorian Reformations: Historical Fiction and Religious Controversy, 1820–1900*. Notre Dame, IN: University of Notre Dame Press, 2014.

Butterfield, Herbert. *The Whig Interpretation of History*. 1931. London: G. Bell and Sons, 1963.

Campbell, Timothy. *Historical Style: Fashion and the New Mode of History, 1740–1830*. Philadelphia: University of Pennsylvania Press, 2016.

Canuel, Mark. *The Fate of Progress in British Romanticism*. Oxford: Oxford University Press, 2022.

Carlyle, Thomas. *On Heroes, Hero-Worship, and the Heroic in History*. Edited by David R. Sorensen and Brent E. Kinser. New Haven: Yale University Press, 2013.

Carlyle, Thomas. "On History." In *Historical Essays*, edited by Chris R. Vanden Bossche, 3–13. Berkeley: University of California Press, 2002.

Carlyle, Thomas. "On History Again." In *Historical Essays*, edited by Chris R. Vanden Bossche, 15–22. Berkeley: University of California Press, 2002.

Carlyle, Thomas. *Sartor Resartus*. Edited by Kerry McSweeney and Peter Sabor. Oxford: Oxford University Press, 1987.

Carpenter, Humphrey. *The Seven Lives of John Murray: The Story of a Publishing Dynasty, 1768–2002*. Edited by Candida Brazil and James Hamilton. London: John Murray, 2008.

Carter, Philip. "Brummell, George Bryan." *Oxford Dictionary of National Biography*, Oxford University Press, 2011. doi: 10.1093/ref:odnb/3771. Accessed 31 Aug. 2023.

Chakrabarty, Dipesh. *Provincializing Europe: Postcolonial Thought and Historical Difference*. New ed. Princeton: Princeton University Press, 2000.

Charise, Andrea. *The Aesthetics of Senescence: Aging, Population, and the Nineteenth-Century British Novel*. Albany: State University of New York Press, 2020.

Chase, Karen. *The Victorians and Old Age*. Oxford: Oxford University Press, 2009.

Chen, Eva. "Dobbin's Corduroys: Sartorial Display and Modes of Masculinities in Vanity Fair." *Victorians: A Journal of Culture and Literature* 124 (2013): 32–53.

Chihaya, Sarah, Joshua Kotin, and Kinohi Nishakawa. "The 'Contemporary' by the Numbers." *Post45*, Feb. 29, 2016, http://post45.research.yale.edu/2016/02/the-contemporary-by-the-numbers/.

Clammer, David. "The Corsican Mischief." *Hardy Society Journal* 2, no. 1 (2006): 43–51.

Cohn, Elisha. *Still Life: Suspended Development in the Victorian Novel*. Oxford: Oxford University Press, 2016.

Cole, Sarah Rose. "The Aristocrat in the Mirror: Male Vanity and Bourgeois Desire in William Makepeace Thackeray's *Vanity Fair*." *Nineteenth-Century Literature* 61, no. 2 (2006): 137–70.

Colligan, Colette. "The Unruly Copies of Byron's Don Juan: Harems, Underground Print Culture, and the Age of Mechanical Reproduction." *Nineteenth-Century Literature* 59, no. 4 (2005): 433–63. JSTOR. doi:10.1525/ncl.2005.59.4.433.

Colvin, Howard. *Essays in English Architectural History*. New Haven: Yale University Press, 1999.

Conary, Jennifer. "'Dreaming over an Unattainable End': Disraeli's *Tancred* and the Failure of Reform." *Victorian Literature and Culture* 38, no. 1 (2010): 75–87.

"conversation, n." *Oxford English Dictionary Online*, Oxford University Press. doi: 10.1093/OED/1997277413. Accessed Sept. 25, 2023.

Cook, Daniel, and Amy Culley, eds. "Introduction: Gender, Genre, and Authorship." In *Women's Life Writing, 1700–1850: Gender, Genre, and Authorship*, 1–8. New York: Palgrave Macmillan, 2012.

Corbett, Mary Jean. *Representing Femininity: Middle-Class Subjectivity in Victorian and Edwardian Women's Autobiographies*. Oxford: Oxford University Press, 1992.

Courtemanche, Eleanor. "Beyond Urgency: Shadow Presentisms, Hinge Points, and Victorian Historicisms." *Criticism: A Quarterly for Literature and the Arts* 61, no. 4 (2019): 461–79.

Cousins, A. D., and Dani Napton. "Historical Romance and the Mythology of Charles I in D'Israeli and Disraeli." In *Disraeli and the Politics of Fiction: Some Reconsiderations*, edited by A. D. Cousins and Dani Napton, 91–108. Boston: Brill, 2022.

Cragg, William E. "Bulwer's *Godolphin*: The Metamorphosis of the Fashionable Novel." *Studies in English Literature, 1500–1900* 26, no. 4 (1986): 675–90. *JSTOR*, www.jstor.org/stable/450618.

Creighton, Alexander. "Tickers and Time-Keepers: *Vanity Fair*'s Competing Temporalities." *Journal of Victorian Culture* 23, no. 4 (2018): 527–41.

Cronin, Richard. *Romantic Victorians: English Literature, 1824–1840*. New York: Palgrave, 2002.

Culley, Amy. *British Women's Life-Writing, 1760–1840: Friendship, Community, and Collaboration*. New York: Palgrave Macmillan, 2014.

Davidoff, Leonore, and Catherine Hall. *Family Fortunes: Men and Women of the English Middle Class, 1780–1850*. Chicago: University of Chicago Press, 1987.

Davis, Lennard J. *Enforcing Normalcy: Disability, Deafness, and the Body*. New York: Verso, 1995.

Dickens, Charles. *Little Dorrit*. Oxford: Oxford University Press, 1989.

Dimock, Wai Chee. "Editor's Column: Historicism, Presentism, Futurism." *PMLA: Publications of the Modern Language Association of America* 133, no. 2 (2018): 257–63. doi:10.1632/pmla.2018.133.2.257.

Dinshaw, Carolyn. "Got Medieval?" *Journal of the History of Sexuality* 10, no. 2 (2001): 202–12.

Dinshaw, Carolyn. *How Soon Is Now? Medieval Texts, Amateur Readers, and the Queerness of Time*. Durham, NC: Duke University Press, 2012.

Disraeli, Benjamin. *Coningsby, or, The New Generation*. Leipzig: Tauschnitz, 1844. Google Books.

Disraeli, Benjamin. "General Preface." *Collected Edition of the Novels and Tales by the Right Honorable B. Disraeli*. London: Longmans, Green, and Co., 1870.

Disraeli, Benjamin. *Sybil: Or The Two Nations*. Edited by Sheila M. Smith. Oxford: Oxford University Press, 2008.

Disraeli, Benjamin. *Vivian Grey*. Edited by Michael Sanders. London: Pickering and Chatto, 2004.

"Dress, Dandies, Fashion, &c." *Fashioning the Victorians: A Critical Sourcebook*. Edited by Rebecca N. Mitchell, 129–34. London: Bloomsbury Academic, 2018.

During, Simon. *Against Democracy: Literary Experience in the Age of Emancipations*. New York: Fordham University Press, 2012.

Edelman, Lee. *No Future: Queer Theory and the Death Drive*. Durham, NC: Duke University Press, 2004.

Elfenbein, Andrew. *Byron and the Victorians*. Cambridge: Cambridge University Press, 1995.

Engberg-Pedersen, Anders. *Empire of Chance: The Napoleonic Wars and the Disorder of Things*. Cambridge, MA: Harvard University Press, 2015.

Erll, Astrid. "Generation in Literary History: Three Constellations of Generationality, Genealogy, and Memory." *New Literary History* 45, no. 3 (2014): 385–409.

Esmail, Jennifer. *Reading Victorian Deafness: Signs and Sounds in Victorian Literature and Culture*. Athens: Ohio University Press, 2013.

Esty, Jed. *The Future of Decline: Anglo-American Culture at Its Limits*. Stanford, CA: Stanford University Press, 2022.

Esty, Jed. *Unseasonable Youth: Modernism, Colonialism, and the Fiction of Development*. Oxford: Oxford University Press, 2011.

"fashionable, adj. and n." def. 4b. *Oxford English Dictionary Online*, Oxford University Press. doi: 10.1093/OED/8270213206. Accessed Sept. 1, 2023.

Fleishman, Avrom. *The English Historical Novel: Walter Scott to Virginia Woolf*. Baltimore: Johns Hopkins University Press, 1971.

Flügel, J. C. "'The Great Masculine Renunciation and Its Causes' from *The Psychology of Clothes* (1930)." In *The Rise of Fashion, a Reader*, edited by Daniel Leonhard Purdy, 102–8. Minneapolis: University of Minnesota Press, 2004.

Foucault, Michel. *Discipline and Punish: The Birth of the Prison*. Translated by Alan Sheridan. London: Vintage Random House, 1977.

Foucault, Michel. "Nietzsche, Genealogy, History." In *The Essential Foucault: Selections from the Essential Works of Foucault, 1954–1984*, edited by Paul Rabinow and Nikolas Rose, 351–69. New York: The New Press, 1994.

Fraiman, Susan. *Unbecoming Women: British Women Writers and the Novel of Development*. New York: Columbia University Press, 1993.

Freedgood, Elaine. "Fictional Settlements: Footnotes, Metalepsis, the Colonial Effect." *New Literary History* 41, no. 2 (2010): 393–411.

Freedgood, Elaine. "'Fine Fingers': Victorian Handmade Lace and Utopian Consumption." *Victorian Studies* 45, no. 4 (2003): 625–47. doi:10.2979/vic.2003.45.4.625.

Freedgood, Elaine. *The Ideas in Things: Fugitive Meaning in the Victorian Novel*. Chicago: University of Chicago Press, 2006.

Friedman, Susan Stanford. "Alternatives to Literary History, Modernism, and the 'New' Temporalities." *MLQ* 80, no. 4 (Dec 2019): 379–402.

Gallagher, Catherine. *The Industrial Reformation of English Fiction: Social Discourse and Narrative Form, 1832–1867*. Chicago: University of Chicago Press, 1985.

Gallagher, Catherine. *Telling It Like It Wasn't: The Counterfactual Imagination in History and Fiction*. Chicago: University of Chicago Press, 2018.

Gallop, Jane. "Sedgwick's Twisted Temporalities, 'or even just reading and writing.'" In *Queer Times, Queer Becomings*, edited by E. L. McCallum and Mikko Tuhkanen, 47–75. Albany: State University of New York Press, 2011.

Gatrell, Simon. *Thomas Hardy Writing Dress*. New York: Peter Lang, 2011.

Gillingham, Lauren. *Fashionable Fictions and the Currency of the Nineteenth-Century British Novel*. Cambridge: Cambridge University Press, 2023.

Gillingham, Lauren. "The Novel of Fashion Redressed: Bulwer-Lytton's *Pelham* in a 19th-Century Context." *Victorian Review* 32, no. 1 (2006): 63–85.

Gilmartin, Sophie. *Ancestry and Narrative in Nineteenth-Century British Literature*. Cambridge: Cambridge University Press, 1998.

Gilmartin, Sophie, and Rod Mengham. *Thomas Hardy's Shorter Fiction: A Critical Study*. Edinburgh: Edinburgh University Press, 2007.

Greenslade, William P. *Degeneration, Culture, and the Novel: 1880–1940*. Cambridge: Cambridge University Press, 1994.

Grener, Adam. "Hardy's Relics." *Modern Philology* 114, no. 1 (Aug 2016): 106–29.

Grener, Adam. *Improbability, Chance, and the Nineteenth-Century Realist Novel*. Columbus: Ohio State University Press, 2020.

Greville, Charles C. F. *The Greville Memoirs (second part): A Journal of the Reign of Queen Victoria, from 1837 to 1852*, Vol. II. London: Longmans, Green, and Co., 1885.

Griffin, Cristina Richieri. "Experiencing History and Encountering Fiction in *Vanity Fair*." *Victorian Studies* 58, no. 3 (2016): 412–35.

Grose, Francis. *Lexicon Balatronicum: A Dictionary of Buckish Slang, University Wit, and Pickpocket Eloquence. Compiled Originally by Captain Grose. And Now Considerably Altered and Enlarged, with the Modern Changes and Improvements, By a Member of the Whip Club*. London: C. Chapell, 1811. Google Books.

Grylls, David. "Thomas Hardy: *Wessex Tales*." In *A Companion to the British and Irish Short Story*, edited by Cheryl A. Malcolm and David Malcolm, 140–8. Malden, MA: Wiley-Blackwell, 2008.

Gullette, Margaret Morganroth. *Aged by Culture*. Chicago: University of Chicago Press, 2004.

Halberstam, Jack. *In a Queer Time and Place: Transgender Bodies, Subcultural Lives*. New York: New York University Press, 2005.

Hammond, Mary. "Thackeray's Waterloo: History and War in *Vanity Fair*." *Literature and History* 11, no. 2 (2002): 19–38.

Handwerk, Gary. "Behind Sybil's Veil: Disraeli's Mix of Ideological Messages." *Modern Language Quarterly: A Journal of Literary History* 49, no. 4 (1988): 321–41. doi:10.1215/00267929-49-4-321.

Hardy, Barbara. "Introduction." In *The Trumpet-Major*, by Thomas Hardy, 11–31. New York: Macmillan, 1973.

Hardy, Thomas. "The Profitable Reading of Fiction." In *Thomas Hardy's Public Voice: The Essays, Speeches, and Miscellaneous Prose*, edited by Michael Millgate, 75–88. Oxford: Clarendon Press, 2001.

Hardy, Thomas. *The Trumpet-Major: John Loveday, a Soldier in the War with Buonaparte, and Robert his Brother, First Mate in the Merchant Service, a Tale*. London: Wordsworth Editions Ltd., 1995.

Hardy, Thomas. "Trumpet-Major Notebook." In *The Personal Notebooks of Thomas Hardy*, edited by Richard H. Taylor, 115–186. New York: Macmillan, 1978.

Hardy, Thomas. *Wessex Tales*. Edited by Kathryn R. King. Oxford: Oxford University Press, 1994.

Harley, Alexis. *Autobiologies: Charles Darwin and the Natural History of the Self*. Lewisburg, PA: Bucknell University Press, 2015.

Hatter, Janine, and Nickianne Moody, eds. *Fashion and Material Culture in Victorian Fiction and Periodicals*. Brighton: Edward Everett Root Publishers, 2019.

Hawkins, Ann R. "Evoking Byron from Manuscript to Print: Benjamin Disraeli's *Venetia*." *Papers of the Bibliographical Society of America* 98, no. 4 (2004): 449–76.

Heath, Kay. *Aging by the Book: The Emergence of Midlife in Victorian Britain*. Albany: State University of New York Press, 2009.

Heitzman, Matthew. "'The Devil's Code of Honor': French Invasion and the Return of History in *Vanity Fair*." *Victorian Literature and Culture* 44, no. 1 (March 2016): 43–57.

Herzog, Toby C. "Hardy's 'Fellow-Townsmen': A Primer for the Novels." *Colby Library Quarterly* 18, no. 4 (1982): 231–40.

Hewitt, Martin. "Why the Notion of Victorian Britain *Does* Make Sense." *Victorian Studies* 48, no. 3 (2006): 395–438.

Hibbard, Andrea. "Vivian Grey and the Silver-Fork Etiquette of Authorship." *Genre* 32, no. 4 (Winter 1999): 249–66.

Hochstrasser, T. J. "Conway, Francis Ingram-Seymour-, Second Marquis of Hertford (1743–1822)." *Oxford Dictionary of National Biography*. Oxford University Press, 2008. doi: 10.1093/ref:odnb/25167. Accessed Sept. 1, 2023.

Hoppen, K. Theodore. *The Mid-Victorian Generation: 1846–1886*. Oxford: Clarendon Press, 1998.

Hotten, John Camden. *A Dictionary of Modern Slang, Cant, and Vulgar Words, Used at the Present Day in the Streets of London; the Universities of Oxford and Cambridge; the Houses of Parliament; the Dens of St. Giles; and the Palaces of St. James*. London: John Camden Hotten, 1859. Google Books.

Huber, Irmtraud. *Time and Timelessness in Victorian Poetry*. Edinburgh: Edinburgh University Press, 2023.

Hughes, Clair. *Dressed in Fiction*. New York: Berg, 2006.

Iggers, Georg G. "Introduction." In *The Theory and Practice of History*. By Leopold von Ranke, edited by Georg G. Iggers, translated by Wilma A. Iggers, xi–xlv. New York: Routledge, 2011.

Ireland, Ken. *Thomas Hardy, Time and Narrative: A Narratological Approach to His Novels*. New York: Palgrave Macmillan, 2014.

Jensen, Anthony K. *Nietzsche's Philosophy of History*. Cambridge: Cambridge University Press, 2013.

Jesse, Capt. William. *The Life of Beau Brummell, Esq., Commonly Called Beau Brummell*. London: Saunders and Otley, 1844. Google Books.

Jewusiak, Jacob. *Aging, Duration, and the English Novel*. Cambridge: Cambridge University Press, 2019.

Jewusiak, Jacob. "Thomas Hardy's Impulse: Context and the Counterfactual Imagination." *Textual Practice* 34, no. 3 (2020): 461–78. doi:10.1080/0950236X.2018.1508493.

Johnstone, Julia. "Confessions of Julia Johnstone." In *Whore Biographies: 1700–1825*, edited by Julie Peakman, Alexander Pettit, and Patrick Spedding, VIII:4–367. London: Pickering and Chatto, 2006.

Jones, Jason B. *Lost Causes: Historical Consciousness in Victorian Literature*. Columbus: Ohio State University Press, 2006.

Jupp, Peter. "Disraeli's Interpretation of English History." In *The Self-Fashioning of Disraeli, 1818–1851*, edited by Charles Richmond and Paul Smith, 131–51. Cambridge: Cambridge University Press, 1998.

Kafer, Alison. *Feminist, Queer, Crip*. Bloomington: Indiana University Press, 2013.

King, Kathryn R. "Introduction." In *Wessex Tales*, by Thomas Hardy, xi–xx. New York: Oxford University Press, 1994.

Kingstone, Helen. *Victorian Narratives of the Recent Past: Memory, History, Fiction*. New York: Palgrave, 2017.

Koselleck, Reinhart. *Futures Past: On the Semantics of Historical Time*. Translated by Keith Tribe. Cambridge, MA: MIT Press, 1985.

Koselleck, Reinhart. *The Practice of Conceptual History: Timing History, Spacing Concepts*. Stanford, CA: Stanford University Press, 2002.

Kristeva, Julia. "Women's Time." In *The Kristeva Reader*, edited by Toril Moi, translated by Alice Jardine and Harry Blake, 187–213. New York: Columbia University Press, 1986.

Kurnick, David. *Empty Houses: Theatrical Failure and the Novel*. Princeton: Princeton University Press, 2012.

Lambert, Miles. "The Dandy in Thackeray's 'Vanity Fair' and 'Pendennis': An Early Victorian View of the Regency Dandy." *Costume* 22, no. 1 (1988): 60–9.

Latham, Sean. *The Art of Scandal: Modernism, Libel Law, and the Roman à Clef*. New York: Oxford University Press, 2009.

Lee, Yoon Sun. "Vection, Vertigo, and the Historical Novel." *NOVEL: A Forum on Fiction* 52, no. 2 (2019): 179–99.

Leighton, Mary Elizabeth, and Lisa Surridge. *The Plot Thickens: Illustrated Victorian Serial Fiction from Dickens to Du Maurier*. Athens: Ohio University Press, 2019.

Lesjak, Carolyn. *The Afterlife of Enclosure: British Realism, Character, and the Commons*. Redwood City, CA: Stanford University Press, 2021.

Levine, George. *The Realistic Imagination: English Fiction from Frankenstein to Lady Chatterly*. Chicago: University of Chicago Press, 1981.

Lewes, George Henry. "Review." In *Vanity Fair*, by William Makepeace Thackeray, edited by Peter L. Shillingsburg, 753–8. New York: Norton, 1994.

Lewis, Michael J. *The Gothic Revival*. London: Thames and Hudson, 2002.

Lindner, Christopher. "Thackeray's Gourmand: Carnivals of Consumption in *Vanity Fair*." *Modern Philology* 99, no. 4 (2002): 564–81.

Litvak, Joseph. "Kiss Me, Stupid: Sexuality, Sophistication, and *Vanity Fair*." *NOVEL: A Forum on Fiction* 29, no. 2 (1996): 223–42.

Logan, Deborah A. "'(Entre nous, please!)': Harriet Martineau's Correspondence." In *Harriet Martineau: Authorship, Society, and Empire*, edited by Ella Dzelzainis and Cora Kaplan, 52–62. Manchester: Manchester University Press, 2010.

Logan, Deborah A. *The Hour and the Woman: Harriet Martineau's "Somewhat Remarkable" Life*. DeKalb, IL: Northern Illinois University Press, 2002.

Longford, Elizabeth. *Wellington: The Years of the Sword*. London: Weidenfeld and Nicolson, 1969.

Looser, Devoney. "Age and Aging Studies, From Cradle to Grave." *Age, Culture, Humanities: An Interdisciplinary Journal* 1, no. 1 (2014): 25–9. doi: 10.7146/ageculturehumanities.v1i.129938.

Looser, Devoney. *Women Writers and Old Age in Great Britain, 1750–1850*. Baltimore: Johns Hopkins University Press, 2008.

Love, Heather. *Feeling Backward: Loss and the Politics of Queer History*. Cambridge, MA: Harvard University Press, 2007.

Lowe, Lisa. *The Intimacies of Four Continents*. Durham, NC: Duke University Press, 2015.

Lukács, Georg. *The Historical Novel*. Translated by Hannah and Stanley Mitchell. London: Merlin Press, 1962.

Lupton, Christina. *Reading and the Making of Time in the Eighteenth Century*. Baltimore: Johns Hopkins University Press, 2018.

Lutz, Deborah. *Relics of Death in Victorian Literature and Culture*. Cambridge: Cambridge University Press, 2015.

McAleavey, Maia. "Behind the Victorian Novel: Scott's Chronicles." *Victorian Studies* 61, no. 2 (2019): 232–9.

Macaulay, Thomas Babington. "History." In *Critical, Historical, and Miscellaneous Essays*, I: 376–432. Boston: Houghton, Mifflin, and Co., 1860.

Macaulay, Thomas Babington. *The History of England from the Accession of James II*. Philadelphia: E. H. Butler and Co., 1861.

Macaulay, Thomas Babington. "John Dryden." In *Critical, Historical,* and *Miscellaneous Essays*, I: 321–75. Boston: Houghton, Mifflin, and Co., 1860.

McLoughlin, Kate. "Missing Letters: Reading the Interstices in Archival Correspondence from the Napoleonic Wars and in Thomas Hardy's the Trumpet-Major." *Textual Practice* 29, no. 7 (2015): 1225–44. doi: 10.1080/0950236X.2015.1095444.

"Manifesto of the V21 Collective." *V21 Collective: Victorian Studies for the 21st Century*, March 2015. http://v21collective.org/manifesto-of-the-v21-collective-ten-theses/. Accessed Sept. 1, 2023.

Markovits, Stefanie. "Form Things: Looking at Genre through Victorian Diamonds." *Victorian Studies* 52, no. 4 (2010): 591–619.

Marshik, Celia. *At the Mercy of Their Clothes: Modernism, the Middlebrow, and British Garment Culture*. New York: Columbia University Press, 2017.

Martineau, Harriet. *Autobiography*. Edited by Linda H. Peterson. Peterborough, ON: Broadview Press, 2007.

Maxwell, Richard. *The Historical Novel in Europe, 1650–1950*. Cambridge: Cambridge University Press, 2009.

Mayer, Sandra. "Portraits of the Artist as Politician, the Politician as Artist: Commemorating the Disraeli Phenomenon." *Journal of Victorian Culture* 21, no. 3 (2016): 281–300.

Mayer, Sandra. "The Prime Minister as Celebrity Novelist: Benjamin Disraeli's 'Double Consciousness.'" *Forum for Modern Language Studies* 54, no. 3 (2018): 354–68.

Melman, Billie. "The Power of the Past: History and Modernity in the Victorian World." In *The Victorian World*, edited by Martin Hewitt, 466–83. New York: Routledge, 2012.

Michaelson, Patricia Howell. *Speaking Volumes: Women, Reading, and Speech in the Age of Austen*. Redwood City, CA: Stanford University Press, 2002.

Michie, Elsie B. "Dressing Up: Hardy's *Tess of the D'Urbervilles* and Oliphant's *Phoebe Junior*." *Victorian Literature and Culture* 30, no. 1 (2002): 305–23.

Mill, John Stuart. "Book VI. On the Logic of the Moral Sciences." In *A System of Logic, Ratiocinative and Inductive, Being a Connected View of the Principles of Evidence and the Methods of Scientific Investigation*, in Collected Works of John Stuart Mill, edited by J. M. Robson, VIII: 831–952. Toronto: University of Toronto Press, 1963.

Mill, John Stuart. "The Spirit of the Age." In *The Spirit of the Age: Victorian Essays*, edited by Gertrude Himmelfarb, 50–79. New Haven: Yale University Press, 2007.

Miller, Andrew H. *The Burdens of Perfection: On Ethics and Reading in Nineteenth-Century British Literature*. Ithaca: Cornell University Press, 2008.
Millgate, Michael. *Thomas Hardy: His Career as a Novelist*. New York: Random House, 1971.
Mistichelli, William J. "The Trumpet Major's Signal: Kinship and Sexual Rivalry in the Novels of Thomas Hardy." *CEA Critic: An Official Journal of the College English Association* 56, no. 3 (1994): 43–61.
Mitchell, Rebecca N., ed. *Fashioning the Victorians: A Critical Sourcebook*. London: Bloomsbury Academic, 2018.
"Modern Beau Brummellism." In *Fashioning the Victorians: A Critical Sourcebook*, edited by Rebecca N. Mitchell, 135–9. London: Bloomsbury Academic, 2018.
Moers, Ellen. *The Dandy, Brummell to Beerbohm*. New York: Viking Press, 1960.
Mole, Tom. *What the Victorians Made of Romanticism: Material Artifacts, Cultural Practices, and Reception History*. Princeton: Princeton University Press, 2017.
Moore, Ben. "Disraeli and the Archi-Textual: Constructions of Authority in *Sybil*." *The Modern Language Review* 110, no. 1 (2015): 47–68.
Moretti, Franco. *Graphs, Maps, Trees: Abstract Models for Literary History*. New York: Verso, 2005.
Morgan, Monique R. *Narrative Means, Lyric Ends*. Columbus: Ohio State University Press, 2009.
Mufti, Nasser. *Civilizing War: Imperial Politics and the Poetics of National Rupture*. Evanston, IL: Northwestern University Press, 2017.
Mullen, Mary L. *Novel Institutions: Anachronism, Irish Novels, and Nineteenth-Century Realism*. Edinburgh: Edinburgh University Press, 2019.
Muñoz, José Esteban. *Cruising Utopia: The Then and There of Queer Futurity*. New York: New York University Press, 2009.
Murray, Alex. "Conservative." *Victorian Literature and Culture* 51, no. 3 (2023): 371–4.
Neill, Edward. "Mixed Modes in *The Trumpet-Major*." *Essays in Criticism* 56, no. 4 (2006): 351–69.
Nemesvari, Richard. "The Anti-Comedy of *The Trumpet-Major*." *Victorian Newsletter* 77 (1990): 8–13.
Nickerson, Charles C. "Disraeli, Lockhart, and Murray: An Episode in the History of the *Quarterly Review*." *Victorian Studies* 15, no. 3 (1972): 279–306.

Nickerson, Charles C. "Vivian Grey and Dorian Gray." *Times Literary Supplement*, Aug. 14, 1969, 909.

Nicolay, Claire. "The Anxiety of 'Mosaic' Influence: Thackeray, Disraeli, and Anglo-Jewish Assimilation in the 1840s." *Nineteenth-Century Contexts* 25, no. 2 (2003): 119–45.

Nietzsche, Friedrich. *On the Genealogy of Morals*. Translated by Walter Kaufmann. London: Vintage Books, 1967.

Nietzsche, Friedrich. "On the Uses and Disadvantages of History for Life." In *Untimely Meditations*, edited by Daniel Breazeale, translated by R. J. Hollingdale, 57–123. Cambridge: Cambridge University Press, 1997.

Observer. "Periodicals." Feb. 7, 1848. *ProQuest Historical Newspapers*, www.proquest.com/hnpguardianobserver.

O'Connell, Lisa. "Authorship and Libertine Celebrity: Harriette Wilson's Regency Memoirs." In *Libertine Enlightenment: Sex, Liberty and Licence in the Eighteenth Century*, edited by Peter Cryle and Lisa O'Connell, 161–81. New York: Palgrave Macmillan, 2004.

O'Kell, Robert. *Disraeli: The Romance of Politics*. Toronto: University of Toronto Press, 2013.

Oliphant, Margaret. *Kirsteen; The Story of a Scotch Family Seventy Years Ago*. Edited by Anne M. Scriven. Glasgow: Association for Scottish Literary Studies, 2010.

Oussaid, Nathalie. "A Reading of *Wessex Tales*." *The Thomas Hardy Journal* 19, no. 2 (2003): 25–32.

Parker, Christopher. *The English Idea of History from Coleridge to Collingwood*. Farnham: Ashgate, 2000.

Parry, Jonathan. "Disraeli, Benjamin, Earl of Beaconsfield (1804–1881), Prime Minister and Novelist." *Oxford Dictionary of National Biography*. Oxford University Press, 2011. doi: 10.1093/ref:odnb/7689. Accessed Sept. 1, 2023.

Peakman, Julie. "Memoirs of Harriette Wilson." In *Whore Biographies: 1700–1825*, edited by Julie Peakman, Alexander Pettit, and Patrick Spedding, VII:1–5. London: Pickering and Chatto, 2006.

Peakman, Julie. "Memoirs of Women of Pleasure: The Whore Biography." *Women's Writing* 11, no. 2 (2004): 163–84. doi: 10.1080/09699080400200226.

Peakman, Julie, Alexander Pettit, and Patrick Spedding, eds. *Whore Biographies: 1700–1825*. 8 vols. London: Pickering and Chatto, 2006.

Peterson, Linda H. *Traditions of Victorian Women's Autobiography: The Poetics and Politics of Life Writing*. Charlottesville: University Press of Virginia, 1999.

Pinker, Steven. *The Better Angels of Our Nature: Why Violence Has Declined*. New York: Viking, 2011.
Plenderleath, William C. *The White Horses of the West of England. With Notices of Some Other Ancient Turf-Monuments*. London: Alfred Russell Smith, 1885.
Plotz, John. *Portable Property: Victorian Culture on the Move*. Princeton: Princeton University Press, 2008.
Polowetzky, Michael. *Prominent Sisters: Mary Lamb, Dorothy Wordsworth, and Sarah Disraeli*. Westport, CT: Praeger, 1996.
Pomeroy, Florence Wallace, Viscountess Harberton. "Rational Dress Reform." In *Fashioning the Victorians: A Critical Sourcebook*, edited by Rebecca N. Mitchell, 77–83. London: Bloomsbury Academic, 2018.
Poovey, Mary. *Making a Social Body: British Cultural Formation, 1830–1864*. Chicago: University of Chicago Press, 1995.
Purdy, Daniel Leonhard. *The Rise of Fashion: A Reader*. Minneapolis: University of Minnesota Press, 2004.
Radford, Andrew. *Thomas Hardy and the Survivals of Time*. Burlington, VT: Ashgate, 2003.
Rainof, Rebecca. *The Victorian Novel of Adulthood: Plot and Purgatory in Fictions of Maturity*. Athens: Ohio University Press, 2015.
Rance, Nicholas. *The Historical Novel and Popular Politics in Nineteenth-Century England*. London: Vision Press, 1975.
Ranke, Leopold von. *The Theory and Practice of History*. Edited by Georg G. Iggers. Translated by Wilma A. Iggers. New York: Routledge, 2011.
Reilly, Jim. *Shadowtime: History and Representation in Hardy, Conrad, and George Eliot*. London: Routledge, 1993.
Reynolds, K. D. "Wilson [née Dubouchet], Harriette [known as Mrs. Q], (1786–1845)." *Oxford Dictionary of National Biography*. Oxford University Press, 2010, doi: 10.1093/ref:odnb/29653.
Ribeiro, Aileen. *The Art of Dress: Fashion in England and France, 1750–1820*. New Haven: Yale University Press, 1995.
Richstad, Josephine. "Genre in Amber: Preserving the Fashionable Novel for a Victorian Decade, Catherine Gore's *Hamiltons* (1834 and 1850)." *Modern Philology* 111, no. 3 (2014): 549–65.
Rickman, Thomas. *An Attempt to Discriminate the Styles of Architecture in England, from the Conquest to the Reformation*. Sixth ed. Oxford: John Henry and James Parker, 1862.
Rignall, J. M. "The Historical Double: *Waverley, Sylvia's Lovers, The Trumpet-Major*." *Essays in Criticism: A Quarterly Journal of Literary Criticism* 34, no. 1 (1984): 14–32. doi: 10.1093/eic/XXXIV.1.14.

Rimmer, Mary. "History and the Bogus Heroine: Gender and Genre in *The Trumpet-Major*." *The Thomas Hardy Journal* 29 (2012): 70–80.

Rivers, Bryan. "'Unnaturally Drawn': Harriette Wilson's Criticism of Shakespeare's Shylock (1811)." *ANQ: A Quarterly Journal of Short Articles, Notes and Reviews* 21, no. 4 (Fall 2008): 34–36. doi: 10.3200/ANQQ.21.4.34-36.

Roberts, Caroline. *The Woman and the Hour: Harriet Martineau and Victorian Ideologies*. Toronto: University of Toronto Press, 2002.

Rosling, Hans, Ola Rosling, and Anna Rosling Rönnlund. *Factfulness: Ten Reasons We're Wrong about the World—And Why Things Are Better than You Think*. New York: Flatiron Books, 2018.

Rousseau, Jean-Jacques. "Discourse on the Origin and the Foundations of Inequality among Men." In *The Discourses and Other Early Political Writings*, edited and translated by Victor Gourevitch, 111–88. Cambridge: Cambridge University Press, 1997.

St. Clair, William. *The Reading Nation in the Romantic Period*. Cambridge: Cambridge University Press, 2004.

Sampson, Jennifer. "*Sybil*, or the Two Monarchs." *Studies in Philology* 95, no. 1 (1998): 97–119.

San Francisco Chronicle. "Original Lord Steyne. Who Was the Model of Thackeray's Character?" 14 Sept 1890. *ProQuest Historical Newspapers*.

Sanders, Andrew. *The Victorian Historical Novel, 1840–1880*. New York: St. Martin's Press, 1979.

Sanders, Michael. "Introduction." In *Vivian Grey*, by Benjamin Disraeli, edited by Michael Sanders, xxxvii–lxv. London, Pickering and Chatto, 2004.

Sanders, Valerie. "Victorian Life Writing." *Literature Compass* 1, no. 1 (2004): 1–17.

Saunders, David. "Copyright, Obscenity, and Literary History." *ELH* 57, no. 2 (1990): 431–44. doi: 10.2307/2873078.

Schaffer, Talia. *Communities of Care: The Social Ethics of Victorian Fiction*. Princeton: Princeton University Press, 2021.

Schoenbach, Lisi. *Pragmatic Modernism*. Oxford: Oxford University Press, 2012.

Schwartz, Daniel R. *Disraeli's Fiction*. New York: Barnes and Noble, 1979.

Schwartz, Daniel R. "General Introduction." In *Vivian Grey*, by Benjamin Disraeli, edited by Michael Sanders, ix–xxxv. London: Pickering and Chatto, 2004.

Schweller, Russell. "'Mosaic Arabs': Jews and Gentlemen in Disraeli's

Young England Trilogy." *Schofar: An Interdisciplinary Journal of Jewish Studies* 24, no. 2 (2006): 55–69.

Scott, Walter. *The Heart of Mid-Lothian*. Edited by Tony Inglis. London: Penguin, 1994.

Scott, Walter. *Ivanhoe*. Edited by Graham Tulloch. Edinburgh: Edinburgh University Press, 1998.

Scott, Walter. *The Journal of Sir Walter Scott*. Edited by W. E. K. Anderson. Edinburgh: Canongate Classics, 1998.

Scott, Walter. *Waverley*. Edited by Peter Garside, with an introduction by Ian Duncan. London: Penguin, 2011.

Setzer, Sharon M. "The Memoirs of Harriette Wilson: A Courtesan's Byronic Self-Fashioning." In *Women's Life Writing, 1700–1850: Gender, Genre, and Authorship*, edited by Daniel Cook and Amy Culley, 150–64. New York: Palgrave Macmillan, 2012.

Shannon, Brent. *The Cut of His Coat: Men, Dress, and Consumer Culture in Britain, 1860–1914*. Athens: Ohio University Press, 2006.

Shaw, Harry E. *The Forms of Historical Fiction: Sir Walter Scott and His Successors*. Ithaca: Cornell University Press, 1983.

Simmons, James C. *The Novelist as Historian: Essays on the Victorian Historical Novel*. The Hague: Mouton, 1973.

Skorupski, John. "The Conservative Critique of Liberalism." *The Cambridge Companion to Liberalism*, edited by Steven Wall, 401–22. Cambridge: Cambridge University Press, 2015.

Small, Helen. *The Long Life*. Oxford: Oxford University Press, 2007.

Smiles, Samuel. *A Publisher and His Friends: Memoir and Correspondence of the late John Murray, with an account of the Origin and Progress of the House, 1768–1843*. London: John Murray, 1981.

Smith, Sidonie. *A Poetics of Women's Autobiography: Marginality and the Fictions of Self-Representation*. Bloomington: Indiana University Press, 1987.

Speare, Morris Edmund. *The Political Novel: Its Development in England and America*. Oxford: Oxford University Press, 1924.

"spencer, n.2." def. 2. *Oxford English Dictionary Online*. Oxford University Press. doi: 10.1093/OED/9366308220. Accessed Sept. 1, 2023.

Steinberg, Oded Y. *Race, Nation, History: Anglo-German Thought in the Victorian Era*. Philadelphia: University of Pennsylvania Press, 2019.

Stendhal (Marie-Henri Beyle). *The Charterhouse of Parma*, translated by Margaret Mauldon, with an introduction and notes by Roger Pearson. Oxford: Oxford University Press, 1997.

Stevens, Joan. "Vanity Fair and the London Skyline." *Costerus: Essays in English and American Literature* 2 (1974): 13–41.
Stewart, Robert Wilson. *Disraeli's Novels Reviewed, 1826–1968*. Metuchen, NJ: Scarecrow Press, 1975.
"swell, n." def. 9a. *Oxford English Dictionary Online*. Oxford University Press. doi: 10.1093/OED/8001201804. Accessed Sept. 1, 2023.
Terdiman, Richard. *Present Past: Modernity and the Memory Crisis*. Ithaca: Cornell University Press, 1993.
Teukolsky, Rachel. "Romanticism on the Right: Benjamin Disraeli's Authoritarian Aesthetics." *Victorian Studies* 64, no. 2 (2022): 214–39.
Thackeray, William Makepeace. *Vanity Fair*. Edited by Peter L. Shillingsburg. New York: Norton, 1994.
Thackeray, William Makepeace. *Vanity Fair*. Edited by Geoffrey and Kathleen Tillotson. Boston: Houghton Mifflin, 1963.
Tillotson, Kathleen. *Novels of the Eighteen-Forties*. Oxford: Clarendon Press, 1954.
"Tipsy, adj." *Oxford English Dictionary Online*. Oxford University Press. doi: 10.1093/OED/5291522726. Accessed 1 Sept. 2023.
Tondre, Michael. *The Physics of Possibility: Victorian Fiction, Science, and Gender*. Charlottesville: University of Virginia Press, 2018.
Trezise, Simon. "Thomas Hardy and the Hieroglyphic Napoleon." *Thomas Hardy Journal* 5, no. 1 (1989): 59–72.
Vanden Bossche, Chris R. "Introduction." In *Historical Essays*, by Thomas Carlyle, edited by Chris R. Vanden Bossche, xix–lxviii. Berkeley: University of California Press, 2002.
Veblen, Thorstein. "The Economic Theory of Women's Dress." In *Fashioning the Victorians: A Critical Sourcebook*, edited by Rebecca N. Mitchell, 53–9. London: Bloomsbury Academic, 2018.
Voskuil, Lynn M. *Acting Naturally: Victorian Theatricality and Authenticity*. Charlottesville: University of Virginia Press, 2004.
Walker, Stanwood S. "A False Start for the Classical-Historical Novel: Lockhart's *Valerius* and the Limits of Scott's Historicism." *Nineteenth-Century Literature* 57, no. 2 (2002): 179–209.
Watson, Nicola J. "Trans-figuring Byronic Identity." In *At the Limits of Romanticism: Essays in Cultural, Feminist, and Materialist Criticism*, edited by Mary A. Favret and Nicola J. Watson, 185–206. Bloomington: Indiana University Press, 1994.
Weintraub, Stanley. *Disraeli: A Biography*. New York: Penguin, 1993.
White, Hayden V. *Metahistory: The Historical Imagination in Nineteenth-Century Europe*. Baltimore: Johns Hopkins University Press, 1973.

Wilde, Oscar. "The Suitability of Dress (1882)." In *The Rise of Fashion, a Reader*, edited by Daniel Leonhard Purdy, 232–8. Minneapolis: University of Minnesota Press, 2004.

Williams, Raymond. *Marxism and Literature*. Oxford: Oxford University Press, 1977.

Wilson, Elizabeth. *Adorned in Dreams: Fashion and Modernity*. Berkeley: University of California Press, 1985.

Wilson, Frances. *The Courtesan's Revenge: Harriette Wilson, the Woman Who Blackmailed the King*. London: Faber and Faber, 2003.

Wilson, Harriette. "Memoirs of Harriette Wilson." In *Whore Biographies: 1700–1825*, edited by Julie Peakman, Alexander Pettit, and Patrick Spedding, VII:7–504. London: Pickering and Chatto, 2006.

Wilson, Harriette. *Memoirs of Harriette Wilson, Written by Herself*. 8 vols. London: J. J. Stockdale, 1831.

Wolfson, Susan J. "Byron's Ghosting Authority." *ELH* 76, no. 3 (2009): 763–92.

Woodward, Kathleen. "Aging." In *Keywords for Disability Studies*, edited by Rachel Adams, Benjamin Reiss, and David Serlin, 33–4. New York: New York University Press, 2015.

Woolf, Virginia. "Modes and Manners of the Nineteenth Century." In *Fashioning the Victorians: A Critical Sourcebook*, edited by Rebecca N. Mitchell, 223–6. London: Bloomsbury Academic, 2018.

Wright, T. R. *Hardy and His Readers*. New York: Palgrave Macmillan, 2003.

Young, Brian W. "History." In *Historicism and the Human Sciences in Victorian Britain*, edited by Mark Bevir, 154–85. Cambridge: Cambridge University Press, 2017.

Young, Brian W. *The Victorian Eighteenth Century: An Intellectual History*. Oxford: Oxford University Press, 2007.

Zemka, Sue. "Progress." *Victorian Literature and Culture* 46, no. 3/4 (Fall/Winter 2018): 812–16.

Zemka, Sue. *Time and the Moment in Victorian Literature and Society*. Cambridge: Cambridge University Press, 2012.

Zlotnick, Susan. *Women, Writing, and the Industrial Revolution*. Baltimore: Johns Hopkins University Press, 1998.

Index

Ackermann, Rudolf, 185–7
Acton, Lord, 4, 35, 37, 43–4, 45, 72, 145, 213, 215
Adams, Edward, 13, 26n
adjunctification, viii, 24, 53
age studies, 11, 17, 46–7; see also youth; middle age; old age
Akel, Regina, 93n
Allen, Amy, 12, 72
Allingham, Philip V., 206n
Anderson, Amanda, 10
Anderson, Benedict, 10, 80
antiquarian history (Nietzsche's concept), 39–41
archaic (Raymond Williams's concept), 8–9, 110, 112
Arrighi, Giovanni, 28
Augustine, St., 30
autobiography see life-writing
Autobiography (Martineau), 7, 18, 20, 131–5, 145–63, 166n, 170, 190, 202, 214, 216

Bagehot, Walter, *English Constitution*, 1–4, 6, 16, 100
Bal, Mieke, 176
Barthes, Roland, 102
Beauvoir, Simone de, 17
Beer, Gillian, 195
Bell, Duncan, 28

Bell's Life in London, 141, 143
Benjamin, Walter, 10, 40–2, 80, 125, 150, 185–6
Bentley, Michael, 5, 6, 25n, 36–8
Bevir, Mark, 5
Bildung, 20, 62, 64, 71, 91
Bildungsroman, 5, 7, 12–13, 18, 49, 64, 70–1, 147
Blake, Robert, 65, 93n
Blanch, Lesley, 135, 164n
Bloom, Allan, 28
Bowler, Peter J., 5, 28, 30, 48
Brady, Kristin, 191, 207–8n, 209n
Brantlinger, Patrick, 72, 92n
Breashears, Caroline, 163n
Broughton, Trev L., 150, 156, 159
Brummell, Beau, 105–6, 128n, 140, 148; see also "Modern Beau Brummellism"
Buckle, Henry Thomas, 29, 35–7, 39, 42, 190, 215
Buckley, Jerome Hamilton, 4–6
Bulwer-Lytton, Edward, 127n
 Godolphin, 94n, 121, 124
 Pelham, 71, 106, 111, 115
Burke, Edmund, 11, 71–2; see also conservatism
Burrow, J. W., 4–5, 30–1, 60, 71
Burstein, Miriam Elizabeth, 13, 26n, 80

Butterfield, Herbert, 4, 30, 32, 33, 43; *see also* whig history
Byron, Lord, 59, 64, 92–3n, 135, 143–5, 164n, 165n

Campbell, Timothy, 16, 101–2
Canuel, Mark, 7, 22, 31, 36
Carlyle, Thomas, 19, 32, 64, 169
  On Heroes, 40, 123, 134, 139, 141, 145
  "On History," 39, 42, 125
  "On History Again," 9, 41
  Sartor Resartus, 15–16
  translation of *Wilhelm Meisters Lehrjahre*, 64
Chakrabarty, Dipesh, 11–12
Charise, Andrea, 17, 48
Chase, Karen, 17, 59
Chen, Eva, 106
Chihaya, Kotin, and Nishakawa, 53
Christian temporalities, 10, 26n, 30, 43, 79–80
chronology, 19, 21, 135–7, 143, 150
clothing, 11, 13–18, 20–1, 26n, 67, 87–8, 97–112, 127n, 170, 174, 177–85, 190, 204, 206n
  men's clothing, 1–4, 99–106, 108–13, 115–18, 128n, 136–7, 139, 179–80, 200
  women's clothing, 14, 97–8, 106–8, 177–85, 210–17
  see also fashion; jacket; knee-breeches; lace; muslin; spencer
Cohn, Elisha, 5
Colligan, Collette, 164n
Colvin, Howard, 89
Comte, Auguste, 20, 35, 134, 146, 149, 152, 155–6, 158, 161–2, 167n; *see also* positivism
Coningsby (Disraeli), 8, 18, 19, 47, 60–1, 65–6, 68, 70–83, 87, 90, 94n, 113, 115, 119–22, 141, 154, 214
conservatism, 10–11, 13, 24, 31, 40, 61–2, 71, 78, 80, 82, 92, 129n, 138
contingency, 13, 21, 123, 134, 148, 170–2, 177, 192, 195–7, 204, 214
conversation, 2, 6, 8–9, 19–20, 45–6, 51, 61, 63, 67–9, 73–4, 77, 80, 84–8, 91, 114, 135, 137, 141–5, 152–3, 159–60, 168n, 195–6, 208n
Cook, Daniel, 132
Corbett, Mary Jean, 131, 163n
Courtemanche, Eleanor, 22–3, 38, 40–1
Cousins, A. D. and Dani Napton, 81–2
Creighton, Alexander, 98
crip time, 24, 57–8n
critical history (Nietzsche's concept), 39–40
Cronin, Richard, 46
Culley, Amy, 132, 136
cyclicality, viii, 4–6, 16, 18, 20–1, 23, 28, 30, 32–4, 37, 40, 43, 48–9, 98–9, 102, 113, 131, 133–4, 138, 145–6, 154, 162, 170, 180, 193, 195, 197, 199, 201–2, 204, 211–2, 215

Dähling, Heinrich Anton, 185
deafness, 150, 157–60, 167–8n
decline, 4, 8–9, 13, 17, 21, 24, 28, 30, 37, 48–51, 60, 88, 90, 102, 120, 125, 157, 160, 190, 204, 213; *see also* regress
development *see* progress
Dickens, Charles, 75, 115
  Little Dorrit, 2–4, 100
Dimock, Wai Chee, 22, 38, 56n
Dinshaw, Carolyn, 133–4

Disraeli, Benjamin, 6, 19, 20, 24, 31, 59–92, 92n, 93n, 98, 113, 126, 163, 170, 215
  Coningsby, 8, 18, 19, 47, 60–1, 65–6, 68, 70–83, 87, 90, 94n, 113, 115, 119–22, 141, 154, 214
  Sybil, 19, 61, 71–3, 79–91, 113–15, 118–19, 122, 141, 190, 192–3, 199–200, 214, 216
  Vivian Grey, 7, 9, 18, 19, 61–71, 86, 93–4n, 117, 133, 143, 194
The Dynasts (Hardy), 205n

Edelman, Lee, 52
Elfenbein, Andrew, 71
Engberg-Petersen, Anders, 13, 169, 195
The English Constitution (Bagehot), 1–4, 6, 16, 100
Enlightenment, 30, 73
empire, 5, 12–13, 24, 28, 41, 59, 86, 102–4, 147, 161
Erll, Astrid, 46–7
Esmail, Jennifer, 159, 167–8n
Esty, Jed, 12, 37, 147

fashion, 1–4, 6, 8–9, 11, 13–18, 20–1, 26n, 59, 63–4, 66–9, 97–113, 115, 125, 137, 145, 178–84, 190, 200, 202, 210–17; *see also* clothing
Fleishman, Avrom, 126n, 127n
Flügel, John Carl, 108
Foucault, Michel, 41–2, 125, 169
Freedgood, Elaine, 13, 102–3, 114, 182–3
Friedman, Susan Stanford, 23

Gallagher, Catherine, 13, 92n, 195
Gallop, Jane, 151

Gatrell, Simon, 181, 183–4
gender, 14, 20–1, 26n, 46, 73, 83–4, 90–1, 100, 103, 111, 126, 131–6, 155, 163n, 166n, 168n, 178–9, 183, 203, 205n, 210–5; *see also* masculinity; women's time
genealogy, 18, 23, 29, 38, 40–2, 44, 47, 79, 81, 91, 100, 112, 115, 118–9, 125, 126n, 131, 133–4, 145, 199, 216; *see also* presentism
generationality, 8, 20, 29–30, 44–9, 51–4, 57n, 61, 69–70, 72–4, 77–8, 81, 86, 117, 119–22, 199, 210
George III (King), 173–6, 187
George IV (King), 82–3, 97, 121, 139
Gibbon, Edward, 28
Gillingham, Lauren, 14–16, 64–5, 84, 87, 101, 113
Gilmartin, Sophie, 69, 81, 192, 198, 207–8n
Glenarvon (Lamb), 135, 144, 164n, 165n
"Glorious Revolution" (1688), 34–5, 61, 71–2, 148
Godolphin (Bulwer-Lytton), 94n, 121, 124
Gothic architecture, 88–90
Grener, Adam, 13, 187, 205n
Greville, Charles, 76–7
Griffin, Cristina Richieri, 114
Grylls, David, 191, 194
Gullette, Margaret Morganroth, 46–7

Halberstam, Jack, 50–1, 57n, 133
Handwerk, Gary, 82, 87
Hardy, Barbara, 204–5n
Hardy, Thomas, 6, 163, 169–204, 211, 215

The Dynasts, 205n
"The Profitable Reading of Fiction," 177–9, 183–4
The Trumpet-Major, 8, 9, 21, 169–95, 203–4, 206n, 208n, 213
Wessex Tales, 7, 13, 18, 21, 24, 169–71, 177, 188, 190–204, 207–8n, 212, 214
Harley, Alexis, 156
The Heart of Mid-Lothian (Scott), 175
Heath, Kay, 17, 215
Heitzman, Matthew, 98
Herrick, Robert, 178–9, 181
Hertford, Third Marquis of, 70, 76–7, 115, 117, 121–2
Hewitt, Martin, 5
historical novel, 7, 12–3, 20–1, 26n, 44–6, 64, 79–80, 97, 99–100, 102–3, 112, 126n, 127n, 169–70, 172, 177, 179–80, 184, 195, 206n, 211–2; see also Scott
historiography, 6, 25n, 28–44, 61–2, 71, 80, 82, 91–2, 100–1, 105, 112, 116, 122, 126, 145, 161, 204; see also progress; whig history
"History" (Macaulay), 9, 33–4
History of England (Macaulay), 34–5
History of the Thirty Years' Peace (Martineau), 161
The Hour and the Man (Martineau), 150–1
Hughes, Clair, 107–8
Hume, David, 30, 101–2, 181

Illustrations of Political Economy (Martineau), 152–3, 156
Ireland, Ken, 176
irregular survival, 4, 6–8, 10–11, 14, 16, 18, 22, 61, 67, 70, 78, 80, 82, 92, 99–100, 160
Ivanhoe (Scott), 87–8, 103

jacket, 1–2, 100, 106–8, 182–3, 210
Jensen, Anthony K., 40
Jewusiak, Jacob, 18, 75–8, 194, 203
"John Dryden" (Macaulay), 32–4
Jones, Jason, 13, 40, 126n
Judaism, 63, 70, 147

Kant, Immanuel, 30, 73
Khaldun, Ibn, 28
Kingstone, Helen, 6, 26n, 174–5
Kirsteen (Oliphant), 8, 21, 211–17
knee-breeches, 16, 108–11, 117, 137, 183, 200
Koselleck, Reinhart, 10, 30, 47–8, 73–4
Kristeva, Julia, 133–4, 138, 140
Kurnick, David, 99

lace, 182–3, 216
Lamb, Caroline, *Glenarvon*, 135, 144, 164n, 165n
Lambert, Miles, 105–6
Lee, Yoon Sun, 44–5
Lesjak, Carolyn, 10
Levine, George, 98
Lewes, George Henry, 107–8
liberalism, 4–13, 18, 23–4, 28, 33, 61, 92, 98–9, 110, 190
Life in the Sick-Room (Martineau), 147, 149, 151
life-cycle, 6, 18, 67, 178
lifespan, 12, 18, 77–8
life-writing, 7, 13, 18, 20–1, 131–63, 169
Logan, Deborah A., 147
Longford, Elizabeth, 141
Looser, Devoney, 17, 46, 132

Lowe, Lisa, 11, 33, 103–4
Lukács, Georg, 64, 97, 100, 126n, 127n; *see also* historical novel

McAleavey, Maia, 45
Macaulay, Thomas Babington, 4, 6, 19, 29, 37, 45, 71–2, 90, 145, 155, 215
　"History," 9, 33–4
　History of England, 34–5
　"John Dryden," 32–4
McLoughlin, Kate, 170
Markovits, Stefanie, 178
Marshik, Celia, 14
Martineau, Harriet, 6, 167–8n
　Autobiography, 7, 18, 20, 131–5, 145–63, 166n, 170, 190, 202, 214, 216
　History of the Thirty Years' Peace, 161
　The Hour and the Man, 150–1
　Illustrations of Political Economy, 152–3, 156
　Life in the Sick-Room, 147, 149, 151
masculinity, 100, 108, 131, 215; *see also* gender
Maxwell, Richard, 127n
Mayer, Sandra, 60, 93n
medieval period, 17, 33–4, 61–2, 71, 79–80, 82, 84, 87–91, 109; *see also* Gothic architecture
Melman, Billie, 5
Memoirs (Wilson), 7, 8, 18, 20, 21, 63, 126, 131–45, 146, 148, 150, 152, 162–3, 163–5n, 170, 183, 215–16
Mengham, Rod, 192, 198, 207–8n
Michaelson, Patricia Howell, 68, 139, 141–2, 163n
Michie, Elsie, 183

middle age, 20–1, 59, 74, 104, 111, 131, 136–7, 140, 147, 154–5, 158, 200–1
Mill, John Stuart, 4, 12, 29, 45, 131, 155
　"The Spirit of the Age," 1–2, 4, 6, 84, 100
　System of Logic, 19, 31–3, 35, 39, 43, 215
Miller, Andrew, 124, 195
Millgate, Michael, 204–5n, 206n
Mistichelli, William J., 205n
Mitchell, Rebecca N., 14, 26n
"Modern Beau Brummellism," 15, 102, 105
Moers, Ellen, 106, 110
Mole, Tom, 46, 72–3
monumental history (Nietzsche's concept), 39–40
monumental time (Kristeva's concept), 133–4, 140, 145–6, 157, 162, 170, 178, 195, 202, 204
monuments, 21, 170, 187–8
Moore, Ben, 82
Moretti, Franco, 57n
Mufti, Nasser, 12, 79, 81
Mullen, Mary, 5, 31, 113
Muñoz, José Esteban, 50
Murray, Alex, 10
Murray, John II, 63–4, 67, 69, 93n
muslin, 179–82, 184, 211–2

Napoleonic Wars, 9, 97, 114, 123–4, 148, 161, 169, 172–3, 176–7, 185–91, 195–6
Nemesvari, Richard, 172, 206n
New Materialism, 14, 26n
new time studies, 23
Nietzsche, Friedrich, 30, 32
　On the Uses and Disadvantages of History for Life, 38–41,

50–3, 56n, 60, 92, 126, 161, 169, 171, 184

objects, 6–9, 11, 13, 16–19, 21, 61, 101–3, 170–1, 184–91, 204, 212, 215; *see also* clothing; monuments; propaganda
O'Connell, Lisa, 138–9, 163n, 164n
old age, 1–3, 8–9, 17–18, 21, 44–53, 59–60, 73–9, 81–2, 91, 117, 122–4, 126, 131, 136, 147, 154, 161, 170, 185, 195–7, 214–5
Oliphant, Margaret, *Kirsteen*, 8, 21, 211–17
On Heroes (Carlyle), 40, 123, 134, 139, 141, 145
"On History" (Carlyle), 39, 42, 125
"On History Again" (Carlyle), 9, 41
On the Uses and Disadvantages of History for Life (Nietzsche), 38–41, 50–3, 56n, 60, 92, 126, 161, 169, 171, 184
Ottoman empire, 121, 187
Oussaid, Nathalie, 208n

Parker, Christopher, 42
Peakman, Julie, 163n
Pelham (Bulwer-Lytton), 71, 106, 111, 115
Peterson, Linda, 131, 146, 148, 155, 156
Piketty, Thomas, 37
Pinker, Steven, 37, 190
Plenderleath, William C., 188
Poovey, Mary, 74, 90, 92n
positivism, 4, 19–20, 22, 29–30, 35–7, 40, 42–3, 55n, 87, 99, 125–6, 155–6, 161–2; *see also* Comte

postcolonialism, 11–13, 24, 37; *see also* empire
presentism, 22–4, 29, 37–44, 56n, 90–2, 99, 125, 134–5
"The Profitable Reading of Fiction" (Hardy), 177–9, 183–4
progress, 4–11, 28–54, 55n
  as inevitable but deferred, 52, 84, 120, 122
  gradualism, 4–11, 15, 17–20, 22, 24–5, 29–32, 35, 44, 60–2, 65, 69–74, 76–7, 80, 84, 88–91, 99, 110, 125, 132, 144–6, 155–7, 160–3, 211, 213–15
  segmentation, 8–9, 18–19, 29, 35, 60–2, 71–2, 80, 91, 133–4, 145–6, 155–7, 162–3
  see also whig history
propaganda, 9, 17, 21, 70, 170, 185–7
Protestantism, 33–6, 55n, 71, 148, 160–1
Purdy, Daniel Leonhard, 15, 16, 211

queer temporality, 11–13, 16–17, 24, 30, 50–2, 57–8n, 111, 133–4, 215

Radford, Andrew, 188
Rainof, Rebecca, 17, 29
Ranke, Leopold von, 36, 39, 42, 51–3, 55n, 77, 199
Regency, 70, 105, 106–9, 112, 145, 181, 211–12
regress, 4, 6, 19, 23, 28–9, 49, 100, 161–2; *see also* decline
Reilly, Jim, 23, 206n
repetition, 1–2, 4, 16, 20–1, 40, 68, 106, 133–4, 149, 154–5, 159–60, 170–1, 173–4, 202–4

The Representative (Murray), 63–4, 93n
residual (Raymond Williams's concept), 8, 10, 86, 99, 110, 198
Reynolds, K. D., 164n
Ribeiro, Aileen, 106, 128n
Richstad, Josephine, 66–7, 126n
Rignall, J. M., 177
Rimmer, Mary, 171–2, 177, 180
Rivers, Bryan, 163n
Roberts, Caroline, 167n
roman-à-clef, 19, 61–2, 70, 99, 113–15, 125, 135
Rosling, Hans, 37
Rousseau, Jean-Jacques, 30, 48–53, 161
rupture, 4, 6, 8–10, 18, 20, 23, 25, 28–9, 35–6, 45, 51, 60–2, 70, 76, 90, 99, 120–1, 125, 134, 145, 155–6, 161–3, 177, 211, 213, 215

St. Clair, William, 164n
Sampson, Jennifer, 83
Sartor Resartus (Carlyle), 15–16
Saunders, David, 164n
Schaffer, Talia, 154–5
Schwartz, Daniel, 59–60
Scott, Walter, 21, 73, 88, 99–100, 127n, 141, 169–70, 185, 212
  The Heart of Mid-Lothian, 175
  Ivanhoe, 87–8, 103
  Waverley, 19, 29, 44–8, 51, 52, 173–4, 205n
secularization, 32, 43, 90, 160, 189–90
  Martineau and, 147–58
Sedgwick, Eve, 151
Setzer, Sharon, 163n
Shannon, Brent, 26n, 108
Shaw, Harry, 97, 126n, 127n
silver-fork fiction, 9, 59–60, 62–5, 67, 84

Skorupski, John, 11
Slote, Michael, 154
Small, Helen, 17, 154
Smith, Sidonie, 168n
spencer, 106–8, 182–3
"Spirit of the Age" (Mill), 1–2, 4, 6, 84, 100
stasis, 3–6, 8, 13, 16–17, 19–21, 23, 28–9, 33, 35–6, 44–5, 49–51, 60–2, 70, 74–7, 88, 90–1, 98–101, 105, 112–13, 116, 120–1, 125–6, 131–4, 139, 141, 145, 148, 155, 159–60, 162–3, 170–1, 175, 190, 192, 195, 197, 199, 201–2, 204, 214–15
Steinberg, Oded Y., 34
Stendhal (Marie-Henri Beyle), 173
Stephen, Leslie, 171, 173
Sybil (Disraeli), 19, 61, 71–3, 79–91, 113–15, 118–19, 122, 141, 190, 192–3, 199–200, 214, 216
System of Logic (Mill), 19, 31–3, 35, 39, 43, 215

Terdiman, Richard, 47
Teukolsky, Rachel, 60, 62, 70–1
Thackeray, William Makepeace, *Vanity Fair*, 6, 13, 16–18, 20–1, 47, 70, 97–126, 126n, 133, 139, 145, 154, 159, 169–70, 179, 182–3, 200, 204–5n, 211–12, 214
Thing Theory, 13–14, 26n
Tillotson, Kathleen, 98, 116, 126n
time *see* Christian temporalities; chronology; crip temporality; cyclicality; decline; progress; queer temporality; regress; rupture; stasis; women's time
"To Dianeme" (Herrick), 178–9, 181
Tondre, Michael, 13, 24, 195–6

The Trumpet-Major (Hardy), 8, 9, 21, 169–95, 203–4, 206n, 208n, 213
Tully, James, 12

V21, 22, 41, 56n
Vanden Bossche, Chris R., 39
Vanity Fair (Thackeray), 6, 13, 16–18, 20–1, 47, 70, 97–126, 126n, 133, 139, 145, 154, 159, 169–70, 179, 182–3, 200, 204–5n, 211–12, 214
Veblen, Thorstein, 14, 16
Victoria (Queen), 82–4, 90, 183
Vivian Grey (Disraeli), 7, 9, 18, 19, 61–71, 86, 93–4n, 117, 133, 143, 194
Voltz, Johann Michael, 185–7

Watson, Nicola, 165n
Waverley (Scott), 19, 29, 44–8, 51, 52, 173–4, 205n
Wessex Tales (Hardy), 7, 13, 18, 21, 24, 169–71, 177, 188, 190–204, 207–8n, 212, 214
whig history, 4–5, 15, 25n, 29–33, 37, 43, 61, 71, 148, 160, 162
White, Hayden, 31, 139
Wilde, Oscar, 16, 93n

Wilhelm Meisters Lehrjahre (Goethe, trans. Carlyle), 64
William IV (King), 82–3
Williams, Raymond, 8, 10, 110, 198
Wilson, Elizabeth, 3, 100–1
Wilson, Frances, 138, 139, 145
Wilson, Harriette, *Memoirs*, 7, 8, 18, 20, 21, 63, 126, 131–45, 146, 148, 150, 152, 162–3, 163–5n, 170, 183, 215–16
Wolfson, Susan, 165n
women's time, 12, 20–1, 90, 126, 131–5, 214–15; *see also* gender
Woolf, Virginia, 14–15
Wright, T. R., 205n

Young, Brian W., 43, 57n
youth, 1–3, 8, 17–18, 21, 44, 48–51, 53, 59–65, 70–4, 76–7, 80–4, 91, 93n, 122–4, 126, 136–8, 145–8, 154, 161, 170–1, 195–6, 199–201, 211–14

zeitgeist, 19, 59, 105, 112, 144
Zemka, Sue, 5, 29
Zlotnick, Susan, 83